Psychosis, Psychoanalysis and Psychiatry in Postwar USA

Covering the last four decades of the 20th century, this book explores the unwritten history of the struggles between psychoanalysis and psychiatry in postwar USA, inaugurated by the neosomatic revolution, which had profound consequences for the treatment of psychotic patients. Analyzing and synthesizing major developments in this critical and clinical field, Orna Ophir discusses how leading theories redefined what schizophrenia is and how to treat it, offering a fresh interpretation of the nature and challenges of the psychoanalytic profession. The book also considers the internal dynamics and conflicts within mental health organizations, their theoretical paradigms and therapeutic practices.

Opening a timely debate, considering both the continuing relevance and the inherent limitations of the psychoanalytic approach, the book demonstrates how psychoanalysts reinterpreted their professional identity by formalizing and disseminating knowledge among their fellow practitioners, while negotiating with neighboring professions in the medical fields, such as psychiatry, pharmacology and the burgeoning neurosciences. Chapters explore the ways in which psychoanalysts constructed – and also transgressed upon – the boundaries of their professional identity and practice as they sought to understand schizophrenia and treat its patients. The book argues that among the many relationships psychoanalysis sustained with psychiatry, some weakened their own social role as service providers, while others made the theory and practice of psychoanalysis a viable contender in the jurisdictional struggles between professions.

Psychosis, Psychoanalysis and Psychiatry in Postwar USA will appeal to researchers, academics, graduate students and advanced undergraduates who are interested in the history of psychoanalysis, psychiatry, the medical humanities and the history of science and ideas. It will also be of interest to clinicians, health care professionals and other practitioners.

Orna Ophir is Adjunct Associate Professor in the Humanities at the School of Arts and Sciences, Johns Hopkins University, Baltimore, USA, and Adjunct Associate Professor in the Doctoral Studies Program in Clinical Psychology at Long Island University, New York, USA. She is a licensed clinical psychologist in Tel Aviv, Israel, and a licensed psychoanalyst in New York, USA.

The International Society for Psychological and Social Approaches to Psychosis Book Series
Series editors: Alison Summers and Nigel Bunker

ISPS (The International Society for Psychological and Social Approaches to Psychosis) has a history stretching back more than fifty years during which it has witnessed the relentless pursuit of biological explanations for psychosis. The tide has been turning in recent years and there is a welcome international resurgence of interest in a range of psychological factors that have considerable explanatory power and therapeutic possibilities. Governments, professional groups, people with personal experience of psychosis and family members are increasingly expecting interventions that involve more talking and listening. Many now regard practitioners skilled in psychological therapies as an essential component of the care of people with psychosis.

ISPS is a global society. It aims to promote psychological and social approaches both to understanding and to treating psychosis. It also aims to bring together different perspectives on these issues. ISPS is composed of individuals, networks and institutional members from a wide range of backgrounds and is especially concerned that those with personal experience of psychosis and their family members are fully involved in our activities alongside practitioners and researchers, and that all benefit from this. Our members recognise the potential humanitarian and therapeutic potential of skilled psychological understanding and therapy in the field of psychosis and ISPS embraces a wide spectrum of approaches from psychodynamic, systemic, cognitive, and arts therapies to the need-adapted approaches, family and group therapies and residential therapeutic communities.

We are also most interested in establishing meaningful dialogue with those practitioners and researchers who are more familiar with biological-based approaches. There is increasing empirical evidence for the interaction of genes and biology with the emotional and social environment, and there are important examples of such interactions in the fields of trauma, attachment relationships in the family and in social settings and with professionals.

ISPS activities include regular international and national conferences, newsletters and email discussion groups. Routledge has recognised the importance of our field in publishing both the book series and the ISPS journal: *Psychosis – Psychological,*

Social and Integrative Approaches with the two complementing one another. The book series started in 2004 and by 2012 had 13 volumes with several more in preparation. A wide range of topics are covered and we hope this reflects some success in our aim of bringing together a rich range of perspectives.

The book series is intended as a resource for a broad range of mental health professionals as well as those developing and implementing policy and people whose interest in psychosis is at a personal level. We aim for rigorous academic standards and at the same time accessibility to a wide range of readers, and for the books to promote the ideas of clinicians and researchers who may be well known in some countries but not so familiar in others. Our overall intention is to encourage the dissemination of existing knowledge and ideas, promote productive debate, and encourage more research in a most important field whose secrets certainly do not all reside in the neurosciences.

For more information about ISPS, email isps@isps.org or visit our website, www.isps.org.

For more information about the journal *Psychosis* visit www.isps.org/index.php/publications/journal

Psychosis, Psychoanalysis and Psychiatry in Postwar USA: On the borderland of madness
Orna Ophir

Meaning, Madness and Political Subjectivity: A study of schizophrenia and culture in Turkey
Sadeq Rahimi

Models of Madness: Psychological, Social and Biological Approaches to Schizophrenia 1st Edition
Edited by John Read, Loren R. Mosher & Richard P. Bentall

Psychoses: An Integrative Perspective
Edited by Johan Cullberg

Evolving Psychosis: Different Stages, Different Treatments
Edited by Jan Olav Johanessen, Brian V. Martindale & Johan Cullberg

Family and Multi-Family work with Psychosis
Gerd-Ragna Block Thorsen, Trond Gronnestad & Anne Lise Oxenvad

Experiences of Mental Health In-Patient Care: Narratives from Service Users, Carers and Professionals
Edited by Mark Hardcastle, David Kennard, Sheila Grandison & Leonard Fagin

Psychotherapies for the Psychoses: Theoretical, Cultural, and Clinical Integration
Edited by John Gleeson, Eión Killackey & Helen Krstev

Therapeutic Communities for Psychosis: Philosophy, History and Clinical Practice
Edited by John Gale, Alba Realpe & Enrico Pedriali

Making Sense of Madness: Contesting the Meaning of Schizophrenia
Jim Geekie and John Read

Psychotherapeutic Approaches to Schizophrenia Psychosis
Edited by Yrjö O. Alanen, Manuel González de Chávez, Ann-Louise S. Silver & Brian Martindale

Beyond Medication: Therapeutic Engagement and the Recovery from Psychosis
Edited by David Garfield and Daniel Mackler

CBT for Psychosis: A Symptom-based Approach
Edited by Roger Hagen, Douglas Turkington, Torkil Berge and Rolf W. Gråwe

Experiencing Psychosis: Personal and Professional Perspectives
Edited by Jim Geekie, Patte Randal, Debra Lampshire and John Read

Psychosis as a Personal Crisis: An Experience-Based Approach
Edited by Marius Romme and Sandra Escher

Models of Madness: Psychological, Social and Biological Approaches to Psychosis 2nd Edition
Edited by John Read and Jacqui Dillon

Surviving, Existing, or Living: Phase-specific Therapy for Severe Psychosis
Pamela Fuller

Psychosis and Emotion: The Role of Emotions in Understanding Psychosis, Therapy and Recovery
Edited by Andrew Gumley, Alf Gillham, Kathy Taylor and Matthias Schwannauer

Insanity and Divinity: Studies in Psychosis and Spirituality
Edited by John Gale, Michael Robson and Georgia Rapsomatioti

Psychotherapy for People Diagnosed with Schizophrenia: Specific techniques
Andrew Lotterman

Creativity and Psychotic States in Exceptional People: The work of Murray Jackson
Murray Jackson and Jeanne Magagna

Psychosis, Psychoanalysis and Psychiatry in Postwar USA
On the borderland of madness

Orna Ophir

LONDON AND NEW YORK

First published in 2015 in English as *Psychosis, Psychoanalysis and Psychiatry in Postwar USA: On the borderland of madness*

by Routledge
27 Church Road, Hove, East Sussex, BN3 2FA

and by Routledge
711 Third Avenue, New York, NY 10017

Routledge is an imprint of the Taylor & Francis Group, an informa business

© 2015 O. Ophir

The right of O. Ophir to be identified as author of this work has been asserted by her in accordance with sections 77 and 78 of the Copyright, Designs and Patents Act 1988.

All rights reserved. No part of this book may be reprinted or reproduced or utilised in any form or by any electronic, mechanical, or other means, now known or hereafter invented, including photocopying and recording, or in any information storage or retrieval system, without permission in writing from the publishers.

First published in Hebrew as *On the Borderland of Madness: Psychoanalysis, Psychiatry and Psychosis in Postwar USA* 2013
by Resling

Trademark notice: Product or corporate names may be trademarks or registered trademarks, and are used only for identification and explanation without intent to infringe.

British Library Cataloguing in Publication Data

A catalogue record for this book is available from the British Library

Library of Congress Cataloging-in-Publication Data
Ophir, Orna.
    Psychosis, psychoanalysis and psychiatry in post war USA :
on the borderland of madness/Orna Ophir.
        pages cm
    Includes bibliographical references and index.
    1. Psychoanalysis—United States—History.   I. Title.
    BF173O546 2015
    616.89'17097309045—dc23
    2014045747

ISBN: 978-1-138-82352-5 (hbk)
ISBN: 978-1-315-74201-4 (ebk)

Typeset in Galliard
by Apex CoVantage, LLC

Contents

Acknowledgments	xi
Introduction	1
1 Freud's dual view of schizophrenia (1894–1940)	13
2 Ravens in white coats: The medicalization of American psychoanalysis (1909–1954)	27
3 Psychoanalysis, psychopharmacology and community psychiatry (1954–1970)	43
4 The "dopamine hypothesis" and evidence of genetic factors in schizophrenia (1971–1980)	69
5 The emperor's new clothes: DSM-III and the abandonment of psychodynamics in favor of the biomedical model (1980–1990)	97
6 The last battle of psychoanalysis? The Decade of the Brain (1990–2000)	133
7 The many faces of Schreber as the face of American psychoanalysis (1954–2000)	171
Epilogue	187
Index	191

Acknowledgments

This book is based on a study conducted at the Cohn Institute for the History and Philosophy of Science and Ideas at Tel Aviv University. I want to thank Professor José Brunner, who at the time of writing was the Director of the Minerva Institute for German History, whose sustained interest and serious investment in this project transformed a troubling question of a clinician working in a mental hospital into a rigorous research project in the history of psychiatry and psychoanalysis. Thanks to the generous support of the School of History at Tel Aviv University, I was able to take time off my other obligations and devote the necessary concentration to this archival and methodological research.

The deep passion I developed for exploring the historical and institutional relationships among psychoanalysis, psychiatry and the phenomenon and treatment of psychosis was largely due to the many years I was an active member on the staff of the Shalvata Mental Health Center in Israel. I will always be in debt to the many patients I met there, to their families and to the dedicated colleagues on the hospital's staff whose total commitment to the humane care of severely ill patients is truly exceptional and exemplary. I am especially grateful to Dr. Shlomo Mendlovic, the Head of Department C, whose energy and involvement in the field of dynamic psychiatry and hospitalized patient care has inspired me ever since I was fortunate enough to meet him. He has inspired many generations of clinicians and continues to do so to this day. I owe a special thanks to Joshua Durban, an exceptional psychoanalyst and mentor, whose psychoanalytic work with primitive states of mind has been essential in writing this book.

I also want to thank my translators Adi Avivi, a sensitive and clearheaded psychologist, and Zvi Weiss, promising Ph.D. student, both of whom are among the finest products of a very special doctoral program in clinical psychology at Long Island University, which has welcomed me among its faculty for the last two years. I want to thank Maryellen Lo Bosco, my copyeditor, who checked and corrected the manuscript with meticulous care. Thanks to Alison Summers and Nigel Bunker, coeditors of ISPS book series, who showed interest in bringing this book to publication, and to Clare Ashworth and Emily Bedford for helping to make it happen.

I am deeply grateful to Professor Danielle Knafo, a faculty member in the Serious Mental Illness concentration of Long Island University's doctoral program in

xii *Acknowledgments*

Clinical Psychology. She demonstrated unwavering faith in my writing and teaching. Her trust and good advice provided important support at a crucial moment, and her paradigmatic role in training young clinicians to use psychoanalysis in the treatment of severe mental illness remains, in my view, unmatched.

Since I arrived in New York in August 2008, I have found two professional homes: the Kleinian clinical group, led by Ms. Karen Proner, and the DeWitt Wallace Institute for the History of Psychiatry at Weill-Cornell Medical College. Ms. Proner and the members of the Klein group, and especially James Peel, Alison Bruce and Aleksandra Wagner, were a constant reminder that psychoanalytic work with very primitive mental states is possible and beneficial.

At Weill-Cornell, I have been privileged to meet many of the people who were an integral part of the very history I was writing. I would like to thank Professor George Makari and Dr. Nate Kravis for the warm hospitality and scholarly feedback, which they have unfailingly offered over these last few years. I have greatly profited from the contributions of all the members of the Richardson Seminar, as well as from deeply motivating conversations with the members of the History of Psychoanalysis Working Group, both at Weill-Cornell. I especially want to thank Larry Friedman, Leni Goopman, Barbara Stimmel, Ted Shapiro, Bob Michaels and Kathy Dalsimer for their curiosity, attentiveness and intellectual generosity.

I'm grateful to my friends at *Das Unbehagen*, a free association of psychoanalysis in New York that collects the finest young minds in psychoanalysis and proves that psychoanalysis is not only alive, but also kicking!

Ruth Weinberg, Antal Tsur, Aya Seker, Efrat Shamgar, Tsibi Geva, Smadar Eliasaf, Sefi Rosen, Daphna Spigelman, Gil Talmi and Shiri Broza have always been there through many years of friendship, which I deeply cherish.

I thank my beloved family members: my husband Hent, whose presence in my life is nothing short of a miracle, my daughters Britt and Alma, whom I absolutely adore and profoundly admire, and my brothers Ori and Arnon, who have always been surprisingly tolerant and forgiving whenever their sister decided to immerse herself more and more deeply in the theorization and treatment of madness.

Most of all I am grateful to my parents, Aliza and Avigdor Ophir, who were always a safe haven in my life, thereby allowing me to take intellectual, emotional and other journeys into the borderlands of madness. This book is dedicated to them with love and gratitude.

Orna Ophir
New York, September 2014

Introduction

The relationship between American psychiatry, psychoanalysis and psychosis belongs to the discourse that Michel Foucault calls the "history of the present." Although this volume offers a historiography of schizophrenia – the paradigmatic form of madness in the modern era of psychiatry as constructed in postwar American psychoanalysis – its concern is with a present in which mentally ill individuals are deprived of psychoanalytical treatment or other forms of psychological therapies. Some might say this is a modern form of the incarceration of the mentally ill, who were first released from their chains by well-known enlightenment figures such as Pinel, Tuke, Chiarugi and Rush.

Since it covers approximately the last four decades of the 20th century, during which psychoanalysts' theoretical approach to psychosis and clinical work with schizophrenic patients underwent a dramatic transformation, this volume seeks to explore a paradox in American psychoanalysis: although psychoanalytic discourse exhibits much concern for the "psychotic parts" of otherwise healthy people, it seems to have very little interest in those who suffer from major psychoses, both in theory and in practice.

Opening with Freud and his discussion of the legendary judge, Daniel Paul Schreber, who complained that his somatic psychiatrists were performing "soul murder" on him, and ending almost 100 years later with the actual murder of Dr. Wayne Fenton, a prominent specialist on psychoanalysis and schizophrenia from the generation of Chestnut Lodge, this book explores a troubling period in the historical development of American psychoanalysis. During the investigated period, the age-old psychiatrists' version of Cartesian dualism (i.e., the somatic versus the psychodynamic paradigm) shaped psychoanalysis's theory of madness and its praxis with psychotic patients to the point where it almost "lost its mind" as it ventured to put "neurons in neurosis."

As it follows psychoanalysis's struggles and competition with somatic psychiatry, as well as its dialogues and negotiations with psychiatry, this volume presents the boundaries between these diverse professional landscapes not only as markers of difference, segregating epistemic and disciplinary jurisdictions, but also as capturing a fundamental social process of fatal osmosis and blurring of boundaries. It further demonstrates how these different interactions between psychoanalysis

2 Introduction

and psychiatry, each in its own unique way, contributed to the various constructions of the idea of schizophrenic madness in psychoanalysis and to the manifold conceptualizations of its treatment.

The eventual transformation of psychoanalytic theory and praxis in its dealings with schizophrenic madness took place during a neosomatic revolution in American psychiatry that spanned four stages, beginning with the emergence of so-called antipsychotic medication during the 1960s and ending with George H. W. Bush's presidential proclamation of the "Decade of the Brain" in the early 1990s. Psychoanalytic journals, which are the archives of professional abstract knowledge, are tracked to determine the ways in which psychoanalysts constructed and articulated, defended and shifted, undermined and transgressed the boundaries of their profession as they sought to deal with schizophrenia, its theory and its patients. This is more than simply a formal analysis. Rather, this volume demonstrates how psychoanalysts enacted their professional identity by articulating and formalizing their knowledge and disseminating it among their fellow practitioners, all the while struggling and negotiating with neighboring professions. It is argued that among the many relationships psychoanalysts entertained with their "strange bedfellows" – that is to say, psychiatrists – some were weakening their own social role as providers of expert service to ameliorate the problem of schizophrenic madness, while others made themselves equal contenders in these jurisdictional struggles between the professions.

Being both a historian of science and a practicing clinician and psychoanalyst, who has worked for many years in psychiatric hospitals with patients suffering from schizophrenia, I locate this book on the borderland between these fields – historical research and its clinical implications. Although this study offers a historical examination of the development of the concept of "madness" in American psychoanalysis, it further crystallizes around questions of sociological history – specifically, of defining the profession.

The metaphor of territories and jurisdictions, which is used in the context of the sociology of professions, led to Andrew Abbott's argument that the "real" history of a profession is the one that focuses on its struggle over jurisdictions with neighboring professions. Taking its lead from this intuition, this study on the development and change of American psychoanalytic theory concerning madness and its praxis with psychotic patients explores psychoanalysis as a profession that is part of a "system of professions," and is thus prone to engage in struggles with its contenders.

Psychoanalysis and psychiatry were struggling over jurisdiction since the very founding of psychoanalysis, and the concept of schizophrenia in American psychoanalysis and its treatment were shaped by a neosomatic revolution that took place in American psychiatry in four stages and spanned four decades, 1960–2000.

The first two chapters of this book mainly cover Freud's corpus and secondary literature concerning Freud and psychoanalysis in America. The first chapter, "Freud's dual view of schizophrenia (1894–1940)," discusses Freud's two theories of schizophrenia: the unitary theory, which sees schizophrenia as only quantitatively different from neurosis, and the specific theory, which sees it as

Introduction 3

qualitatively different and thus unsuitable for psychoanalytic treatment. This distinction evolved as part of Freud's efforts to professionalize psychoanalysis and a consequence of his attempts to prove psychoanalysis's supremacy over psychiatry. Since he aspired to explain the mind in part by studying its pathologies, Freud was preoccupied with formulating a theory of schizophrenia. However, because of his belief that schizophrenic patients were incurable – immune to a technique that sought to establish the "ego where id was" – he could not afford for them to spoil his initial claim to have a successful therapeutic method vis-à-vis psychiatry, and he declared schizophrenic patients as not analyzable. In his later writings, when Freud became more realistic about the psychoanalytic "cure," he gradually also became more optimistic about the analyzability of schizophrenic patients and in fact supported Ernest Simmel, the Berlin psychoanalyst and founder of the first psychoanalytic sanatorium at Schloss Tegel, in his efforts to establish a psychoanalytic sanatorium in the United States for this population.

The second chapter, "Ravens in white coats: The medicalization of American psychoanalysis (1909–1954)," argues that the medicalization of psychoanalysis in America was the royal road of the profession to the "homeland" of psychiatry – that is to say, to psychiatric hospitals where schizophrenic patients were being treated. But both American eclecticism and pragmatism, which together allowed this process to run its course, were trends that also transformed psychoanalysis into dynamic psychiatry. The resulting confusion of boundaries between psychoanalysis and psychiatry initiated a process in which both professions regressed into themselves to try to better define their expertise. As a result of this regression, psychoanalysis withdrew from psychiatric hospitals and its schizophrenic patients and focused on private practice with the "worried well," whereas psychiatry returned to its origins, notably somatic medicine, but in a new guise as neosomatic psychiatry, armed with a winning, quick and cheap treatment for schizophrenics – namely, neuroleptic drugs.

Each of the four chapters that follows opens with a short discussion of the formative event in somatic psychiatry in the field of schizophrenia during the decade it explores. These chapters analyze the reaction of American psychoanalysis to these major events, as it is found in the primary literature – that is to say, in the archives of psychoanalysis as a profession. This discursive analysis puts special emphasis on the theoretical construction of schizophrenia, as well as on the suggested therapeutic techniques developed for treating those suffering from it. Because this is a panoramic view of the psychoanalytic approach to schizophrenia in each decade, it examines the way in which psychoanalysis was described by different analysts, both prominent and peripheral, and used more than just the canonical works. This study draws on articles that are explicitly about schizophrenia, as well as some that touch on the subject secondarily. Other sections of journals were also examined, such as "at issue" discussions, book reviews and the like. Perusal of all journal materials allowed for a comprehensive conceptualization of schizophrenia during those years – and both implicit and explicit perceptions among American analysts.

4   *Introduction*

The primary literature consists of some 1,000 articles on the subject of schizophrenia, published during these 40 years in the most popular American psychoanalytic journals: the *Journal of the American Psychoanalytic Association* (*JAPA*), the *Journal of the American Academy of Psychoanalysis and Dynamic Psychiatry* (*Journal of the Academy*) and *Psychoanalytic Dialogues* (*Dialogues*). Articles by American psychoanalysts published in the *International Journal of Psychoanalysis* (*IJP*) are also examined, in addition to articles on psychoanalysis in *Schizophrenia Bulletin* (*The Bulletin*). These journals are treated as the archive of American psychoanalysis's abstract knowledge; that is to say, as the very same knowledge that, according to Abbott, construes it as a field of expertise. Indeed, occupations turn into professions not only through associations, licensure procedures, ethical codes and the like, but also by constructing so-called expert knowledge. This discourse is used as one of the strategies to determine and institute professionalization. The formalization of this abstract knowledge, as part of a scientific discourse that includes logic and rigorous diagnosis, as well as comprehensive academic research based on high standards of rationality, is a crucial part of jurisdictional struggles between different professions. By means of these discursive strategies, which are at once cognitive and social processes, the professional group creates a scholarly discourse that simultaneously legitimates the group from within and is used externally in its jurisdictional struggles with other professional groups. For this reason, this discourse serves in my study as a repository of the ways in which psychoanalysts constructed, articulated, defended, shifted, undermined or transgressed the boundaries of their profession in the very borderland of schizophrenic madness.

The third chapter, "Psychoanalysis, psychopharmacology and community psychiatry (1954–1970)," discusses the first stage of the neosomatic revolution in American psychiatry, which followed the introduction of neuroleptic medication as the cheapest and most effective therapy for schizophrenic patients. The use of neuroleptics, a formative event in American psychiatry, was part of a much wider revolution initiated by John F. Kennedy's "New Frontier," in which the mentally ill were deinstitutionalized and community psychiatry grew as a method for treating schizophrenic patients in day programs. Two versions of American psychoanalysis for schizophrenia were formed in this period. The first one, using mostly "ego psychology," was heavily influenced by the psychoanalytic struggles over jurisdiction and, like its competitor (neosomatic psychiatry), identified a sick "organ" of its own – the ego – while marking its defective functions. Just like medicine, this school of psychoanalysis used classifications, empirical laboratory research, etiological formulation, an explanation of the mechanism involved when drugs successfully took effect and so forth.

The danger inherent in the effort of psychoanalysts to stay relevant to the field of schizophrenia – by re-medicalizing their profession – was deserting their unique psychoanalytic method of research. There was also a risk in adapting the psychoanalytic therapeutic method to the so-called "defect theory" of schizophrenia, to such an extent that it became virtually impossible to distinguish psychoanalysis from supportive therapy used with drugs. In this process of accommodation,

Introduction 5

psychoanalysts developed a rhetorical hybrid that mixed up the abstraction of its own discourse with the concreteness of medical jargon. For example, psychoanalysts now claimed that drugs treat the ego and that libido was quantifiable.

The second version of psychoanalysis that developed during this period, traces of which can be found mainly in *IJP*, published in London, was largely based on clinical encounters with patients with schizophrenia. Instead of using their competitor's metaphors and methods, these psychoanalysts dwelled on their own terms and concepts. The method of research was the psychoanalytic method, the "laboratory" was the analyst's room and the only "manipulation" was classic psychoanalytic therapy. Aside from explicitly distancing itself from medicine and criticizing the somatic treatment of schizophrenia in general and "drug therapy" in particular, this response provided a psychoanalytic alternative to understanding, studying and treating the schizophrenic patient as part of a wider ethical commitment. This version of psychoanalysis respected the complexity of schizophrenia, which was properly understood as being more than a merely somatic condition, and its response emerged from within psychoanalysis itself and formed a productive and creative synthesis among its different voices. By distancing itself from medicine while emphasizing its unique research and therapeutic tools, this alternative strategy proved to be beneficial both to the profession and its patients. Very few case studies of patients with schizophrenia or vignettes drawn from analysis of these patients are found in published articles representing the "fusion with medicine," but many clinical encounters were reported in articles reflecting the opposite trend of distancing psychoanalysis from medicine and criticizing neosomatic methods.

The fourth chapter, "The 'dopamine hypothesis' and evidence of genetic factors in schizophrenia (1971–1980)," deals with the reaction of psychoanalysts to Snyder's "dopamine hypothesis" of schizophrenia and Kety's genetic findings concerning schizophrenic patients, both of which reinforced the neosomatic trend in psychiatry in the field of schizophrenia. Whereas in previous decades somatic psychiatry was touted as cheaper and more effective than psychoanalysis in treating schizophrenia, 10 years later somatic psychiatry introduced brain phenomenology and genetic etiology as explanations of the problem at hand.

During these years psychoanalysts who were "confined" within the boundaries of mainstream American journals responded to this strengthening of the grip of somatic psychiatry on the field of schizophrenia by distancing themselves from this very field and its presuppositions. There were fewer discussions of this kind of madness, and when schizophrenia was rarely mentioned, the hybrid language of the last decade gave way to an extremely "purist" one, this time based on an exclusively biological approach. While discussing schizophrenia during the 1970s, psychoanalysts began to describe in detail the different structures of the brain, the functions of different neurotransmitters and the effect of neuroleptic drugs on them. Freud, the neurologist, the scientist and the "doctor," was "resurrected," and texts in which he had distanced psychoanalysis from the study and treatment of schizophrenia – and, indeed, had predicted a future biological basis for psychoanalysis – gained new attention.

6 Introduction

Meanwhile, a very different response could be found in the *Journal of the American Academy for Psychoanalysis and Dynamic Psychiatry*. Analysts in the Academy who had resigned from the American Psychoanalytic Association published many of their articles on the subject of schizophrenia. Alongside the rebellious attitude characterizing the Academy from its very beginning was its eclecticism, expressed in the field of schizophrenia by the wide variety of theoretical explanations of the condition. On one hand, published articles showed acceptance and internalization of the genetic findings, but, on the other, they also offered to move from the defect hypothesis of schizophrenia to the vulnerability hypothesis, suggesting that under a fair amount of stress anyone can become schizophrenic. Analysts proposed to pay attention to the "sick society" and to the "corrupted world," both of which, in their view, fostered conditions that produce sick individuals. Therapeutic proposals were affected by the counterculture of the 1960s and 1970s, which shaped the Academy. As a consequence, both the somatic therapies (neuroleptic drugs) and psychoanalytic methods (object-relations theories, as well as regression into therapeutic symbiosis with the analyst) were criticized for their "infantalization" of the schizophrenic patient.

Beyond the borders of American journals, in the 1970s' international arena of psychoanalytic discourse, American analysts responded to the strengthening of somatic psychiatry by situating themselves on either pole of the split between somatic and predominantly social explanations of illness, as they attempted to unite the divisions that existed within psychoanalysis. They sought to integrate Freud's two theories of schizophrenia, which had created two "schools" within psychoanalysis based on the unitary and the specific theory. This integration pertained not only to theory at its most abstract level, but also to the concrete view of individual patients. By integrating Freud's two theories of schizophrenia, patients with schizophrenia were now viewed as having both mad and sane parts, "psychotic" and "nonpsychotic" personalities, defects and conflicts, and as such falling within the jurisdiction of psychoanalysis. Also covered in this chapter are the views expressed in the *Schizophrenia Bulletin*, where psychoanalysis was transformed into a "light" version of itself, dealing mainly with behaviors and much less with the mysteries of the intra-psychic world.

The main thrust of Chapter 5, "The emperor's new clothes: DSM-III and the abandonment of psychodynamics in favor of the biomedical model (1980–1990)," is that the DSM-III ushered in the third stage of the neosomatic revolution as it incorporated the field of schizophrenia. The publication and wide acceptance of this manual convinced the public and authorities that schizophrenia was to be controlled by somatic psychiatry and hence fell under its jurisdiction. The publication of "psychiatry's new bible" declared dynamic psychiatry (i.e., psychoanalysis) to be obsolete. The move from Freud to Kraeplin, from dynamic thinking to descriptive psychiatry and from the search for what is "behind the symptom" to obsession with visible behavior changed the focus from the "mind" to the "brain." One of the neo-Kraeplinian hypotheses was that "the brain is the organ of the mind" and, hence, that core schizophrenic symptoms ought to be

Introduction 7

conceptualized as a manifestation of brain dysfunction. The DSM-III, characterized by its critics as the "emperor's new clothes" – was a very effective tool for new players in the field. Consequently, a strong, "unholy" alliance evolved between psychiatry, the psychopharmaceutical industries and insurance companies paying for the treatments. This alliance claimed an expanding realm of jurisdiction, pushing psychoanalysis further away from the treatment of schizophrenic patients.

American psychoanalysts writing in the mainstream journal *JAPA* responded to the manual and its impact in three different ways. For one thing, they criticized descriptive psychiatry and its narrow and limiting system of diagnosis. In its place they proposed an alternative system of psychoanalytic diagnosis that highlighted the inner psychic world and, instead of emphasizing binary dichotomies such as sane-mad, healthy-sick and neurotic-psychotic, offered a developmental and dynamic or dialectical approach. These authors suggested that psychoanalysts return to psychiatric departments to teach psychoanalysis to the next generation of psychiatrists or, alternatively, open the doors of their psychoanalytic institutes to more mental health professionals – notably, clinical psychologists – who would be psychotherapeutically oriented in the first place.

Yet another response can be found in the writings of American analysts who simply offered "more of the same" and who merely attempted to mimic the views and practices of their competitors, just as they had done in the 1960s. In this spirit, analysts not only showed psychiatrists that they accepted the "new developments" and that they had taken stock of the scientific findings in somatic psychiatry; they also offered their treatment as supportive to medications and helping with non-complaint patients. At the same time, however, these analysts insisted that patients with borderline personality disorder were not suffering a biological condition and hence should remain firmly within the jurisdiction of psychoanalysis. A third reaction, finally, was to attempt to find new alliances for psychoanalysis by giving up psychiatry and its neosomatic fashions altogether in favor of alternatives such as communication theories, cybernetics, literary criticism, art, anthropology and the like.

Whatever the nature of these different responses, it is worthwhile noting that during the whole decade, in what was considered to be the journal of mainstream American psychoanalysis, not a single case study of a schizophrenic patient – not one vignette or excerpt from sessions – was to be found. In contrast, American psychoanalysts in the *Journal of the Academy* were responding indirectly to the fashionable DSM-III by bringing back the age-old question of the "ghost in the machine." They insisted that, even if there was an agreement on the somatic determinants of schizophrenia, the human individual should still be viewed as a meaning-seeking creature, whose search for the implication of his brain defect could find its place only within psychoanalysis. Although analysts in the Academy were promoting an "integration movement within psychiatry" by combining somatic and psychodynamic approaches, when it came to therapy they were very much in defense of their own psychoanalytic technique and attacked the somatic technologies that were said to relate to schizophrenic patients as "broken, malfunctioning machines." In this

8   Introduction

sense, psychoanalysts constructed schizophrenia far less as a disease than as a human condition whose similarities to creative processes seemed undeniable.

American analysts publishing during the 1980s in the international psychoanalytic arena (*IJP*) were walking a tightrope between biological theories and hermeneutic schools of thought. Yet both excluded schizophrenia from the jurisdiction of psychoanalysis. The biological theorists did so because there seemed to be no meaning that could be ascribed to schizophrenic symptoms, while the hermeneutic theorists followed suit because, in their view, the person as such was, in a schizophrenic state, not yet created as a self invested with agency. Only those analysts who were integrating into their works the insights of their British colleagues – notably those who emphasized object relations and dealt with pre-Oedipal development – were able to keep schizophrenia within the jurisdiction of the psychoanalytic profession. Avoiding both the "flight" from the phenomena suggested by biology, which assumed that schizophrenia was a brain disease for which psychoanalysis has nothing to offer, and its hermeneutic counterpart that aspired to rid itself of the term "patient" altogether, these psychoanalysts followed in the footsteps of their British colleagues by analyzing the most primitive layers of the schizophrenic patient's psyche.

During this decade, the *Schizophrenia Bulletin* showed that psychoanalytic therapies for schizophrenia were under increasing attack by proponents of empirical research. During the 1980s, the pharmacotherapy of schizophrenia became an indisputable reality, and neosomatic psychiatry established itself with uncontested authority. The only question researchers allowed themselves to investigate was: "Which psychological treatment will be most effective as an *adjunct* therapy to the drug therapy?" Somatic psychiatry created a psychological treatment whose aim was to turn the schizophrenic patient into a compliant, productive and well-adjusted subject. This implied that the value of finding and understanding meaning, required by the psychodynamic paradigm, was replaced by the value of productiveness that merely supportive therapies implied.

Chapter Six, "The last battle of psychoanalysis? The Decade of the Brain (1990–2000)," follows psychoanalysts struggling with a new argument for somatic psychiatry's claim for jurisdiction in the field of schizophrenia. This fourth and last stage of the neosomatic revolution in psychiatry was announced in the beginning of the 1990s by President George H. W. Bush's proclamation of the "Decade of the Brain." This proclamation determined that schizophrenia was a brain disease and that brain scientists should "conquer" it. This was the same presidential spirit that supported the shift of federal financial resources reserved for therapy for the mentally ill to biological research in this field during the previous decade. Supportive of the pharmaceutical companies, the proclamation concluded that advanced studies in genetics and brain imaging would now tackle the phenomenon of schizophrenia. Based on these findings, the pharmaceutical companies that financed most of these research projects were expected to produce more effective drugs for the use of schizophrenic patients. The nation's determination to "conquer brain disease" went hand in hand with turning away from disciplines, such as psychoanalysis, interested in the phenomenology of the mind and that respected the functional autonomy of mental processes. The president's proclamation implicitly declared which professions were "in" and which were "out" in the field of schizophrenia. Exacerbating the compromised position of psychoanalysis were the "Freud Wars" of the early 1990s and the subsequent "Freud bashings" that made psychiatry all the more eager to rid itself of psychoanalysis once and for all.

American analysts responded to what looked like a knockout blow to their aspirations and struggles in three different ways. First, they attempted to master the language of the conquering profession and avoid their "father tongue." Second, they tried to hold onto other, more "friendly" territories that were not yet declared to be in the realm of "brain diseases," such as borderline and narcissistic disorders. Finally, they attempted to protect the uniqueness of psychoanalysis and prove its relevance in the field of schizophrenia, insisting on the efficacy of psychoanalytic treatment as richly evidenced in analysts' practices. Analysts publishing in *JAPA*, for example, represented mostly hopeless efforts to survive in the field of schizophrenia – rather than strengthening psychoanalysis's overall standing, they weakened it even more. Their attempts, which included integrating biological findings with psychoanalytic discourse, fell on a slippery slope in which psychoanalytic language became first a hybrid nonsensical discourse and then a biological dialect that left no room for the basic tenets and idiom of psychoanalysis itself (which had always insisted on drives, anxieties, conflicts and defense mechanisms). This biological trend in psychoanalysis seemed to exclude schizophrenic patients from psychoanalytic praxis. There were almost no reminders of clinical encounters with these patients, and the articles that did mention them resembled "elegies for a dying art."

As Freud once wrote, psychoanalysis is like a hydra monster: once it is beheaded, it grows more heads than it had before. Beheaded by somatic psychiatry, American psychoanalysis established a new school during this decade, called the relational school of psychoanalysis. Although formed during the 1980s, the first issue of its founding journal, *Psychoanalytic Dialogues*, appeared at the very beginning of the Decade of the Brain. The relational school distanced itself from medicine and showed no interest in schizophrenic patients; it was very interested in psychosis, but not in psychotic patients. Indeed, articles of relational psychoanalysts were filled with references to "psychotic parts," "psychotic elements," "psychotic defenses," "psychotic dynamics" and similar characterizations, but references to schizophrenic patients were almost totally absent. An exception to this rule formed the dialogue between British analysts and American analysts in 1998, when a British author presented a case study of a psychotic patient and some American analysts published their comments.

The Decade of the Brain brought an exclusive focus on biology even into the international psychoanalytic arena, which up until then seemed to serve as an "asylum" for American psychoanalysts who had wished to retreat from the fashionable developments in neosomatic psychiatry in their own country. In this international arena, too, Freud the scientist was resurrected, and the DSM-III,

10 *Introduction*

as well as other characteristics of descriptive psychiatry, became a common theme in published articles. The only journal in which American psychoanalysts showed pride in psychoanalysis and touted its uniqueness and supremacy over other methods was the *Journal of the Academy*. Unlike the relational psychoanalysts, analysts in the Academy stressed the singularity of the schizophrenic condition. Their main interest was clinical, practical and much less theoretical, and the threats they experienced during the Decade of the Brain were not so much the waning prestige of psychoanalysis but, rather, their own praxis with schizophrenic patients, which was less likely to be covered by the health insurance companies and less supported by medical institutions.

Evidence that analysts in the Academy were effectively protecting their jurisdictional ambition for psychoanalysis to include schizophrenic patients can be found in the numerous case examples from contemporary clinical practice. These were quite different from the "McDonald's-like" approach of somatic psychiatry and exemplified an ethical commitment to the very otherness of the schizophrenic patient. Instead of viewing the schizophrenic as a person who suffers a brain disease, analysts argued in these articles against simplifying the complexity of the schizophrenic condition. They stressed the unique character of the condition, which, although posing great difficulties for the analyst in the clinical encounter, offered a psychic, professional and ethical challenge that could potentiality enrich both the patient and analyst.

The fifth stage of the neosomatic revolution in psychiatry failed as a result of the intervention of a task force of the International Society for the Psychological Treatment of Schizophrenia and Other Psychoses (ISPS) and the publication of a special edition of the *Journal of the Academy* that contained articles supporting psychoanalytic interventions in schizophrenia. These endeavors were a response to the Schizophrenia Patient Outcomes Research Team (PORT) study, published in 1998 and endorsed by governmental authorities, which recommended that psychotherapies based on psychoanalytic principles should never be conducted with schizophrenic patients. The PORT study provoked yet another escalation in the struggle over jurisdiction between psychoanalysis and somatic psychiatry. But, this time, the reaction of psychoanalysts against the PORT study proved both determined and effective. The aforementioned task force not only succeeded in convincing policy makers to change their recommendations, with the result that psychoanalysis was no longer declared to be "dangerous" and "forbidden" as a therapy for schizophrenics, but also obtained a new recommendation that in the therapy of these patients psychopharmacology should not be prescribed to the exclusion of other methods and that psychosocial intervention could be needed just as much.

In the final chapter of this book, "The many faces of Schreber as the face of American psychoanalysis," my perspective is that of a therapist, clinical psychologist and psychoanalyst. I recount the story of one of my patients who resembled Schreber and who suffered not only from schizophrenia but also from the neosomatic treatment of his illness. The chapter goes on to explore the different readings of the case of Judge Schreber by American psychoanalysts, during the four periods covered by this study, to further illuminate the shift in psychoanalytic ethos, theory and practice with respect to schizophrenic madness.

The history of psychoanalysis's jurisdictional struggles was still being written as I was completing this book. Two weeks before writing its conclusion, Dr. Wayne Fenton, a well-known and highly esteemed American, psychoanalytically oriented psychiatrist from the legendary generation of Chestnut Lodge, where psychoanalysis was offered to schizophrenic patients and on which the famous book *I Never Promised You A Rose Garden* was written, was murdered in his practice by a psychotic patient as he tried to persuade the patient to comply with his medication regimen. Psychoanalytic work with serious mental illnesses is a difficult and risky task, which became even more challenging as psychoanalysts left the hospitalized patient. With these patients, more than with others, the ethical demand on the analyst is to carry inside herself the pain producing, unprocessed, destructive, terrifying, hostile, dead, shameful and meaningless aspects of the patient. It is the analyst's task to transform these elements and offer them back to the patient in a processed form so that the patient can grapple with them. Analysts' willingness to host inside their psyche, their minds and their offices such psychotic contents, laden with agonizing anxiety and tormenting psychic pain, is the core of psychoanalytic ethical practice. This becomes much harder and even impossible when psychiatric hospitals, those referred to by the British analyst Henry Rey as "The Brick Mother," continuously disappear and leave the analyst unprotected and uncontained while she takes in psychotic patients.

As is shown throughout this study, psychoanalysis was in danger not only of being excluded from the territory of schizophrenia by external forces, but was just as much a victim of its own internal mechanisms that exposed it to divisions and splits. Only drawing on the profession's own inner resources while staying faithful to its unique qualities as a theory of the mind, a research method and a therapeutic technique might ultimately prove effective in the unending jurisdictional conflict over the treatment of schizophrenia. Therefore, this study offers a cautionary tale in the current scholarly debate in which repeated attempts have been made to take Freud's work – and, notably, the early "project" (1895) – as a specimen of neuroscientific bias. But, for both theoretical and clinical reasons, Freud decided not to follow that path. Psychoanalysis as a method and ethical commitment to patients came into its own only after this realization that minding the gap between the mind and the brain requires one to resist the temptation to forget that Freud ultimately stood by his first intuitions. Schizophrenia is a very complex human condition, and all endeavors to understand it should be encouraged. Thus, although this study found that some strategies analysts have used in their jurisdictional struggles over schizophrenia did a far greater service in keeping psychoanalysis relevant in this field, this conclusion by no means contradicts or undermines, much less disparages, the enormous intellectual efforts of all those whose conceptual strategies fared less well or came at a price.

12 Introduction

This book is written with a deep love for psychoanalysis and with a firm belief in its power to transform psychotic misery into common unhappiness, to paraphrase Freud. There is an urgent need to rethink psychoanalysis's involvement with severe mental illness and to ensure that its healing techniques are not lost to those who are most in need of them.

1 Freud's dual view of schizophrenia (1894–1940)

> *"Finally I confessed to myself that I do not like these sick people, that I am angry at them to feel them so far from me and all that is human."*
>
> (Freud 1928 in Gay 1998, p. 537)

The unique and intriguing paradox inherent in the psychoanalytic approach to schizophrenia is that while it seeks to deepen an understanding of psychosis in general and schizophrenia in particular, it also assigns itself a reduced role in treating schizophrenic patients. This stance is at least partly due to the jurisdictional struggles that have historically occurred between psychoanalysis and the medical professions, especially psychiatry and neurology, which held social and cultural control over the treatment of mental ailments. The roots of this struggle can be traced back to Freud's own efforts to professionalize psychoanalysis and to his writings on psychosis and schizophrenia.

As part of the institutionalization of psychoanalytic knowledge, Freud sought to appropriate for psychoanalysis areas of treatment that, during his time, were under the control of psychiatry and neurology. Thus, in his efforts to ensure a place for psychoanalysis among the trusted methods of healing, he sought to explain all pathological conditions (including psychosis and schizophrenia), using his newly formulated psychoanalytic theory. Although Freud is better remembered for assigning modest aims to psychoanalysis – a method of cure to merely turn neurotic misery into common unhappiness (Freud 1893, p. 305) – a very different ambition is evident in his lesser known writings. In a letter to his lover (and later wife), Martha Bernays, about his future plans, Freud wrote, ". . . and I will cure all the incurable nervous cases . . ." (June 20, 1885 in Gumbrich-Simitis 2011). Because the onus was on psychoanalysis to prove its superiority to the already established fields of psychiatry and neurology, Freud offered a theoretical explanation of schizophrenia and asserted that psychoanalytic theory could explain even the most psychotic condition. However, since schizophrenic patients presented an ever-looming threat of incurability to a young profession in need of proving its efficacy, the "father of psychoanalysis" did not like these patients and did not assume them to be part of the psychoanalytic clinical endeavor (Freud 1928 in Gay 1998).

14 *Freud's dual view of schizophrenia*

Even though some of Freud's patients turned out to be psychotic (one even exhibiting signs of schizophrenia), Freud refused to diagnose them as such, openly insisting that such patients were indeed unable to be treated by psychoanalysis. It seems that in its pursuit of jurisdiction in the mental health field, psychoanalysis included schizophrenic patients, but did so only in theory, excluding these individuals from clinical psychoanalytic treatment.

The jurisdictional struggles of psychoanalysis

One of the most important statements Freud made about the struggle between psychoanalysis and the medical professions to control mental health appeared in his book, titled *The Question of Lay Analysis* (1926). This was written in response to the failed attempt by the Viennese government to enact legislation against charlatanism and quackery. The government's actions were largely an attempt to shut down the popular practice of Theodore Reik, a Viennese analyst who was not a trained or licensed physician. According to Winter (1999), it was through writing this text that Freud took a strategic step in developing psychoanalysis as a profession, by defending those analysts who were not medical doctors but who were adequately trained in the art and science of psychoanalysis. Freud sought to convince the public (both laypeople and professionals) that medical training was not an essential component of analytic expertise. He argued that psychoanalytic understanding is a field of knowledge unto itself and that it cannot be properly practiced by those who are not wholly engrossed in it. Conversely, those who acquired psychoanalytic knowledge through rigorous training in psychoanalytic institutes, through guidance from older and experienced analysts or from years of handling actual cases under the watchful eye of skilled senior analysts were no longer laymen in the field of psychoanalysis (Freud 1926, p. 228).

In his attempt to popularize the perception of psychoanalysis as superior to psychiatry, Freud argued that having psychoanalytic knowledge was better than having medical expertise alone in the treatment of mental illnesses. A qualified analyst, in his opinion, would have a broad knowledge of the history and culture of the field, derived from the analyst's feeling "at home" in many disciplines and enjoying expertise in multiple academic fields. In Freud's opinion, doctors who attempted analysis without receiving appropriate psychoanalytic training were the laymen and thus should seek psychoanalytic training to achieve true competence, regardless of a national or state conferral of a medical degree (Freud 1926). In this same text Freud also warned that psychoanalysis should not be "swallowed up" by medicine,

> to find its last resting-place in a text-book of psychiatry under the heading "Methods of Treatment", alongside of procedures such as hypnotic suggestion, autosuggestion, and persuasion, which, born from our ignorance, have to thank the laziness and cowardice of mankind for their short-lived effects.
>
> (p. 248)

In commenting on the competition between psychoanalysis and the medical professions over the control and treatment of mental illnesses, the Cambridge-based historian of psychoanalysis, John Forrester (1985), argued that psychoanalysis capitalized on an opportune moment in medical history in which the relative professional authority of medicine was weakened. The psychoanalytic movement used this opportunity to advocate its clinical technique and expertise. Psychoanalysis, as presented by Freud, was marketed as being superior to these medical professions in the field of mental health, and, like surgery, psychoanalysis was said to be able to effectively cure a disease rather than simply diagnose it. The package that Freud presented, therefore, was the most complete in terms of what a profession can offer: a personal and personalized service of a trained specialist who could mediate the demands of society, the family and the individual. Based on that claim, the psychoanalytic technique had to prove itself to be a more effective cure than what was being offered by its competitors. Thus, Freud could not afford to analyze schizophrenic patients because they threatened to contradict his principle of cure ("where Id was, there shall Ego be," or "Wo Es war, soll Ich werden") (1933, p. 80). His renunciation of schizophrenic patients left them under the care of medicine, especially psychiatry and neurology, the two professions that treated them somatically. Another reason schizophrenic patients were excluded from psychoanalysis was because it was largely done in private practices, not in medical institutions, where schizophrenic patients were treated.

Aside from garnering public recognition and appreciation of its expertise, a profession must target its services to a specific clientele. Towards this end, Freud took two steps: first, he created a new jurisdiction for psychoanalysis – the "personal problems" of those in the educated, upper middle-class social circles he traveled in. Second, he challenged medical doctors by setting his professional sights on the "hysterical" clientele whom he declared suffered from reminiscence (Winter 1999). He attempted to eject psychiatry and neurology from this jurisdiction by asserting that these disciplines did not truly understand hysteria, and that they, in this regard, were laymen. Freud's categorical assertion that only psychoanalysis could adequately treat hysteria not only attacked the process of psychiatric diagnosis; it went beyond hysteria and questioned the fundamental capability of the medical field, which specialized in bodily ailments, to treat mental disorders. Nonetheless, although Freud questioned psychiatry's ability to render psychological treatment generally, he seemingly did not attempt to claim jurisdiction over psychotic and schizophrenic patients.

In what may have been an additional attempt to distance psychoanalysis from neurology and psychiatry, Freud did write about these disorders, and even coined the term "paraphrenia" to describe the phenomenon that Emil Kraepelin, the father of modern scientific psychiatry, psychopharmacology and genetic psychiatry, referred to as "dementia praecox," and which the Swiss psychiatrist Eugen Bleuler called "schizophrenia." And although Freud used these terms interchangeably and was not overly impressed with psychiatric nosology, in a letter to

16 Freud's dual view of schizophrenia

Carl Jung he criticized the psychiatric term: "I write paranoia and not dementia praecox because I regard the former as a good clinical type and the latter as a poor nosographical term" (Freud 1908, p. 121).

Despite the fact that he applied his theoretical framework to psychotic patients in his struggle with psychiatry over professional jurisdiction, Freud clearly did not want to treat psychotic patients in his clinical practice. In 1913, in his paper "On Beginning the Treatment," Freud suggested that analysts provide a "trial period" of two weeks when beginning treatment with a new patient to ascertain whether he or she is suitable for analysis – namely, if he or she did not exhibit any hint of psychotic tendencies. In such cases, Freud recommended that such a patient (suffering from paraphrenia) would not be an ideal candidate for analysis and should not be treated with his method. When Freud defined the jurisdiction of psychoanalysis, he targeted first the educated, upper-middle classes who suffered from personal conflicts and life stressors. Only secondarily did he include hysterical clients whom he attempted to wrest from the psychiatric camp. Finally, Freud also declared who could not be helped by psychoanalytic treatment, and he purposefully left individuals suffering from schizophrenia within the domain of medical professionals by dint of their inability to be effectively cured by psychoanalysis.

Freud's treatment of psychotic patients

Nonetheless, among Freud's patients were a number who were later diagnosed as psychotic, as well as one diagnosed with schizophrenia. Further, among Freud's writings is a collection of unpublished clinical articles on a number of these patients. In some of these articles, Freud focuses on applying the psychoanalytic method and practice to the treatment of these psychotic and schizophrenic patients. David Lynn (1993), a psychiatrist at Harvard University who examined the entire corpus of Freud's 133 cases, identified one as a case of paranoia and ten as cases of psychosis, despite Freud's own explicit recommendations against treating schizophrenics through psychoanalysis. Lynn's conclusions were based on a perusal of hospital files, interviews with psychiatrists, a discussion by Freud in 1927 in his paper "Fetishism" and Freud's correspondence with Oskar Pfister, a psychoanalyst and Swiss priest, about his analysis of a young psychotic man. As Lynn (1993) noted that the patient, A.B., from a wealthy American family, was diagnosed by Bleuler as suffering from mild schizophrenia. After five years of treatment with Freud, he was hospitalized and diagnosed with chronic paranoid schizophrenia and remained there until his death. Lynn posited that Freud's conflicting stance regarding the treatment of schizophrenics, and particularly his treatment of the young American man, can be viewed from three different perspectives, each associated with different implications for the psychoanalytic treatment of this patient group:

1   Freud as a pessimistic doctor who felt remote from his schizophrenic patient and wanted to terminate his contract with him;

2 Freud as an optimistic psychoanalyst who sought to understand the patient
   through concepts such as resistance, repression and catharsis through analytic revelation; and
3 Freud as a humanist with a personal style of thinking, who believed that even
   if the patient's behavior is "far from normal," his personality is "worth any
   amount of trouble" (Freud 1925 in Lynn, p. 68).

Lynn's article concluded that Freud's recommendation of setting a trial period of
treatment before deciding whether to accept a person in psychoanalysis was established, not to disqualify psychotic patients, as Freud argued, but rather to explore
the interaction between analyst and patient. Freud's affection for A.B., said Lynn,
is what prompted him to continue with his analysis, despite the patient's psychotic symptomatology. While A.B. was not ultimately cured with psychoanalysis
and actually deteriorated over the years (culminating in his spending his final
years in a psychiatric hospital), it was Freud's analysis, according to Lynn, that
prevented him from an even earlier institutionalization. Lynn is unclear whether
A.B.'s decline was due to the fact that Freud terminated treatment in 1930 or
that the deterioration was the *cause* of termination. In any case, despite his own
recommendations, even Freud selected his patients not so much based on diagnosis, but rather on his personal interests and rapport. His famous "Wolf Man"
patient, although diagnosed by Freud as an obsessive neurotic, exhibited delusional thinking, which would fulfill today's diagnostic criteria for schizophrenia.
His psychotic symptoms did not stop Freud from analyzing him (Muslin 1991;
Lang 1997).

The libido theory of schizophrenia

Despite Freud's reluctance to use psychoanalysis to treat psychosis and schizophrenia, he wrote extensively about these illnesses. In the 1890s he viewed neuroses and psychoses as defenses against repressed memories. He saw schizophrenia
as defending against severe forms of conflict and unacceptable desires. For the
early Freud the difference between psychosis and neurosis was based on the types
of defenses being used, as well as the degree to which patients could process their
unacceptable desires.

Freud's libido theory of schizophrenia was published in 1911 in his essay
on Judge Daniel Paul Schreber, titled "Psycho-Analytic Notes on an Autobiographical Account of a Case of Paranoia (Dementia Paranoides)." Freud used the
judge's personal account, *Memoirs of My Nervous Illness* (1903/2000) – which
included a description of his psychosis and hospitalization, his delusional attitude towards his psychiatrist, Dr. Paul Flechsig (who Schreber alleged committed "soul murder") and his erotic relationship with God – to form theories about
psychosis and schizophrenia.

Freud continued to theorize about paranoia and schizophrenia even after he
wrote his famous notes on Schreber (Freud 1914, 1915a), and in three specific
works (1916, 1917, 1922) he claimed there could be one theory to explain the

18 Freud's dual view of schizophrenia

clinical phenomena of schizophrenia. In these papers Freud developed a theory that claimed that sexual and libidinal energy progress from autoeroticism in early childhood (during which a child's body, especially his mouth, anus and genitals, are the source of sexual satisfaction), to narcissism (in which the entire body or self of the child becomes the object of sexual desire) and eventually to a love object (represented by a significant person or caregiver in the child's life). During development, certain amounts of sexual energy may be left behind and may create fixations as a result. Fixation is a condition in which the libidinal energy remains invested in one of the first two stages of development (autoeroticism or narcissism) and, therefore, is not fully available to be invested in other people, objects or ideas (as is necessary for *cathexis*, which requires attachment to an external object).

At this stage of Freud's theory, the phenomenon of experiencing the "end of the world," as described by Schreber and numerous other schizophrenic patients, was a projection of the inner catastrophe, accompanied by the libidinal withdrawal (regression) from the world and its objects. According to Freud, megalomania, manifesting in Schreber as a delusion that God impregnated him to create a new race of people, was a libidinal regression from the world in which one invested oneself entirely in the self rather than the external world (Freud 1911). Due to the nature of libidinal regression, the schizophrenic patient was perceived by Freud as being unable to establish transferential relationships and thus incapable of transferring his libidinal energy from himself to the analyst (Freud 1915a). Since transference plays such a crucial role in the psychoanalytic process, psychotic and schizophrenic patients were, not surprisingly, considered to be poor candidates for psychoanalytic treatment (Freud 1917).

In two 1915 essays, Freud filled in a gap in his theory of schizophrenia by explaining the processes of schizophrenic thinking (Freud 1915b, 1915c). In these articles he developed the notion of reduced cathectic capacity and distinguished between cognitive representations of an object and cognitive representations of the word for that object, suggesting that with schizophrenia, both cognitive representations of the object and the word for that object undergo decathexis. In their attempts to "recover," schizophrenics connect to an object by using its verbal representation. However, they then find themselves committed to and confined by the word in which they invested their energy, as opposed to the object itself, and so they treat words as if they were objects themselves (Freud 1915a).

Although Freud had already formulated his theory of aggression in "Beyond the Pleasure Principle" in 1920, its application to schizophrenia was first explicated in 1925 in his article "Negation." Freud argued that the general wish of psychotics to negate is probably a sign that the instincts were defused due to a withdrawal of the libidinal components. Freud further discussed schizophrenia in his seminal book, *The Ego and the Id*, in 1923, and in two additional articles in 1924: "Neurosis and Psychosis" and "The Loss of Reality in Neurosis and Psychosis." In the latter articles he described a situation in which the ego

Freud's dual view of schizophrenia 19

(i.e., the structure defined as representative of the external world, responding to the "reality principle," attuned to perceptions of the world and associated with logic and sanity) is in conflict with the id (i.e., the structure that contains the instinctual drives and that responds to the "pleasure principle"), the super-ego (i.e., the structure representing one's conscience and morality) and reality itself. The extent of pathology depends upon how well the ego navigates the outside world and is able to silence the id. Freud wrote, ". . . in a neurosis the ego, in its dependence on reality, suppresses a piece of the id (of instinctual life), whereas in a psychosis, this same ego, in the service of the id, withdraws from a piece of reality" (Freud 1924, p. 183). He argued that psychosis is first and foremost an escape from reality, and only secondarily an active restructuring of that reality. The concept of denial (or disavowal) was similarly introduced in these writings as the specific defense used in psychosis to deny reality and instead create one anew (Freud 1924).

Splitting in psychotic patients

In his 1927 article "Fetishism," Freud expressed dissatisfaction with his 1924 analysis and tried to reformulate the difference between neurosis and psychosis by introducing the idea of splitting. He suggested that two contradictory positions exist simultaneously in the psyche: one responds to urges and desires and the other responds to reality. This split, much like denial and disavowal, is often used as a defense by the schizophrenic ego (Freud 1940). In his book, *Moses and Monotheism* (1939), Freud argued for "a state within a state," in which the inaccessible, psychotic part of the personality, with which cooperation is impossible, overcomes the "normal" part of the personality and forces it into its service.

In his later years, Freud's writings on the subject allowed him to question whether schizophrenic patients were in fact more "analyzable," and this position was further studies and developed by followers in the United States and Great Britain. In his book, *An Outline of Psycho-Analysis* (1938), he wrote,

> even in a state so far removed from the reality of the external world as one of hallucinatory confusion, one learns from patients after their recovery that at the time in some corner of their mind (as they put it) there was a normal person hidden, who, like a detached spectator, watched the hubbub of illness go past him.
>
> (p. 202)

With this suggestion of a "nonpsychotic" part nested even in a patient with the most acute psychotic disorder, Freud paved the way to psychoanalysis with psychotic patients.

Freud did not propose a theory for the etiology of schizophrenia, and the theory that he did suggest for its phenomenology (behavioral manifestations)

20   *Freud's dual view of schizophrenia*

never gained traction. At various points, concordant with developments in psychoanalytic theory, Freud's phenomenology was adapted and revised to fit with general psychoanalytic theory. In different places Freud described psychotic and schizophrenic patients as qualitatively similar to neurotic patients, different only in the quantitative nature of behavioral "deviations," and hence included them as possible recipients of psychoanalytic treatment. At other points, however, Freud described them as completely different from neurotic patients, excluding them from the jurisdiction of psychoanalysis.

Two theories of schizophrenia

Preeminent in examining this oscillation in Freud's writings is Nathaniel London (1973a, 1973b), analyst and past president of the Western New England Psychoanalytic Society. London proposed that Freud had a complex, at times contradictory, and unresolved theory of psychosis. Although he viewed Freud as mostly interested in the study of the psychoses and not in their treatment, London traces within Freud's psychoanalytic theory "two theories of schizophrenia," which resulted in two clinical orientations – to treat or not to treat schizophrenic patients psychoanalytically. Based on London's arguments it seems that the theory, which eventually placed schizophrenia within the realm of psychoanalytic treatment, sprouted from a combination of Freud's desire for synthesis and the scientist's tendency to favor one theoretical framework through which many perspectives can be explained (1973a). According to London, a unified theory that was designed for "theoretical and scientific elegance" (p. 6) – seamlessly organizing and synthesizing complex (and perhaps somewhat contradictory) data – also served the purpose of strengthening psychoanalysis as a profession and establishing it as a legitimate scientific and clinical discipline. Abbott (1988) noted that science- and research-based expertise strengthens a given discipline in its pursuit of professional jurisdiction, and Freud used his study of schizophrenia as a means to strengthen his discipline. But schizophrenia became the "Cinderella of psychoanalysis," in the words of New York psychoanalyst Michael Eigen (1993); Freud used schizophrenia for psychoanalysis's growing theory, but did not embrace it as one of the illnesses he aspired to cure.

London suggested that Freud's theory of schizophrenia in fact contained two theories, which he calls the unitary and specific theories (1973a). The unitary theory, according to London, sought to create a formula to explain and account for all mental phenomena. The same formula would apply to understanding psychosis and neurosis (London 1973a): an internal conflict arises (among the agencies of the mental structure, namely, the id, ego and superego), which results in anxiety (aimed at activating defense mechanisms for keeping the material out of consciousness), which in turn creates a defensive struggle (to reduce anxiety), which finally culminates in regression to the point of fixation (i.e., the patient's safe space). The only difference between psychosis and neurosis is the points at which fixation occurs (and where patients return during

Freud's dual view of schizophrenia   21

such a defensive regression), with schizophrenics regressing to earlier development stages, as well as to more primitive defense mechanisms. London's unitary theory of schizophrenia, which he attributed to Freud, rests on the following assertions:

1   Schizophrenic behavior lies on a continuum, from neurotic to psychotic. Although schizophrenic behavior is considered to be more severe than neurotic behavior, it is actually the polarized manifestation of the same behavior.
2   The theory of schizophrenia is part of the theory of unconscious conflict and defenses, and schizophrenia is seen as motivated by unconscious processes. Although traumatic factors are significant in the development of both neuroses and psychoses, the trauma tends to be more significant in schizophrenia, more pronounced, and usually occurs earlier in life. According to this theory, every person possesses the potential to develop schizophrenia, given a certain threshold of internal conflict without a resolution (catharsis). Delusional thinking, hallucinations, increased preoccupation with the body and somatization and narcissism (all common symptoms of schizophrenia) can be explained in terms of conflict and defense. Severity of schizophrenic symptoms can be viewed as stemming from ego weakness and regressed ego functioning, or from an excess of aggressive internal conflicts, which are uniquely different from libidinal conflicts that more often lead to neuroses (London, 1973a).

London assumed that this theory was the springboard from which analytic praxis with schizophrenic patients began.

Freud's specific theory of schizophrenia removed schizophrenic patients from the professional and clinical jurisdiction of psychoanalytic practice and included the following assertions:

1   Schizophrenic behavior is unique and qualitatively different from more usual behaviors, despite the fact that schizophrenic behaviors do occur concurrently with the latter behaviors and, thus, are not easily delineated or demarcated.
2   Among the clinical features considered to be unique to schizophrenia, the schizophrenic's inability to engage in transference is key to the psychoanalyst's inability to successfully analyze such a patient. Every manifestation of schizophrenia is thought to be a withdrawal of libido from representations of objects, and schizophrenic behavior is conceptualized as a reaction to an internal catastrophe that results in a relative loss of connection with reality. Schizophrenic symptomatology (such as delusions and hallucinations) is created to compensate for the psychological deficiency states created by the withdrawal (London, 1973a).

Although London never specified whether Freud himself explicitly favored one of these theories over the other, he did argue that Freud believed the specific theory

22 Freud's dual view of schizophrenia

was superior. London argued that Freud did not easily embrace the idea of a continuum of behavior from neuroses to schizophrenia, and especially as it would apply to clinical treatment (London 1973a). Freud believed that the psychotic's thought disturbances and complicated object relations would not allow patients to free associate effectively or develop transferential relationships, both of which are essential components of the psychoanalytic process. He also highlighted the differential response to danger in schizophrenics, and the excessive presence of primitive thinking and fantasy.

Summary

When Freud (1905) claimed at the outset that psychoanalytical treatment was suitable only for educated patients suffering from neurosis (since their education would motivate them to alleviate their suffering through treatment), who are past adolescence, who are not in any state of psychological emergency and whose mental state is normal, he was seeking patients who were most likely to achieve success in therapy, and who could be pointed to as success stories in his pursuit of professional jurisdiction. Freud was dissatisfied with his controversial 1928 statement to the Hungarian psychoanalyst Istvan Hollos that he "did not like psychotics" (Freud 1928 in Gay 1998). He thought that it was a "strange sort of intolerance" and added, in resignation, "in the course of time, I have ceased to find myself interesting, which is surely incorrect analytically" (p. 537). Yet, as Gay (1998) suggested, he did find himself interesting enough to speculate about his failure: "Might it be the consequence of an ever more evident partisanship for the primacy of the intellect, a hostility toward the id? Or what else?" (p. 537). Thus, it seems that in his efforts to understand his own "symptom," Freud found that the possible cause of his refusal was the "victory of the id" – that is, the primal part of the psyche that includes impulses and desires and that psychoanalysis is designed to subdue as part of its therapeutic promise.

Freud's early decision to include schizophrenia in psychoanalysis only "in theory" but leave these patients outside its practical, clinical endeavor stemmed from his need to establish his psychoanalytic "empire." But near the end of his life, when his empire had already been secured, Freud published two articles, "Analysis Terminable and Interminable" (1937a) and "Constructions in Analysis" (1937b), which opened the door to treating schizophrenic patients. It seems that at that stage in the development of psychoanalysis, in which it had already been institutionalized through international training institutes, associations and publications, and along with Freud's anticipation of his own death, he began to allow himself to admit that his professed treatment was indeed imperfect and, as such, allowed patients previously considered to be a threat to the profession's aspiration to cure to enter the jurisdiction of psychoanalytic treatment. "It almost looks as if analysis were the third of those 'impossible' professions in which one can be sure beforehand of achieving unsatisfying results" (Freud 1937a, p. 248), he wrote in "Analysis Terminable and Interminable," and this sober recognition, along with his realization that the work never ends – so different from his previously unwavering belief in the healing power of his method – allowed Freud to revisit his previous antagonism towards these patients.

Paradoxically, Freud's pessimism and skepticism about the terminability of psychoanalytic treatment led to his optimism about applying psychoanalytic treatment to schizophrenics. In writing about delusional thinking in the essay "Constructions in Analysis," Freud (1937b) asserted that "the essence of it is that there is not only *method* in madness, as the poet has already perceived, but also a fragment of historic truth" (p. 267), and that it may be worthwhile to analyze historical instances of diseases to test assumptions made about its management and treatment. He noted,

> The vain effort would be abandoned of convincing the patient of the error of his delusion and of its contradiction of reality; and, on the contrary, the recognition of its kernel of truth would afford common ground upon which the therapeutic process could develop . . . I believe that we should gain a great deal of valuable knowledge from work of this kind upon psychotics even if it led to no therapeutic success.
>
> (Freud 1937b, pp. 267–268)

Furthermore, in the same article, Freud argued that mankind as a whole "developed delusions which are inaccessible to logical criticism and which contradict reality" (Freud 1937b, p. 269). Freud seemed to have noticed very early that delusions were lurking all around him, and he did not exclude that psychoanalysis, too, was afflicted by thought disorders. As far back as the Schreber case, Freud wrote that only the future would decide whether there was more delusion in his theory than he would like to admit, or whether "there is more truth in Schreber's delusion than other people are as yet prepared to believe" (Freud 1911, p. 79). It seems his disillusionment with the perhaps delusional grandiosity of psychoanalysis in its early days made Freud less "resistant" to bringing psychoanalysis to schizophrenic patients during his last years.

Freud bequeathed to his successors and followers his theoretical division, and one path led to treating schizophrenic patients psychoanalytically, while the other led to excluding them or at least encouraging the implementation of a "more flexible" clinical method with these patients. Freud's attempt to distance psychoanalysis from medicine and its institutions, along with the theoretical duality presented above, are both relevant in mapping the fate of psychoanalytic treatment of schizophrenia in the United States. The next chapter will briefly review the relationship between psychoanalysis and psychiatry in the United States up until the 1960s. It will follow the reception of Freud's ideas in America and argue that the manner in which psychoanalysis was adapted in the United States contradicted *both* of Freud's stances toward the treatment of schizophrenia. Psychoanalysis in the United States underwent medicalization and for a long time was "subsumed"" under psychiatry, which is exactly what

24 Freud's dual view of schizophrenia

Freud had sought to avoid. Concurrently, where Freud cautioned against treating psychoses and schizophrenia, psychoanalysis became both attractive and dominant among American psychiatrists, in part because it offered hope in a field full of despair for the humane treatment of the mentally ill in psychiatric hospitals, which were considered in the first half of the 20th century as the "Shame of the States" (Deutsch 1948).

References

Abbott, A., 1988. *The system of professions. An essay on the division of expert labor.* Chicago, IL: University of Chicago Press.

Deutsch, A., 1948. *The shame of the States.* New York: Harcourt, Brace.

Eigen, M., 1993. *The psychotic core.* Northvale, NJ: Jason Aronson.

Forrester, J., 1985. Contracting the disease of love: Authority and freedom in the origins of psychoanalysis. In: W. F. Bynum, R. Porter, and M. Shepherd, eds., *The anatomy of madness: Essays in the history of psychiatry*, Volume 1. London: Tavistock. pp. 255–256.

Freud, S., 1893. The psychotherapy of hysteria from *Studies in hysteria*. In: *The standard edition of the complete psychological works of Sigmund Freud*, Volume 2. London: Hogarth Press. pp. 253–305.

Freud, S., 1905/1904. On psychotherapy. In: *The standard edition of the complete psychological works of Sigmund Freud*, Volume 7. London: Hogarth Press. pp. 263–268.

Freud, S., 1908. Letter from Sigmund Freud to C.G. Jung, February 17, 1908. In: *The Freud/Jung letters: The correspondence between Sigmund Freud and C.G. Jung.* Princeton, NJ: Princeton University Press. pp. 57–59.

Freud, S., 1911. Psycho-analytic notes on an autobiographical account of a case of paranoia (dementia paranoides). In: *The standard edition of the complete psychological works of Sigmund Freud*, Volume 21. London: Hogarth Press. pp. 1–82.

Freud, S., 1913. On beginning the treatment. In: *The standard edition of the complete psychological works of Sigmund Freud*, Volume 12. London: Hogarth Press. pp. 121–144.

Freud, S., 1914. On narcissism. In: *The standard edition of the complete psychological works of Sigmund Freud*, Volume 14. London: Hogarth Press. pp. 67–102.

Freud, S., 1915a. The unconscious. In: *The standard edition of the complete psychological works of Sigmund Freud*, Volume 14. London: Hogarth Press. pp. 159–215.

Freud, S., 1915b. A metapsychological supplement to the theory of dreams. In: *The standard edition of the complete psychological works of Sigmund Freud*, Volume 14. London: Hogarth Press. pp. 217–235.

Freud, S., 1915c. A case of paranoia running counter to the psycho-analytic theory of the disease. In: *The standard edition of the complete psychological works of Sigmund Freud*, Volume 14. London: Hogarth Press. pp. 261–272.

Freud, S., 1916. Introductory lectures on psycho-analysis. In: *The standard edition of the complete psychological works of Sigmund Freud*, Volume 15. London: Hogarth Press. pp. 1–240.

Freud, S., 1917. Introductory lectures on psycho-analysis. In: *The standard edition of the complete psychological works of Sigmund Freud*, Volume 16. London: Hogarth Press. pp. 241–463.

Freud, S., 1920. Beyond the pleasure principle. In: *The standard edition of the complete psychological works of Sigmund Freud*, Volume 18. London: Hogarth Press. pp. 1–64.

Freud, S., 1922. Some neurotic mechanisms in jealousy, paranoia and homosexuality. In: *The standard edition of the complete psychological works of Sigmund Freud*, Volume 18. London: Hogarth Press. pp. 221–232.

Freud, S., 1923. The ego and the id. In: *The standard edition of the complete psychological works of Sigmund Freud*, Volume 19. London: Hogarth Press. pp. 1–66.

Freud, S., 1924. The loss of reality in neurosis and psychosis. In: *The standard edition of the complete psychological works of Sigmund Freud*, Volume 19. London: Hogarth Press. pp. 181–188.

Freud, S., 1925. Negation. In: *The standard edition of the complete psychological works of Sigmund Freud*, Volume 19. London: Hogarth Press. pp. 233–240.

Freud, S., 1926. The question of lay analysis. In: *The standard edition of the complete psychological works of Sigmund Freud*, Volume 20. London: Hogarth Press. pp. 177–258.

Freud, S., 1927. Fetishism. In: *The standard edition of the complete psychological works of Sigmund Freud*, Volume 21. London: Hogarth Press. pp. 147–158.

Freud, S., 1933. New introductory lectures on psycho-analysis. In: *The standard edition of the complete psychological works of Sigmund Freud*, Volume 22. London: Hogarth Press. pp. 1–182.

Freud, S., 1937a. Analysis terminable and interminable. In: *The standard edition of the complete psychological works of Sigmund Freud*, Volume 23. London: Hogarth Press. pp. 209–254.

Freud, S., 1937b. Constructions in analysis. In: *The standard edition of the complete psychological works of Sigmund Freud*, Volume 23. London: Hogarth Press. pp. 255–270.

Freud, S., 1938. An outline of psychoanalysis. In: *The standard edition of the complete psychological works of Sigmund Freud*, Volume 23. London: Hogarth Press. pp. 139–208.

Freud, S., 1939. Moses and monotheism. In: *The standard edition of the complete psychological works of Sigmund Freud*, Volume 23. London: Hogarth Press. pp. 1–38.

Freud, S., 1940. Splitting of the ego in the process of defence. In: *The standard edition of the complete psychological works of Sigmund Freud*, Volume 23. London: Hogarth Press. pp. 271–278.

Gay, P., 1998. *Freud: A life for our time.* New York: Norton.

Gumbrich-Simitis, I., 2011. *Seeds of core psychoanalytic concepts. On the courtship letters of Sigmund Freud and Martha Bernays.* Contribution to the Opening Ceremony of the 47th Congress of the International Psychoanalytical Association. Mexico City, 3–6 August 2011.

Lang, H., 1997. Obsessive-compulsive disorders in neurosis and psychosis. *Journal of the American Academy of Psychoanalysis and Dynamic Psychiatry*, 25, pp. 143–150.

London, N. J., 1973a. An essay on psychoanalytic theory: Two theories of schizophrenia. Part I: Review and critical assessment of the development of the two theories. *International Journal of Psychoanalysis*, 54, pp. 169–178.

London, N. J., 1973b. An essay on psychoanalytic theory: Two theories of schizophrenia. Part II: Discussion and restatement of the specific theory of schizophrenia. *International Journal of Psychoanalysis*, 54, pp. 179–193.

26 *Freud's dual view of schizophrenia*

Lynn, D. J., 1993. Freud's analysis of A.B., a psychotic man, 1925–1930. *Journal of the American Academy of Psychoanalysis*, 21, pp. 63–78.

Muslin, H. L., 1991. The role of the transference in the wolf man case. *Journal of the American Academy of Psychoanalysis and Dynamic Psychiatry*, 19, pp. 294–306.

Schreber, D. P., 1903. *Memoirs of my nervous illness*. New York: New York Review Book.

Winter, S., 1999. *Freud and the institution of psychoanalytic knowledge*. Stanford, CA: Stanford University Press.

2 Ravens in white coats
The medicalization of American psychoanalysis (1909–1954)

> *In Europe I felt as though I were despised; but over there I found myself received by the foremost men as an equal. As I stepped on to the platform at Worcester to deliver my Five Lectures on Psycho-Analysis it seemed like the realization of some incredible day-dream: psycho-analysis was no longer a product of delusion, it had become a valuable part of reality.*
>
> (Sigmund Freud, "An Autobiographical Study" 1925, p. 52)

> *. . . the American and psychoanalysis are often so ill-adapted for one another that one is reminded of Grabbe's parable, "as though a raven were to put on a white shirt."*
>
> (Sigmund Freud, in a letter to Franz Wittels; Wittels 1928/1995, p. 130)

Freud was ambivalent not only about psychiatry and psychosis; the father of psychoanalysis also had a complex relationship with America and the American (Falzeder 2012). On one hand, Freud believed America would transform psychoanalysis from a "delusion" into a viable part of professional and scientific reality, but on the other, he was anxious about American culture, saying: "These primitives have little interest in science not directly convertible into practice." He was mostly concerned about what he found "the worst of the American way"; that is, "their so-called broadmindedness through which they even feel themselves to be magnanimous and superior to us narrow-minded Europeans . . ." (Freud in Falzeder 2012, p. 92). Freud's hopes and concerns about the future of psychoanalysis in America were realized to a large extent: although his ideas became a conspicuous part of American culture, psychoanalysis in the United States was transformed into a dynamic and eclectic branch of psychiatry, and, in the name of pragmatism, American practitioners turned psychoanalysis into merely another method of treating the severely mentally ill – whose treatment up to that point had repeatedly failed.

Despite these close encounters between psychoanalysis and schizophrenic patients, made possible by American eclecticism and pragmatism, it was precisely these two tendencies that were also responsible for the decline in American psychoanalysts' encounters with these patients. The broad-mindedness

28 *Ravens in white coats*

that characterized dynamic psychiatry, the American scion of psychiatry and psychoanalysis, created confused identities for both professions and led to a retreat and then a renewed, narrower definition of both specialties. Psychoanalysis withdrew to psychoanalytic institutes and private practices, moving away from hospitals and schizophrenic patients and focusing on the original clientele – those with "personal problems," or the "worried well." In an effort to remove itself from the dominance of psychoanalysis, which threatened its medical and scientific identity, psychiatry withdrew to its natural environment – the field of somatic medicine – and focused on the use of antipsychotic medication as the primary method of treatment. As a result of its "abandonment" by its "parents," dynamic psychiatry, which had become the psychoanalytic treatment of primarily schizophrenic patients in hospital settings, withered and shrunk.

Early psychiatry in medical institutions

The medicalization of American psychoanalysis occurred as part of its appropriation by psychiatry on American shores. Andrew Abbott (1988), who studied the development of psychiatry in America, explained that in the mid-19th century, the insane from workhouses and jails were gradually transferred to institutions created especially for them. These institutions, first called "lunatic asylums," then "mental hospitals" and eventually "mental health centers," were originally created by people who were not medical doctors. Nonetheless, these institutions were led and administered by medical men. Although two specialties treated the same group of patients during the 19th century – patients whose problem seemed to be "in their mind" – neurology defined these patients by their lack of response to standard treatment, while psychiatry defined them as incipiently insane. Unlike other fields of medicine, psychiatry was not based on diagnosing a specific problem and treating it; rather, it concerned itself solely with treatment. Yet the moral treatment it offered to the insane, promising complete healing of insanity if the patient adhered to a detailed regimentation of activities, emotions and the environment, proved to be a complete failure towards the end of the 19th century. However, since there was no effective alternative to their prescribed treatment, psychiatrists retained jurisdiction over treatment of the mentally ill. The national decision to create larger centers to care for these patients revolutionized the profession, leading to the growth of another class of physicians, the assistant physicians, who carried out the medical work in those asylums under the guidance of the superintendent of these institutions, which were psychiatrists (Abbott 1988, p. 22). Thus, most psychiatrists were able to move within the profession and distance themselves from the asylums, where the cure of the insane proved impossible to accomplish. Abbott, who believed psychiatrists had many good reasons to move out of the asylums, not least because "the insane had proved resiliently intractable to half a century of serious scientific work" (p. 294), detailed psychiatrists' justification of invading other professional jurisdictions, such as neurology, in order to prevent the

Ravens in white coats   29

supposed (yet never proved) degeneration of less severe pathology into psychosis. By assigning itself to the treatment of disorders of the mind outside lunatic asylums, psychiatry became a subspecialty of neurology.

The situation in Europe was not much different. While the experience and knowledge accumulated over the years in clinical psychiatry led to the establishment of the first system of psychiatric classification and diagnosis, psychiatry still lacked an overarching theory of mental illness and method of cure and had to rely on other disciplines.

Locating mental illness in the body

Nathan Hale (1971, 1995), in his extensive research on psychoanalysis in the United States, found that neurology, which began its ascendency in the United States in the 1870s, following the Civil War, held jurisdiction over mental illness for a long while through its somatic approach, which represented "scientific purity." Armed with a high socioeconomic status and upscale professional training from prestigious European or American medical schools, neurologists claimed the important discovery of localization of brain functions. Despite the fact that this discovery actually came from Europe, "ubi est morbus" (namely, "where is the disease?") became the mode of inquiry within neurological research centers in America. Medicine was advancing with the help of tissue staining, better and more powerful microscopes and the discovery of bacteria, and it seemed only natural to extend the somatic model to mental illness. According to the neurology of the day, paranoia was the result of irreversible general atrophy of the brain, mania and melancholia were caused by cortical irritation; hallucinations from abnormal subcortical functions; psychotic symptoms of nerve weakness (for example, the inability to concentrate) was seen as resulting from cerebral malfunction (Hale 1971, p. 52); and so forth. Predispositions to mental illness, according to neurologists who adhered to the somatic model, resulted from inferior hereditary genetics.

The emphasis on the genetic basis of mental illness spawned two movements with radically different approaches: the mental hygiene movement and the eugenics movement. The perception that a human being can overcome or neutralize inherited traits or tendencies – through early training in healthy physical habits, control of passions, avoidance of unnecessary stress and brain training – was the basis for the mental hygiene movement. Founded in 1908, its goal was the promotion of research on causes of mental illness, and the movement advocated for better hospitals for the mentally ill. Meanwhile, the eugenics ("well-born") movement, the brainchild of Sir Francis Galton, asserted that nature was more important than nurture in development. From 1905 to 1917, when the influence of American eugenics psychiatry reached its peak, it was suggested that people with chronic mental illness should be sterilized so their "poisonous germ plasm" would prevent from spreading like a plague (Whitaker 2002). While both movements were based on the idea that madness had a genetic origin, they advocated

30 *Ravens in white coats*

radically different approaches to treatment, with one emphasizing prevention along with environmental and social interventions, and the other advocating severe physical treatment aimed at the elimination of madness and, occasionally, the elimination of the patients themselves.

American psychiatry was challenged to offer an alternative to these somatic approaches (Hale 1971, p.83) and it appears that this challenge motivated psychiatry's flirtation with psychoanalysis. Although American psychiatrists expressed interest in psychoanalysis early on, 1911 is considered to be the official year in which psychoanalysis was received in America, commencing with Freud's visit in 1909 to Clark University and followed by the establishment of the first two American psychoanalytic associations. Both Hale (1971) and Abbott (1988) agreed that American psychiatry incorporated psychoanalysis into its practice in reaction to the prevailing notions concerning the neurological and biological bases of mental illness. But Hale (1971) believed that psychiatrists did so in an attempt to address hospital patients' distress when somatic treatment failed to fully effect a cure. Abbott (1988), however, believed that while distress was a concern of psychiatrists, they turned to psychoanalysis primarily as a means to move out from insane asylums, break away from the dominance of neurology and claim jurisdiction over a domain of less severe pathology – those suffering from personal problems. Both approaches taken by psychiatry eventually created two types of American practitioners: those who left the hospital and later created ego psychology, the American version of psychoanalysis used to treat the neurotic population, and those who remained in the insane asylums and used psychoanalysis as an alternative to somatic treatment of severe mental illness, thus creating dynamic psychiatry.

Freud and American eclecticism

In line with Freud's concerns and as Hale (1971) suggested, psychoanalysis in America became simpler, more didactic, more moralistic and more popular (p. 332). Although Freud and the American psychiatrists held similar positions about many subjects (for example, development of the individual parallels the development of society, progress will be achieved through scientific and cultural achievements made by extraordinary people, conflict is an unavoidable aspect of any evolutionary process), there was a large theoretical gap between Freud and the eclectic Americans on the subject of drives and instincts. For Freud, drives could neither be domesticate nor tamed; for America's eclectic psychiatrists, however, who struggled over professional jurisdiction and had to prove therapeutic efficacy, it was exactly the "taming" of these drives or instincts that brought about healing. With this theory, eclectic psychiatrists working in hospitals not only attacked neurology over its unproven theories of localization, but also claimed that, unlike neurologists, they were in fact able to cure mental illness. Thus, Adolf Meyer, the Swiss born psychiatrist who is considered to be one of the fathers of modern American psychiatry, criticized the chronicity that

Kraepelin's classification (an early system of classification of mental illness) argued for and claimed that after many years of mental illness, patients had been healed by dynamic psychiatry and had become rational citizens contributing to society (Hale 1971, p. 86). Like Meyer, Abraham Brill, an Austrian-born psychiatrist who worked under Meyer in the New York state psychiatric hospital system and was a prominent proponent of psychoanalysis in the United States (even translating some of Freud's writings into English), claimed that psychoanalysis could offer hope to cure these mental illnesses. Brill cited a neurologist's report that noted that "the patient is stupid, lazy, and demented" and claimed that many of these reports concluded with "the patient died suddenly" (Hale 1971, p. 86). Brill argued against rigid classifications grounded in the somatic perception of schizophrenia, which offered few, if any, effective treatment options. Other psychiatrists also criticized somatic pessimism and advocated for psychotherapeutic approaches. William Alanson White, of St. Elizabeth's Hospital in Washington, D.C., rejected the neurologists' theory of localization of mental disorders and undermined the trusted somatic understanding of psychopathology and madness, instead promoting the notion that not only the brain, but the entire person should be of interest to the doctor when considering a cure (Hale 1971, p. 71).

Opposing views of neurologists and psychiatrists

Thus, at the time of Freud's lecture at Clark University in 1909, American neurology and psychiatry were divided into two camps: those who took a somatic approach (especially neurologists, whose narrow vision of psychological problems focused mostly on brain functioning) and those who took an eclectic systemic approach (mainly psychiatrists) who were advocating psychotherapies. According to Abbott (1988), this dispute was largely about the degree to which mental illness had a somatic explanation (pp. 300–308). However, for Hale (1971) the debate was more fundamental, with one side relying on somatic explanations of mental illness and the other on a broader, more systemic explanation of pathology that incorporated body and mind (pp. 71–98). Since psychoanalysis was primarily used by dynamic psychiatrists, it became, just as Freud predicted, one of many treatment modalities for the mentally ill. As such, research funds (for example, at the Menninger Foundation of Topeka, Kansas) that supported studies and treatment of the mentally ill simultaneously promoted both psychoanalytic treatment and radical somatic treatments, such as electroconvulsive therapy (ECT). In the same vein, psychiatrists such as Edward Strecker (who ran the Pennsylvania Hospital) performed lobotomies (Whitaker 2002, p. 107–139), a notorious treatment method for schizophrenic patients (depicted in such memorable films as *One Flew Over the Cuckoo's Nest*), while using psychoanalysis to explain the underlying conflicts and dynamics in which the illness was rooted (Strecker 1944).

In the United States, their link to psychiatry allowed American psychoanalysts entry to psychiatric hospitals (for example, at Johns Hopkins and the Phipps Clinic

32 *Ravens in white coats*

in Baltimore, St. Elizabeth's Hospital in Washington, D.C., and the state hospitals of New York) and, thus, access to the schizophrenic population. Moreover, hospitals affiliated with universities exposed to psychoanalytic influence began to explore psychological factors associated with somatic influences and began using psychoanalytic concepts to explain symptoms of schizophrenic madness. The influence of psychoanalysis on psychiatric training was evident in the appearance, for the first time, of a chapter on psychopathology and psychoanalysis in a psychiatric textbook, called *Diseases of the Nervous System* (1915). Written by William Alanson White and Smith Ely Jelliffe (a preeminent psychiatrist who helped popularize psychoanalysis and psychosomatic medicine in the United States in the early 20th century), the book criticized genetic theories of mental illness, claiming that they weakened therapeutic efforts and were vague, contradictory and not based on the scientific method (p. iii). Alongside this seminal publication, psychoanalysis became central to the field of mental illness between 1909 and 1917, and at least 24 references related to psychoanalysis appeared in the *American Journal of Insanity*, with 12 of them generated by psychoanalysts (Hale 1971, p. 448).

After World War I, many hospitals and clinics were established to train professionals in the psychoanalytic approach. Hale (1995) argued that encounters with soldiers suffering from "shell shock" led medical personnel to believe that only those able to engage with the irrational aspects of human nature, to which these soldiers had been exposed during the war, could perform psychiatric services.

Three factors contributed to the complex relationships developed between medicine and psychoanalysis during the treatment of soldiers returning from the war: a lack of systematic psychoanalytic training for medical doctors, the eclecticism that characterized the American version of psychoanalysis and the popularity of psychoanalysis among laymen (Hale 1995, p. 27). Although Hale believed that the distancing of American psychoanalysis from its Freudian roots was due to the development of the new ego psychology, which promised a more "scientific" approach to psychoanalysis, it seems that its transformation into "psychiatric psychoanalysis," also known as "dynamic psychiatry," also contributed to this trend.

Although dynamic psychiatry is based on the investigation of emotional processes, their sources and the underlying mental structures, it is not purely psychoanalytic. According to Elizabeth Roudinesco (1999), a French historian and analyst, dynamic psychiatry was actually the name given to the many schools of thought recommending dynamic treatments of mental illness – namely, those that included transference between the doctor and patient. Nevertheless, dynamic psychiatry, which grew out of medicine, preferred mental processes over physical explanations of psychological phenomena and was predicated upon four models that explain the human personality and psyche (p. 24):

1   The nosographic model is an outgrowth of psychiatry, which enables a universal sorting of diseases and pathology.
2   The psychotherapeutic model, a remnant of clinical antiquity, attaches efficacy of treatment to suggestive power.

3 The philosophical/phenomenological model allows for an understanding of the meaning of mental disorder in light of the subject's existential experience (conscious and unconscious).

4 The cultural model attempts to discover the diversity in mental processes based on social, religious, and anthropological understanding of the subject.

Opposing views of dynamic and ego psychology

The schism in American psychoanalysis – between dynamic psychiatry and ego psychology – became more pronounced in the 1930s. As a result of the Great Depression, dynamic psychiatry became stronger because it offered a pragmatic response to difficulties of daily living. However, ego psychology gained momentum as a result of the great migration of European analysts (especially from Vienna) to the United States after the rise of Nazism. The "psychoanalytic civil wars," as Hale (1995, chapter 6) called them, are relevant in exploring the relationship between psychiatry, psychoanalysis and the psychoses. American analysts who opposed analysis by those who were not medical doctors claimed that only physicians could diagnose whether a patient's symptoms were due to psychological neurosis or an organic illness such as a brain tumor, and hence only those with medical training would be able to differentiate between neurosis and psychosis. Using this argument in their resolution about membership, the American Association for Psychoanalysis enacted new laws in 1938 dictating that only those who had completed a psychiatric residency at an accredited institution could become members. Thus, the psychoses were used as an argument against lay analysts, even though physician analysts were already showing less interest in this group of patients.

The second psychoanalytical civil war, which broke out in 1939 and ended in a split between the orthodox/classical psychoanalysts and the revisionists who established their own training organizations, was set against a similar background. Classical psychoanalysis, or ego psychology as it was called, was threatened by a prominent eclectic psychoanalyst, Harry Stack Sullivan, who was inextricably linked with the view that psychoanalysis could be used to treat schizophrenia. A psychiatrist who worked in the hospitals of Baltimore and Washington, D.C., Sullivan established with other psychoanalysts an informal group called "The Zodiac Club," which represented the neo-Freudian trends later established through institutes such as the American Academy of Psychoanalysis and Dynamic Psychiatry.

Despite the disagreements between the classical American and revisionist psychoanalysts, both supported the medicalization of psychoanalysis and its joining with medicine. Psychiatry embraced psychoanalysis after it was used to help care for the shock victims of World War I, and the psychodynamic model was adapted to view emotional factors as the cause of many diseases, from ulcers to schizophrenia. The psychiatric establishment began using experimental psychoanalytic

34 *Ravens in white coats*

psychotherapy in treating psychoses, and psychoanalysis became an important subdiscipline in medical schools. Due to this bond between psychiatry and psychoanalysis, from the 1930s to the 1950s psychoanalysts held prestigious positions at universities and hospital departments (Shorter 1997). At that time all department directors of psychiatry argued that the psychodynamic framework should be the dominant one in the treatment of psychiatric patients (Grob 1991). Psychoanalysts held directorships of 60% of psychiatric departments in the United States, required texts read in these wards were psychoanalytic and all medical schools (save one) taught psychoanalysis. Analysts were also dominant in the American Psychiatric Association, and in the postwar years, the senior positions in the organization (including the presidency) were held by psychoanalysts.

Can psychoanalysis cure severe mental illness?

Although, and perhaps due to the fact that psychoanalysis has gained so much political strength in psychiatry, its success in curing mental illness was put to the test. In 1934, with the establishment of a special division for psychoanalysis in the American Psychiatric Association, the success of psychoanalysis in treating psychoses became the subject of debate (Shorter 1997). While a psychiatric unit without psychoanalysis was considered to be incomplete, psychoanalysts had difficulty working with psychotics. This was partially due to the nature of hospital work: each psychiatrist was responsible for a caseload averaging 30 patients, which did not allow for proper and intensive psychoanalytic treatment. Moreover, the budgets in hospitals were too low to attract psychoanalysts to work there (Leveille 2002).

Although Freud was concerned with American pragmatism, Hale (1971) asserted that the American pragmatists William James, Charles Pierce and John Dewey had a positive impact on adopting psychoanalysis into psychiatric eclecticism. This type of psychiatry provided an understanding of the role of cognitive skills, such as language and attention, the importance of the relationship between therapist and patient and the role of community in mental health treatment. The perception that patients did not suffer from a disease, but rather from a syndrome that developed during specific life experiences, led Sullivan, for example, to determine that there is not as sharp a gap between the healthy and the schizophrenic as was previously conceived, and that schizophrenia could be healed through psychotherapy. Sullivan claimed that the pessimistic view psychoanalysis held with regard to schizophrenia resulted not from the condition itself, but rather from the fact that patients became resistant to treatment and change due to their extended stay in an institutional system. In Sullivan's version of psychodynamic therapy, which included the role of the environment in creating mental disease, psychiatry began to reject Freud, and especially his hypothesis that schizophrenics were unable to create transferential relations. Sullivan argued that psychosis was a human process, a psychobiological response to a life situation, and his famous dictum became the premise of his "new American theory" of schizophrenia, positing, "we shall assume that everyone is much more simply human than otherwise, be we happy and successful, contented and detached, miserable and mentally disordered, or whatever . . ." (Sullivan 1940/2006).

Hale (1995) argued that the success of psychoanalysis in the United States was based upon its provision of timely instruments to deal with two crises in American society in the early 20th century: the crisis in sexual morality and the state of mental health, in which a large population of vulnerable people suffering from nervous and mental disorders were being neglected (p. 4). Therefore, when Sullivan asserted that mental illnesses were caused by American sexual-religious moralism and that psychoanalysis could bring relief to and cure these illnesses, he provided a response to both pressing problems. Because medical theories of mental illness were not sufficiently developed to present an etiology of brain disorder, and because no therapeutic response to these disorders was suggested, Sullivan's emphasis on environmental factors (which can be changed) ensured that the American version of psychoanalysis would be considered the key to correcting the problem and curing the patients. If the source of the problem was external (i.e., social and environmental in nature), then dynamic psychiatry, which views these factors as central to both creating mental illness and treating it, would have a solution superior to those offered by other medical specialties. American psychiatry and its version of psychoanalysis had put more emphasis on society, targeting social factors as primary causes of disorders of the mind, thus distancing itself both from the more orthodox version of Freudian psychoanalysis and from the more somatically oriented medical disciplines.

Sullivan's version of psychoanalysis was not easily accepted by either the *Journal of American Psychiatry* or classical institutions of psychoanalysis. In the spirit of establishing neo-Freudian psychoanalysis within psychiatry, a new magazine called *Psychiatry* was published in 1936. This journal was associated with the Washington School of Psychiatry, which trained doctors, anthropologists and psychologists to become psychoanalysts. It was apparent that Sullivan's interpersonal psychoanalysis, which tried to move away from medicine and attach itself to other areas of the social sciences, distanced itself from medicine and eventually from psychoanalysis with its emphasis on the internal unconscious world of drives and phantasies. Sullivan and his successors greatly promoted psychodynamic therapy for schizophrenics in the United States through work in hospitals such St. Elizabeth's and Sheppard Pratt, where Sullivan established a department of psychoanalysis in 1920 that pioneered treatment for schizophrenic patients. But the question of whether dynamic psychiatry gave up on the essence of psychoanalysis in favor of understanding the social role in the development and treatment of mental disorders remains to this day.

Eclectic dynamic psychiatry was strengthened during World War II and reached its peak of influence in the postwar years. In 1946, significant government funds were funneled to the National Institute of Mental Health (NIMH) in Washington, D.C., with the purpose of training psychiatrists to treat veterans. NIMH was established in 1949, when President Truman signed the National Mental Health Act, and was officially recognized as one of the four National Institutes of Health. One example of governmental support of psychoanalysis was the transfer

36 Ravens in white coats

of money from the NIMH to various training programs for psychoanalytically oriented psychiatrists. Through such programs, the Menninger Clinic, Yale University and the University of California in Los Angeles (where analysts ran the department of psychiatry) received generous financial support from NIMH.

Despite financial support from NIMH, many psychiatrists began to distance themselves from psychiatric hospitals, the very heart of psychiatric jurisdiction, as private clinics began to flourish. By 1947, more than half of American psychiatrists were working in private clinics, a 20% to 30% increase from 1940. By 1958, only 16% of American Psychiatric Association members worked as full-time employees in psychiatric hospitals (Hale 1995, p. 339). Psychiatrists who practiced in the public sector earned significantly less than those in the private sector and worked in psychiatric hospitals with the chronically sick and elderly, which was both more difficult and less profitable. Most of the public psychiatric hospitals were in rural areas far away from the universities and the analytic institutes, and treatment in these institutions was considered to be second- and third-class treatment. As the years passed, psychiatrists continued to distance themselves from psychiatric hospitals, and the rise of community mental health contributed to this trend. For the most part, those left to treat schizophrenic patients in state psychiatric hospitals were the older somatic psychiatrists who mainly used ECT and medications as their methods of treatment (Hale 1995).

Nonetheless, some private hospitals became home to psychoanalytic treatment for schizophrenia, where it was further developed and refined. According to Hale (1995), the continued investment of psychoanalysis in the treatment of schizophrenic patients stemmed from a belief that the somatic treatments that were in use at the time – such as insulin coma, ECT and lobotomies – had questionable results, and that there was no clear protocol for the use of these treatments. Psychoanalytic psychotherapy was perceived by psychoanalysts as superior to somatic treatments for schizophrenia, since the latter were successful only in symptom reduction, whereas psychoanalysis had the potential to remove the conflict that led to disorder and to help break psychopathological patterns while regenerating psychological powers to regain lost ground (Arieti 1959).

Even if dynamic psychiatry in America tried to keep schizophrenic patients within its jurisdiction, most practitioners working in hospital settings found that Freud's psychoanalytic technique was often not applicable to their patients. As institutionalized schizophrenic patients challenged the classical psychoanalytic method, other forms of treatment were developed for these patients. From the variety of treatments, which still considered themselves to be psychoanalytic, two controversial approaches in particular formed the basis for the attack on the use of psychoanalysis to treat schizophrenic patients. These approaches seem to have developed as part of the jurisdictional struggle between psychoanalysis and somatic medical psychiatry. Both approaches were struggling with conventional medical classification, both believed that something in the medical atmosphere (e.g., the hospitals) turned schizophrenia into a chronic condition and both blurred the lines between "sick" and "healthy." One of these controversial analytic approaches to schizophrenia was developed by John Rosen (Hale 1995).

Ravens in white coats 37

A psychiatrist and an analyst, Rosen believed that it was possible to "penetrate" the world of the schizophrenic patient and communicate with the person's unconscious through direct interpretation. Rosen blurred the lines between "sick" and "healthy" and suggested that schizophrenic symptoms could be decoded in the same way that symbolism in dreams is deciphered. He believed that given the right environmental stressors, any person could become schizophrenic. Unconcerned with diagnostic categories, he believed that mental illness only rarely had a physical basis. Rosen understood Kraepelin's conceptualization of the deterioration and decay in schizophrenia (dementia praecox) not as part of the illness itself but instead as resulting from the patient's long years of being institutionalized in a psychiatric setting. For Rosen, psychosis is like a nightmare, and analytic interpretation helps to awaken the "dreaming schizophrenic" (pp. 265–266).

Frieda Fromm-Reichmann, a German-born American psychiatrist, mostly known as Dr. Fried in Hannah Green's (Joanne Greenberg's) novel *I Never Promised You a Rose Garden* (1964), proposed yet another alternative psychoanalytic technique for analysts working in psychiatric hospitals with schizophrenic patients. A prominent figure at Chestnut Lodge, a private psychiatric hospital in Rockville, Maryland, Fromm-Reichmann's technique deviated from "classical psychoanalysis," as well as from standard medical conceptualization. Fromm-Reichmann claimed that analysts, unlike their fellow professionals in other medical fields, did not heal a disease; rather, they were like "mothers raising children" (Fromm-Reichmann 1950). For Fromm-Reichmann, judicious doses of affection and the creation of a primary attachment could serve the patient during the acute stage of the illness. The book written by Fromm-Reichmann's patient was a testament to the success of this approach. The work at Chestnut Lodge was an ambitious attempt to use the psychodynamic approach to psychiatry, preserving the framework of analytic treatment while altering the technique as necessary. In this hospital directed by psychoanalysts, residents were also candidates in analytic institutes in Washington, D.C., and Baltimore, and the goal for them was nothing less than recovery. The means to that end was that they received intensive psychoanalytic therapy with minimal use of psychopharmacology or restraints. The "Lodge" was a hospital in that it was identified with the medical establishment, but unlike other hospitals, distinctions between doctors and patients were blurred, a process that progressively weakened the stature of psychoanalysis in the treatment of psychoses in America. The attempt to characterize themselves as different from somatic psychiatrists, as well as from classical psychoanalysts, brought the psychoanalytic psychiatrists to blur the lines between "healthy" and "sick," between "analyst" and "mother" and between psychoanalysis and other forms of psychotherapy. *The Mental Hospital* (1954), written by psychiatrist Alfred Stanton and sociologist Morris Schwartz, posited that the Lodge developed a psychoanalytic subculture in which the belief that "everyone is crazy" obscured the reality of the disability of mental disease. Even though their research had shown that patients were benefitting from treatment (even chronic patients showed significant improvements and developed increased insight into at least some of their symptoms), the price of hospitalization at the Lodge was three times the

38 *Ravens in white coats*

average family salary ($850 per month in 1950), and only wealthy patients were able to afford it. Although there were attempts to implement psychoanalytic psychotherapy with psychotic patients in some public hospitals in New York, Massachusetts, California and Kansas, psychotherapy was given to only 29% of the patients. However, in private hospitals nearly all patients were treated with the use of psychotherapy, and 10% of those patients were treated using psychoanalysis (Hale 1995, p. 270). Most of the public hospitals did not agree to implement psychoanalysis with schizophrenic patients, and even those who believed in psychotherapy thought that these patients required somatic therapy as well. Thus, apart from a few enclaves of psychoanalysis in psychiatric hospitals, somatic psychiatry continued to be the treatment of choice, particularly in public institutions and especially for schizophrenic patients.

The place of psychoanalysis in a changing therapeutic landscape

According to Hale's historiography (1971, 1995), the popularity of psychoanalysis in the United States began a debate between loyal Freudians who wanted psychoanalysis to be a unique and separate discipline and those who wanted Freudian psychoanalysis to be assimilated into the medical schools and universities. The loyalists argued that extensive expansion of psychoanalysis in America resulted in losing what was unique about Freudianism and replacing it with an institutionalized version of a medical discipline. Despite this claim, by the mid-1950s the number of non-physician psychoanalysts had multiplied. Interestingly, of the two versions of psychoanalysis developed in the United States, eclectic psychoanalysis, associated with hospitals and treatment of schizophrenics, held a more liberal position, supporting analysis by non-doctors, whereas more orthodox psychoanalysis, which was not related to institutions of medicine and whose founders were themselves not necessarily all doctors, was opposed to analysis by laymen (that is, non-physician analysts). In this regard, John Leveille (2002), a West Chester University sociologist, argued that psychoanalysis became dominant in American psychiatry as a way for psychiatrists to extend their jurisdiction over less severe disorders (those not requiring hospitalization) in their struggle with clinical psychologists over therapeutic turf. According to his argument, private practice, made possible after World War II, provided psychiatrists who sought to leave hospitals a broad client base, from the neurotic housewife to the deviant criminal or chronic schizophrenic. Exposure to such a wide range of patients led to a wealth of theories and treatment practices, with neurotic housewives receiving psychoanalytic treatment at a time when psychotic patients were treated at the clinics with ECT and lobotomies. Outside of hospitals, the public did not distinguish between psychotherapy given by psychologists, psychiatrists and psychoanalysts; thus, the profession of psychiatry, fearing the loss of medical prestige, found itself under pressure to define and defend its unique professional identity by retreating to a purer scientific environment, a strategy a profession under pressure will often adopt (Abbott 1988). Since psychoanalysis, too, had to define its professional boundaries, psychiatrists who were trained as psychoanalysts turned to analytic training institutes. Although this helped them define their identity as separate from medicine, it created yet another problem: defining their jurisdiction in relation to clinical psychologists and social workers who occupied many positions in the field of mental health after World War II. Clinical psychologists particularly threatened the analytic psychiatrists because they treated the same clientele – neurotic patients – and the early 1950s saw psychiatrists and psychologists battling in court over the psychologist's role among mental health professionals. Leveille (2002) argued that to ensure that "subpar practice" would not bleed into reputable institutions, the American Medical Association, the American Psychiatric Association and the American Psychoanalytic Association issued a joint statement in 1954 which declared that psychotherapy should be practiced only by those who were medical doctors. Towards the end of the 1950s, psychologists were awarded the legal right to engage in psychotherapeutic practice. Even so, analysts involved in the struggle over therapeutic turf, such as the president of the American Psychiatric Association, Leo Bartemeier (1952), claimed that psychotherapy offered by clinical psychologists should be regulated and organized by the most qualified physicians in this field, namely, psychiatrists (p. 790). Much to their chagrin, analytic psychiatrists working outside of hospitals found themselves to be merely therapists, just like other professionals in the field of mental health. However, the socioeconomic ranking of mental healers remained: psychiatrist-analysts for the rich, psychologists for the middle class and social workers for the poor (Winter 1999). As a result of this struggle between psychiatry and psychology, many psychiatrists simply left the practice of psychotherapy and returned to a more narrow medical somatic practice.

Up until 1950 somatic psychiatry had seen very little progress, and after World War II the hereditary explanations it offered of mental illness were linked by many to Nazi Germany and its destructive eugenics theories. However, in 1954, neosomatic treatments were offered for psychosis when neuroleptic or "antipsychotic" drugs were released to the public. These were intended to replace cruel and outdated somatic treatments of the past. Psychotherapies used with patients suffering from the psychoses began incorporating these new treatments, and neurological and biological research into the phenomenon of schizophrenia became more common.

Psychiatry revisits the role of psychoanalysis

One other reason that American psychiatry began to rid itself of psychoanalysis – in addition to the fact that the terms "psychiatrist" and "psychoanalyst" became interchangeable and other non-medical professionals could be confused with medical doctors – was the criticism of philosophers with regard to the scientific claims of psychoanalysis. In 1958, just two years after the centennial of Freud's birth, a symposium on "Psychoanalysis and Science" was held at New York University, and Adolf Grünbaum (who later became one of the major critics

40 *Ravens in white coats*

of psychoanalysis) argued that even if psychoanalysis was an empirical science that could legitimately make generalizations about human nature, gaining confirmation of analytical hypotheses based on clinical evidence was an error in logic and empirically incorrect (Grünbaum in Hale 1995). Hale (1995) claimed that psychoanalysis had to prove within its American context of medicine that it was a science. It seems that ego psychology, a branch of psychoanalysis that made a large investment in empirical laboratory research, complied with this demand. However, dynamic psychiatry, the version of psychoanalytic treatment applied in hospitals, could not meet these standards, since it was busy treating patients and relying on individual case studies. As a result, psychiatry began divesting itself of psychoanalysis while producing an alternative somatic method. It is ironic that psychiatry itself attacked the somatic method earlier in the century, using psychoanalysis as its superior alternative. However, by the late 1950s the wheel had come full circle.

Psychoanalysis was beset by the strengthening of somatic treatments for the mentally ill, along with criticism that it was unscientific; meanwhile, governmental support for psychoanalysis also began to wane. Although it received much support in its early years, psychoanalysis began receiving fewer and fewer grants from NIMH. Funds allocated for psychotherapy research were awarded less and less to psychoanalytic researchers and more and more to somatic projects (Hale 1995, p. 332). In the late 1950s, the use of drugs, as well as research of the brain, neurological functioning and genetics, became the dominant trends within psychiatry. Beginning in the late 1950s, psychiatry strengthened its foundations with psychopharmacology and seemed to no longer have any need of psychoanalysis. Because treatment of psychosis became more focused on pharmacotherapy (not psychotherapy), competition with psychology or other mental health professions became irrelevant.

Summary

In the late 1950s, psychoanalysis, which had gained power in the early part of the 20th century as an alternative approach to harsh somatic treatments of the mentally ill (for example sterilization, malarial and bacterial injections, ice baths, insulin injections, electroconvulsive therapy and lobotomies), lost its place to a somatic cure and supportive care. The American version of psychoanalysis, which advocated dynamic psychiatry for schizophrenic patients – with its eclectic approach and exaggerated emphasis on the effect of society and the environment in the development of the disease – actually led to the weakening of psychoanalysis in the United States. Concepts like the "schizophrenogenic mother" (Fromm-Reichmann 1948) and "refrigerator mother" (Kanner 1949), as well as theories about how environment can cause or exacerbate mental disease, led to the belief that a better environment with more communal support would provide healing power to the mentally ill. Thus, indirectly, dynamic psychiatrists came to support medication to allow for a more rapid release of the mentally ill from institutions and into the community. This move, as subsequent chapters will show, turned out to be a colossal failure. In 1940, psychiatrists engaging in somatic treatments established the Association of Biological Psychiatry, which laid the foundations for the establishment of psychiatry in psychopharmacology (Levielle 2002). As the wheel turned, those in the somatic camp argued that psychoanalysts failed to cure schizophrenia, and that only biological psychiatry, with its pharmacological technology, could offer a solution to the problem of schizophrenia.

References

Abbott, A., 1988. *The system of professions. An essay on the division of expert labor.* Chicago, IL: University of Chicago Press.

Arieti, S., 1959. *American handbook of psychiatry.* New York: Basic Books.

Bartemeier, L. H., 1952. The president page: Clinical psychology. *American Journal of Psychiatry*, 108, p. 790.

Falzeder, E., 2012. "A fat wad of dirty pieces of paper": Freud on America, Freud in America, Freud and America. In: J. Brunham, ed., *After Freud left: A century of psychoanalysis in America.* Chicago, IL: University of Chicago Press. ch.3.

Freud, S., 1925. An autobiographical study. In: *The standard edition of the complete psychological works of Sigmund Freud*, Volume 20. London: Hogarth Press. pp. 1–74.

Fromm-Reichman, F., 1948. Notes on the development of treatment of schizophrenics by psychoanalytic psychotherapy. *Psychiatry*, 11(3), pp. 263–273.

Fromm-Reichmann, F., 1950. *Principles of intense psychotherapy.* Chicago, IL: University of Chicago Press.

Green, H., 1964. *I never promised you a rose garden.* New York: Holt, Rinehart and Winston.

Grob, G. N., 1991. *From asylum to community: Mental health policy in modern America.* Princeton, NJ: Princeton University Press.

Hale, N. G., 1971. *Freud and the Americans. The beginnings of psychoanalysis in the United States, 1876–1917*, Volume 1. New York: Oxford University Press.

Hale, N. G., 1995. *The rise and crisis of psychoanalysis in the United States. Freud and the Americans 1917–1985.* New York: Oxford University Press.

Jelliffe, S. E., and White, W. A., 1915. *Diseases of the nervous system: A textbook of neurology and psychiatry.* New York: Lea and Febiger.

Kanner, L., 1949. Problems of nosology and psychodynamics in early childhood autism. *American Journal of Orthopsychiatry*, 19(3), pp. 416–426.

Leveille, J. J., 2002. Jurisdictional competition and the psychoanalytic dominance of American psychiatry. *Journal of Historical Sociology*, 15, pp. 252–280.

Roudinesco, E., 1999. *Why psychoanalysis.* New York: Columbia University Press.

Shorter, E., 1997. *A history of psychiatry from the era of the asylum to the age of Prozac.* New York: Wiley.

Sullivan, H.S., 1940/2006. *Conceptions of modern psychiatry.* Whitefish, MT: Kessinger Publishing.

Stanton, A. H., and Schwartz, M. S., 1954. *The mental hospital: A study of the institutional participation in psychiatric illness and treatment.* New York: Basic Books.

Strecker, E. A., 1944. Psychoanalytic perspectives. *American Journal of Psychiatry*, 22, pp. 481–489.

42 Ravens in white coats

Whitaker, R., 2002. *Mad in America – Bad science, bad medicine and the enduring mistreatment of the mentally ill.* New York: Basic Books.

Winter, S., 1999. *Freud and the institution of psychoanalytic knowledge.* Stanford, CA: Stanford University Press.

Wittels, F., 1995. *Freud and the child woman: The memoirs of Fritz Wittels.* In: E. Timms, ed., New Haven, CT: Yale University Press. Ch. 9.

3 Psychoanalysis, psychopharmacology and community psychiatry (1954–1970)

> *The future may teach us to exercise a direct influence, by means of particular chemical substances, on the amounts of energy and their distribution in the mental apparatus. It may be that there are other still undreamt-of possibilities of therapy. But for the moment we have nothing better at our disposal than the technique of psycho-analysis, and for that reason, in spite of its limitations, it should not be despised.*
>
> (Sigmund Freud. "An Outline of Psychoanalysis" 1938, p. 192)

The first stage of the neosomatic revolution in psychiatry saw the use of antipsychotic medications with schizophrenic patients, along with their release from psychiatric institutions, and psychoanalysis responded with its theoretical formulation of schizophrenia and treatment with these drugs. The modern practice of treating schizophrenia with drugs began in May 1954, when Smith, Kline, and French Laboratories introduced chlorpromazine into the U.S. market under the name Thorazine. This drug, which was the first antipsychotic developed, began a major revolution in psychiatry, often equated with the one that penicillin wrought within general medicine (Whitaker 2002). It was claimed that with this medication, schizophrenic patients could be released from their confinement in institutions and lead a relatively normal life in their communities. The psychiatrist who first prescribed chlorpromazine in America, Heinz Lehmann (1954), went as far as claiming that the drug would prove itself useful as a pharmacological substitute for lobotomy, which in that era was one of the foremost techniques of somatic psychiatry for treating psychiatric patients, but also considered to be one of the most notorious medical procedures ever to have been developed.

Chlorpromazine reflected psychiatry's presumption of offering a chemical control of schizophrenia. This outcome, in the enervating atmosphere of the psychiatric hospitals of the 1950s, with its dearth of professional staff, overcrowded wards and financial deficits, was considered a great success. Hospitals that until then were not able to properly care for patients, especially given the volatile nature of schizophrenia, could, with the help of the neuroleptics, render schizophrenic patients quieter, more manageable and less hostile individuals. This new

44 *Psychoanalysis, psychopharmacology*

drug allowed somatic psychiatrists to reassert their grip on their schizophrenic clientele, and unlike the somatic practitioners of the previous generation, who used controversial, harsh, physical therapeutic techniques, these neosomatic psychiatrists provided what seemed to be an effective treatment of the schizophrenic state, which was supposed to allow for the quick release of patients from hospitals to their communities.

No other profession at the time could offer such a solution. The promise that, with the use of "miraculous" neuroleptics, the mentally ill could be calmed, soothed and released back into the community was so alluring to the public that some professionals (non-somatic psychiatrists, psychoanalysts and the like) publicly protested against this pledge of a psychiatric "redemption" and brought to light the potential dangers of such a plan. For example, Gregory Zilboorg, a psychiatrist, psychoanalyst and historian of psychiatry in New York, said to the press that the public has been "shamefully misled" and that the only purpose of drug therapy was to make patients more "comfortable and more manageable" (Kaplan 1956).

Drug treatments were supposed to both solve the individual patient's problem and address the social and economic problem of the continued weakening of overcrowded, poorly financed mental institutions. But instead of investing federal money in strengthening and supporting these mental institutions, the new treatment allowed for the release of patients with the promise that the "new drug" would enable them to engage in proper conduct within the community and eliminate their need to use these institutions. It was probably not coincidental that in 1955, just one year after the advent of neuroleptic drugs, the federal government passed the Mental Health Study Act, which called for a reassessment of social and economic problems in the mental health system. The Joint Commission on Mental Illness and Health issued a final report, titled "Action for Mental Health," in 1961, which served as the background to a 1963 special message to the Congress by President Kennedy. The message announced a radical move to release mental patients from formal institutions and establish community mental health centers. Kennedy said,

> I propose a national mental health program to assist in the inauguration of a wholly new emphasis and approach to care for the mentally ill. This approach relies primarily upon the new knowledge and new drugs acquired and developed in recent years, which make it possible for most of the mentally ill to be successfully and quickly treated in their own communities and returned to a useful place in society.
>
> (1963, n.p.)

Broken promises

The summary of the committee's report on which the President based his message referred to neuroleptics as "moral treatment in pill form" (Whitaker 2002, p. 288). On October 31, 1963, three weeks before he was assassinated, President

Kennedy signed into law a bill that meant to "free" many thousands of Americans with mental illnesses from life in institutions. The Community Mental Health Act envisioned building 1,500 outpatient mental health centers that would offer community-based care. This law, based primarily on the promise of the new drugs, contributed to the most significant release of patients from institutions since Pinel freed patients from their chains in the Salpêtrière in Paris 168 years earlier. The Community Mental Health Act was neosomatic psychiatry's finest hour, as the profession finally regained the legal right, through governmental authority, to return to its natural jurisdiction, this time holding proof of effective and cost-efficient treatment. And unlike the many psychotherapies that were offered by psychologists, social workers and counselors, this new treatment was offered exclusively by psychiatrists.

However, the promise of neosomatic psychiatry's miraculous drug to provide effective and humane treatment to schizophrenic patients was not ultimately kept. Reports of the harsh side effects of neuroleptics became more frequent, and community solutions to the schizophrenic condition proved to be inadequate. Poor financial planning plagued community mental health centers, and due to lack of funds they were dependent on local support for their upkeep. Moreover, psychiatrists in these centers diagnosed upper-class and wealthy patients with neurotic conditions and treated them with psychotherapy or psychoanalysis, while the poor were diagnosed with schizophrenia and treated with medications or sent back to the hospital (Hale 1995). Although the establishment of community mental health centers was part of Kennedy's larger "New Frontier" program, Hale (1995) claimed that the dramatic depopulation of state mental hospitals in the United States in the 1960s was probably the result of the efforts of idealistic psychiatrists, who wanted to shut down custodial institutions, and fiscal conservatives, who wished to cut budgets (pp. 337–339). Abbott (1988) pointed out that this deinstitutionalization led to a new problem of homelessness among the schizophrenic population, which itself created a new struggle among other professions to determine jurisdiction (p. 311).

Because somatic treatment and community mental health centers began to be perceived as a failed solution to the problem of mental disorders, analysts continued to think about possible techniques to treat schizophrenia. As psychoanalytic sources show, many analysts struggled with theoretical and practical questions regarding schizophrenia and the patients suffering from this severe mental illness. An examination of texts written by American psychoanalysts in the most prominent psychoanalytic journal in the United States, the *Journal of the American Psychoanalytic Association* (*JAPA*), demonstrates how these professionals were theorizing the schizophrenic condition and what their attitudes were toward its treatment.

History of *JAPA*

The American Psychoanalytic Association, founded in 1911, is one of the most powerful American psychoanalytic organizations and is affiliated with the International Psychoanalytic Association (IPA), the largest and most central organization

46 *Psychoanalysis, psychopharmacology*

of psychoanalysis in the world. The American Psychoanalytic Association began establishing itself between 1907 and 1909, with the first translations of Freud's writings into English by Abraham Brill. In May 1911, the first meeting of the organization was held in Washington, D.C. The association initially was open to anyone interested in psychoanalysis, but became increasingly medically oriented and eventually allowed only physicians to be members. Its first journal, the *Bulletin of the American Psychoanalytic Association*, was published in 1937 and 1938, and was terminated with the outbreak of World War II. The *Journal of the American Psychoanalytic Association* picked up where the *Bulletin* left off and has been continuously published since 1952.

The fact that articles published in this journal represented the spirit and philosophy of the American Psychoanalytic Association was noted by John Frosch (1987), the first editor of *JAPA* who examined the journal in a retrospective article. He said, "this publication should be representative of the viewpoint of the psychoanalytic philosophy of the American Psychoanalytic Association," and "suitable provisions, methods and means must at all times be made available to the association to see that the journal does function as a true representative of the Association's psychoanalytic philosophy" (p. 309). An anecdote about a proposed picture to appear on the cover of *JAPA* (photos of either Freud or Brill) can serve to illustrate how the journal sought to convey the spirit of psychoanalysis. Those who wanted to emphasize the American nature of the journal advocated for Brill's picture to appear on the cover, while supporters of Freud's picture wished to emphasize the connection of the American Psychoanalytic Association to its European father and the authentic practice of psychoanalysis in general. (Ultimately, neither of their pictures appeared on the cover.)

With the advent of *JAPA*, American psychoanalysts who had been publishing in the *International Journal of Psychoanalysis* (*IJP*), the flagship publication of the International Psychoanalytic Association, now had to choose in what context to publish their articles, American or international. *JAPA* remained throughout the years the most prominent psychoanalytic journal in North America, both in terms of the number of subscribers and the number of citations from and in other professional works. It publishes on a quarterly basis original articles, lectures, panel reports, editorials, correspondences and new literature reviews. As such, it will be used here as a textual source to examine the American Psychoanalytic Association's theoretical and clinical practice with schizophrenia during this first period of the neosomatic revolution in psychiatry, in which its two main achievements were the massive use of antipsychotic medication and deinstitutionalization with alternative community psychiatric care.

Ego psychologists' view of schizophrenia

The dominant voice regarding schizophrenia in journal articles of the 1960s was that of analysts of ego psychology, one of the two versions of American psychoanalysis discussed in previous chapters. Ego psychology, which fits nicely with the spirit of American pragmatism, sought to connect human experience more with adaptation to reality and less with fantasy and unconscious impulses. Schizophrenia, which, according to Freud (1914), "will give us an insight into the psychology of the ego" (p. 182), was viewed as a disruption in a person's adaptation to reality. Freud's conception of schizophrenia (specifically as he formulated it in the case of Schreber), was that the cause of psychosis was the withdrawal of libido from external objects into the ego. In contrast, ego psychologists did not focus on the instincts but rather on the ego, which they saw as defective in schizophrenia. Perhaps as they were influenced by the trend to medicalize psychoanalysis, ego psychologists "treated" the ego as if it were a physical organ. Just as neosomatic psychiatrists identified the defective organ in schizophrenia as the brain, ego psychologists designated the ego as a sick organ. Thus, Paul Federn, an Austrian-born American analyst, suggested that schizophrenia was a disorder that is caused by a defect in ego boundaries. The boundaries between this organ and the id, as well as between the ego and reality, were defective, so he claimed (Bergmann 1963). Formulation of schizophrenia as stemming from various other ego defects, including impairments in the function responsible for relationships with others, served psychoanalysts in their attempt to offer a theoretical explanation, as well as technical ways of working out issues related to schizophrenia. Like Federn, Robert Wallerstein (1967), an American analyst and past president of the International Psychoanalytic Association, who is known for his writings about psychoanalysis as a profession, suggested that the lack of ego boundaries, the lack of an integrated identity and the difficulty in the economy of object libido should be the focus of analytic treatment for all schizophrenics. Rudolph Loewenstein (1967), who is regarded as one of the founding fathers of ego psychology in the United States, along with Ernst Kris and Heinz Hartmann, argued that the speech impediments often found in schizophrenia are also an expression of an ego defect, expressed in an inability to organize sensory stimuli into verbal categories. Pointing to the ego as the defective "organ" in schizophrenia and claiming that the development of the ego depends, at least in part, on an optimum level of verbal stimulation, psychoanalysts declared schizophrenia to be a problem that belonged within the jurisdiction of psychoanalysis: appropriate verbal stimulation (a treatment provided by psychoanalysis), as opposed to somatic treatment, could change the structure of the ego organ and strengthen its many functions.

Diagnosis, treatment and inference all serve professions in assuming a cultural authority. The argument of psychoanalysts identified with ego psychology, that they could diagnose the defected organ in schizophrenia and offer an efficient treatment, was a claim for jurisdiction. In this context, it appears that ego psychology tried to produce a psychoanalytic system that would be more attractive to the American public: one asserting that psychoanalysis is not solely interested in diagnosing the deep, inner world of impulses and conflicts, but also (and mainly) invested in the external manifestations of human adaptation to reality. American ego psychology's perception was that the purpose of psychological functioning (like biological functioning) is the survival of organisms through adaptation to the real world, people, organizations, ideas and purposes. Adaptation to reality,

48 *Psychoanalysis, psychopharmacology*

which could be argued as being synonymous with mental health, was the subject of practice and research by ego psychologists, who revived the long-neglected study of health and normality. Ego functions were used by American psychoanalysts to promote a more scientific notion of psychoanalysis, since these ego functions are both visible and measurable, and their strength or weakness can be used as a measure of mental health or illness, which then can be more transparently diagnosed.

Beyond pointing to a defective organ in schizophrenia, which they offered to cure, American psychoanalysts also expressed their desire to medicalize their profession in the considerable effort expended by ego psychologists to create their own nosographic classification of mental disorders. Criticizing the nonanalytical psychiatric classification system, which was based on phenomenological clusters of symptoms, and expressing their dissatisfaction with the dynamic classification based on stages of psychosexual development, analysts in the American Psychoanalytic Association established an alternative analytical nosology (Ross 1960). The system that Emil Kraepelin had conceived was relatively incoherent, contradictory and vague, according to dissidents, and the "new psychoanalysis" (nonmedical, albeit striving for more scientific legitimization) was required to compile a classification system of its own as an alternative. To this end, ego psychologists reached a consensus, saying that the core disturbance within schizophrenia was indeed a defect of the ego, but this defect was categorically different from other ego deficiencies reflected in other disorders, such as homosexuality, psychosomatic disorders, melancholy, depersonalization, hysteria, "as-if personality" disorder, borderline personality disorder and so forth (Socarides 1960; Gosliner 1960; Lipton 1961, among others).

The search for an etiology of schizophrenia is also evidence of the medicalization of American psychoanalysis. As somatic psychiatry at the time was unable to offer any etiology for the disease, ego psychology sought to differentiate between a normal and abnormal childhood in dictating the etiology of schizophrenia. Thus, according to Phyllis Greenacre (1960), an analyst at the New York Psychoanalytic Institute, ego disturbances manifesting in schizophrenia are caused by traumatization – the sources of which are either innate or to be found in persistent, destructive, external elements.

What appears from texts published in *JAPA* at that time on the subject of schizophrenia is that analysts were occupied in attempting to offer an alternative to somatic psychiatry, but by using somatic psychiatry's own tools. They tried to provide a phenomenology to describe the patterns they observed in schizophrenia – namely, to delineate the nature of the injury to the ego and its functions. The ego psychologists attempted to formulate the ego in physical terms, claiming, for example, that during development, the ego is "hurt" and "wounded"; they offered a psychoanalytic nosographic system through which the difference between the ego disturbance in schizophrenia and that in other disorders was delineated. Most important, they offered a therapeutic technique and proposed a promising prognosis for schizophrenic patients. Armed with these theories, psychoanalysts from the American Psychoanalytic Association sought to market psychoanalysis as having a more effective and nuanced understanding of and specialization in schizophrenia, in comparison to somatic psychiatry.

Applying the scientific method to psychoanalysis

In an additional venture to establish its jurisdiction, as somatic psychiatry was gaining power, American psychoanalysis turned to rigorous scientific methods to ensure that its expertise was based on science, and to lend the profession the validity and legitimacy needed in its jurisdictional struggles. To compete in the scientific milieu of general medicine and somatic psychiatry during that era, analysts argued that if provided with the right laboratory conditions, they could create a microcosm of the phenomena observed and discussed by psychoanalysis. Though the stated purpose for collecting data from these studies was to provide a general theory of psychoanalysis, such studies were specifically done in the areas in which analysts were attempting to prove their unique contribution and superiority over somatic psychiatry. Parent-child interactions were one such area of exploration, which allowed for the study of early development and its potential link to the development of schizophrenia. Since there was no neosomatic psychiatric theory of schizophrenia at the time, studies conducted by the psychoanalysts attempted to provide such a theory (Fries 1961; Settlage 1964, among others).

Another area of study was the unconscious mind and the possibility of influencing behavior through its manipulation using subliminal stimulation. These studies could enable psychoanalysts to assert that not only did they understand the etiology of schizophrenia, but also that they had the means to influence the schizophrenic patient through direct access to the affected areas of his unconscious conflict (Silverman 1967). Research on dreams was a third area of scientific study through which psychoanalysis could claim jurisdiction over schizophrenia. Analysts could do so indirectly by first showing that a phenomenon that contained physiological expression, such as dreams, might also contain emotional expression, and then relating these findings to historical attempts to understand psychosis through the understanding of dreams ("A dream, then, is a psychosis, with all the absurdities, delusions and illusions of a psychosis" [Freud 1938]). Analysts similarly showed that their ability to use technology to record electrical activity of the brain, the area generally dominated by somatic psychiatrists, helped them to learn that some normal behavior corresponded to that of schizophrenic psychosis (Fisher 1965). These types of empirical laboratory studies, in addition to psychoanalytic studies on the effects of somatic treatments on schizophrenic patients, allowed analysts to explain positive effects rendered by such therapies as electroconvulsive therapy (ECT) or neuroleptic drugs – explanations which, up to that point, could not be offered by neosomatic psychiatry. What follows is a more detailed analysis of one of the many topics American psychoanalysts set out to study in a "scientific" way, using laboratories and empirical methods more common among their competitors, the somatic psychiatrists.

50 *Psychoanalysis, psychopharmacology*

The scientific study of child development

As part of their mission to distance themselves from the traditional psychoanalytic research methodology, which was based mainly on case studies of patients in the analytic situation, and in their attempts to imitate the research methodologies of the hard sciences, psychoanalysts publishing in *JAPA* in the 1960s commonly reported on their findings based on direct observation of children. Since during this period the early relationship between mother and baby was seen as critical to normal or pathological development, research was conducted to find a correlation between early developmental activities and later clinical syndromes that were considered to be a result of interactions between congenital predispositions and parental pathology. These researchers expressed not only support for the psychoanalytic etiology of schizophrenia, but also for the option of "preventative" care which, as shown in previous chapters, was already part of psychiatric expertise at the turn of the century. Moreover, with the advent of the Community Mental Health Act and Kennedy's declaration in 1963 that "an ounce of prevention is worth more than a pound of cure," mental health became a goal of the nation. In terms of the parent-child relationship, psychoanalysts argued that they could potentially prevent schizophrenia by treating the family at birth and by guiding and consulting at child development centers (Fries 1961).

Observations made by psychoanalysts observation of schizophrenic children, disturbed adolescents and normally developing children became more prevalent. The book, On human symbiosis and vicissitudes of individuation (1968) by the preeminent psychoanalyst Margaret Mahler, was a result of comprehensive research and psychoanalytic work with psychotic children. Observations like Mahler's allowed psychoanalysis to create theoretical terms for the course of development of the early mental life of the newborn, to create a more specific and nuanced etiology for the schizophrenic state and to bring about earlier prevention interventions based on empirical evidence. The transition from case study and reconstruction of the past to the use of conventional methodologies of the time (direct observation, controlled clinical trials and so forth) allowed psychoanalysis in its jurisdictional struggle to demonstrate its scientific competency.

The preoccupation with studying developmental stages (particularly the mother's influence on the child during this period) allowed for analysts to study the significant effects of the environment, family and society on normal and abnormal development. Research done by Ruth and Theodore Lidz (1949), a pioneer couple from the Psychoanalytic Institute of Washington-Baltimore, focused on families of schizophrenic patients. Later, Lidz and his colleagues, Stephen Fleck and Alice Cornelison (1965), published findings of a long-term study on schizophrenic and nonschizophrenic families. This research derived from the concept that the mother-child relationship and the society-mother-child relationship have a recognized influence on the development of schizophrenia. These approaches (as opposed to the approaches that placed most of the emphasis on unconscious mental functioning) also introduced the possibility that

Psychoanalysis, psychopharmacology 51

psychoanalysis could use research methodologies other than the psychoanalytic one in theory formulation.

Psychoanalysis moves away from its roots

It is worthwhile to note that the tension existing in the struggle between psychoanalysis and somatic psychiatry that motivated psychoanalysis to formulate its own etiology of the schizophrenic state was sometimes perceived as distancing American psychoanalysis in postwar years from its psychoanalytic roots. Along with the emphasis on studying environmental factors leading to the disease, which is evident in *JAPA* articles during the 1960s, toward the end of the decade a review of the 1969 book, *Psychopathology of the Psychoses*, by Thomas Freeman, an Irish psychiatrist and psychoanalyst, brought a different view and warned that the approaches that emphasize environmental factors myopically avoid seeing the individual who is suffering from the illness (Book Notices 1970). Although Freeman (1969) did not perceive psychoanalysis as able to offer a perfect etiological formulation of psychosis, he mentioned British writers like Herbert Rosenfeld and Wilfred Bion as analysts who continued to base their understanding of schizophrenia on the unique psychoanalytic understanding of the internal world of conflict, anxiety and regression. His suggestion not to neglect the internal psychic world in favor of the more observed, measured and "objective" external world was also a warning for analysts who, in their eagerness to produce alternatives to "scientific" somatic psychiatry, might drop the fundamentals of psychoanalysis.

In the same spirit of empirical inquiry, analysts published research on the unconscious in *JAPA*, which was done through subliminal stimulation and which they declared to be equivalent to a double-blind procedure (Silverman 1967), the norm in controlled drug studies. This type of research led to hybrid conclusions of analysts who posited that electrical shocks (a treatment using electrical impulses) led to the merger of the object and the self (Silverman 1970), as if the "object" and the "self" were physical materials like electrical impulses. Thus, as part of the struggle for jurisdiction, analysts not only explicated their theories, using somatic psychiatry's (monopolistic) technology and terminology; they also, if indirectly, claimed they could achieve the same results as their rivals while using benign subliminal stimulation instead of notorious electric shock treatment, with its devastating side effects.

Laboratory research on dreams and dream states also began to be conducted with schizophrenics in the 1960s. Resurrecting Freud the "scientist," evident in his "Project for a Scientific Psychology" (1895/1950), in which he attempted to develop a general psychology along the lines of neurophysiology, the dream researchers attempted to reconnect psychoanalysis with the concrete physiological body. A radical example of this tendency can be seen in an article about nightmares and psychosis, in which the author compares the electrical activity of the brain in the throes of a nightmare with a brain in the midst of psychosis. Instead of the more psychoanalytic interpretation of the dream's content, symbolization and meaning, the author presented the recording of electrical activity

52   *Psychoanalysis, psychopharmacology*

along the scalp (using electroencephalography [EEG]) as it was measured during a nightmare, as compared to psychosis (Fisher 1965). Even though Freud ultimately discontinued the "project," as he admitted that a theory of behavior should be psychological, one can argue that he never gave up on the belief that a relationship would eventually be found between psychoanalysis and biochemical processes, and analysts, in their attempt to present themselves as experts in areas where somatic psychiatry showed strength, were attempting to follow in Freud's early footsteps.

Analysts also attempted to remain relevant within the neosomatic trend in psychiatry by adding psychoanalytic understanding to the mechanism of their rival's new, excited mode of "cure" – psychotropic medications. One example is from a report of a symposium held at the annual meeting of the American Psychoanalytic Association in May 1962, chaired by Robert Waelder (Nierenberg 1963). In this report analysts such as Mortimer Ostow, whose book, *Drugs in Psychoanalysis and Psychotherapy* (1962), otherwise promoted the idea that psychotherapy was essential even with very disturbed patients who were treated with drugs, used in arguments psychoanalytic concepts such as the ego and the libido to understand the mechanisms of psychiatric drugs. Thus, he offered that tranquilizers can cause an emptying of libido from the ego and that antidepressants can fill the ego with libido (p. 162). Ostow's argument met with objection from at least two panelists: Natheniel Ross, an analyst from New York, who declared that his own experience with medication was confusing and disappointing (p. 164); and Robert Bak, a Hungarian-born analyst from New York, who felt that Ostow had reduced the number of variables too sharply and that the causal relationships between libido content and administration of drugs could not be correlated (p. 165). When Ostow replied to Ross's criticism of drugs, he suggested that the reason Ross failed to use the efficient psychiatric drugs was that he didn't know how drugs worked (meaning how they presumably affected the levels of libido [p. 166]). It seems, from this kind of discussion that went on during the 1960s, that psychoanalysts had to respond to the victorious technological cure of somatic psychiatry. They did it either by arguing that they had what somatic psychiatry lacked at the time – the explanatory power regarding the mechanism of the drugs – or by dismissing the drugs' efficacy or its relevance to psychoanalysts' superior understanding.

Empirical proof of the worth of treatment?

It was not only their explanatory powers, however, that psychoanalysts used in their jurisdictional struggles with somatic psychiatry. Psychoanalysis also had to empirically prove its worth in the field of treatment. This kind of research rapidly developed in the decades after World War II, but while clinicians after the war published their results of treatment based only on their therapeutic work, in the 1960s analysts had to base their evidence on controlled clinical trials (similar to the methodology used in trials on medications). The demand from analysts to conduct systematic research on treatment and to use an empirical methodology to study the impact of drugs on psychotherapy was evident in articles published in *JAPA* during the decade of the 1960s. Robert Wallerstein (1966), who led the Psychotherapy Research Project at the Menninger Foundation and was president of the International Psychoanalytic Association in the 1980s, claimed that empirical research in the field of psychotherapy would mark the continuing progress in the "march of psychological knowledge" and that psychoanalysis needed more research like that in light of the strengthening of somatic psychiatry.

An identity crisis

In *JAPA* the study of psychoanalysis as an alternative therapeutic method in competition with somatic psychiatry was explored from another angle as well – that is, within the context of the history of science. Maxwell Gitelson (1964), a Russian-American psychiatrist and analyst who was also the president of the International Psychoanalytic Association, used the lens of Kuhn's paradigm shifts, which Kuhn discussed in his famous book *The Structure of Scientific Revolutions*, in order to discuss "the identity crisis" of psychoanalysis. Although he supported adjustment of psychoanalysis according to new knowledge and novel technologies, Gitelson suggested that accommodations should be made within the psychoanalytic body of knowledge and that the entire paradigm should not be rejected. The search for a scientific basis of psychoanalysis would not be what proved its efficacy, he suggested; rather, only the experience of psychoanalysis could be proof of its effectiveness. Distancing psychoanalysis from medicine and its new "scientific" trend, he also mentioned that Freud already asserted that psychoanalysis was not a special branch of medicine, and that essential to any analytic training program were elements of psychology, history, culture, sociology, anatomy, biology and evolution. Further, in defining the difference between the psychoanalyst and the medical doctor, Gitelson argued that although certain emotional and humanist qualities are fundamental to the practice of medicine, psychoanalysts need additional intellectual capabilities and scientific sophistication that is not required from medical doctors.

Gitelson questioned the tendency to view medicine as the parent of psychoanalysis, asking whether this notion was still accurate. He returned to the question of analysis by lay analysts and suggested that the time had come for psychoanalysis to view itself (and have others view it) as a separate, scientific discipline, and called for a separation of psychoanalysis from psychiatry, seeing their relationship as "marriage of convenience" (p. 470). Due to this "marriage" Gitelson claimed that psychoanalysts in the United States were having an identity crisis – caught between psychiatry, which is a therapeutic specialty of medicine, and psychoanalysis, which is a basic science. For Gitelson, the psychoanalyst was superior to the psychiatrist, since doctors of medicine whose calling stems from the healing impulse could not recognize, or refused to accept, the classical model of psychoanalysis as the only method for conducting a controlled study of human individual psychology in its deepest sense. Thus, while the primary function of psychiatry is

54 *Psychoanalysis, psychopharmacology*

mental healing, it is only a part of the psychoanalytic endeavor. Gitelson argued that psychoanalysis is much more that what is known as psychoanalytic therapy, and he called on analysts to accept their separate scientific identity and their role as "various kinds of intellectually qualified persons who are humanly qualified for the human experiment which is the psychoanalytic situation" (p. 474).

The divorce called for in Gitelson's article seemed to have been occurring already. In an article on schizophrenia, Phyllis Greenacre (1960) recalled how, due to the Great Depression of the 1930s, psychoanalysts in the United States worked mainly in hospitals, because very few neurotic patients could afford psychoanalytic treatment. Working with many psychiatric patients allowed her and her colleagues to observe psychiatric patients for long periods of time. Greenacre noticed that this opportunity did not present itself in the reality of the 1960s, since patients in hospitals were treated mainly with somatic treatments such as electroconvulsive therapy and tranquilizers. This reality in which psychoanalysts were no longer a vital part of the psychiatric profession, whose "motherland" was the mental hospitals, contributed to psychoanalysts' identity crisis and their questions regarding their jurisdiction.

It is probably not coincidental that an article on Freud's correspondence with Ernst Simmel, a Berlin psychoanalyst best known for his efforts in Germany to establish the first sanitarium to use psychoanalytic treatment with psychiatric inpatients, appeared in *JAPA* at a time when psychoanalysts were looking for alternatives to psychiatric inpatient institutions. From the correspondence during Simmel's years in Los Angeles, it appears that he aspired to establish a similar psychoanalytic sanitarium in Southern California to continue the work of the Schloss Tegel in Berlin (Deri and Brunswick 1964). In correspondence with Freud, Simmel would update Freud of his plans, who in return expressed interest and encouraged the continuation of the project. In one of his letters, Freud argued that although he was skeptical about the effectiveness of analytic therapy for psychoses, he recognized that effective treatment could be possible only in an institution (Freud 1931 in Deri and Brunswick 1964, p. 106). Although Simmel's plan of opening a psychoanalytic sanitarium in California did not materialize, his influence was indeed felt in the United States, where the Menninger Clinic in Topeka, Kansas, and the Austin Riggs sanitarium in Stockbridge, Massachusetts, were established based on the Schloss Tegel model. Since psychoanalysis places heavy emphasis on confronting anxiety-provoking conflicts with severely regressed patients, such work could be done only in the protective environment of institutions, the very institutions from which psychoanalysis was "divorcing."

Treating schizophrenia with psychoanalysis

The articles reviewed thus far were largely theoretical or historical. Both kinds were concerned with the jurisdictional struggle between psychoanalysis and somatic psychiatry. The theoretical approach expressed in these articles attempted to compete with somatic psychiatry by resembling it in the portrayal of the ego as a damaged organ, by creating diagnostic classifications or by trying to prove psychoanalysis's explanatory power of the mechanism of somatic cures. The historical approach reviewed or called for a divorce between these professions, but also pointed to the price this separation entailed. In articles on schizophrenia in which the main concern was treatment, the psychoanalytic understanding of schizophrenia was maintained, along with traditional psychoanalytical concepts such as impulses, conflict, anxiety and defenses that explained both the disorder and the therapy. Analysts focusing on clinical issues viewed psychosis as only quantitatively different from neurosis and professed the use of psychoanalytic treatment with psychotic individuals. Harold Searles (1962), psychiatrist and psychoanalyst known for his analytic work with schizophrenic patients at Chestnut Lodge, was a notable example of this type of contribution to *JAPA* during the 1960s. In what seemed like an attempt to draw analysts back to the treatment of schizophrenic individuals, which was more and more occupied by neosomatic psychiatrists, he noted that most writings on treating the schizophrenic patient characterized them as concrete thinkers "hopelessly apart from [their] fellow human beings" (p. 23). It was rare that analysts wrote about a rewarding, "even exciting" experience of seeing a schizophrenic patient. To correct this view, Searles presented two clinical cases of analytic treatment of these patients, one of which was an inpatient schizophrenic in a locked ward.

The portrayal of the ego in such treatment-focused texts was vastly different from that presented in the more research-focused articles of that time. The reader can sense that both of Freud's theories of schizophrenia continued to "haunt" analysts' thinking about schizophrenia. While ego psychology claimed that schizophrenia was the result of a defective ego functioning, Searles and other psychoanalysts, who conducted psychoanalytic psychotherapy with schizophrenics in institutional settings, emphasized the conflicts that aroused anxiety and activated defense mechanisms in these patients (similar to what happens in neurosis, perhaps, but to a different degree) as in Freud's unitary theory. This latter conceptualization portrayed schizophrenics not as "damaged objects" with whom the analyst could be no more than compassionate and empathetic, but rather as individuals full of an unbridled energy, which could be channeled toward potential growth and change.

According to Searles, the patient's impulses, conflicts, anxieties and defenses should be explored and analyzed, and the schizophrenic condition in his view was amenable to the traditional psychoanalytic method. While Searles felt that psychoanalysts were distancing themselves from schizophrenic patients because they envisioned them as "defective objects," Otto Kernberg (1965), the Austrian-born New York analyst who worked for years at the Menninger Clinic, pointed to the possible, painful countertransferential response as the source of this disengagement. Countertransference with schizophrenic patients was especially intense, as severely regressed patients often evoked complicated countertransference responses, which triggered regressive areas within the analyst. The analyst could experience an emotional disconnect, find himself or herself unrealistically reliant upon the patient or develop microparanoid attitudes toward the patient. Kernberg argued that psychoanalytic institutes do not prepare the future analyst to deal

56 *Psychoanalysis, psychopharmacology*

with these mental states, as they discourage candidates from treating regressed patients during training. Kernberg claimed that psychoanalytic institutes pressure candidates to fulfill certain requirements for their certification. This pressure often precluded future analysts from freely engaging with difficult therapeutic situations, instead vying for "easier" cases that could more readily propel them toward graduation.

Although both Searles and Kernberg emphasized the difficulties presented to the analyst offering psychoanalytic treatment to regressed patients, they both believed it was an efficient treatment for these patients. This therapeutic approach professed by Kernberg and Searles was in many ways contrary to both the somatic psychiatric approach, which saw these patients as suffering from a neurochemically imbalanced brain, and to ego psychology's approach, which saw schizophrenic individuals as suffering from a defect in their ego. These two approaches were both risking viewing patients with schizophrenia as defective and broken objects, just as these patients seemed to view themselves. Thus, the alternative view of Searles and Kernberg, rarely offered in *JAPA*, represented an ethical commitment to the schizophrenic patient's humanity, even when the patient did not experience himself or herself as part of the world of humans.

American psychoanalysis in the international arena

Whereas in *JAPA* most articles by American psychoanalysts on schizophrenia focused on the theory and research of the disorder while the minority dealt with its treatment, the *International Journal of Psychoanalysis* (*IJP*) presented an opposite picture, with most of the articles based on clinical work and discussing treatment, while a minority of authors were struggling with questions about the scientific stature of psychoanalysis and its roots in medicine. American analysts seemed to take refuge from jurisdictional struggles with somatic psychiatry in the international arena. Publishing articles on schizophrenia, deepening their understanding of their own psychoanalytic theory and growing in sophistication in the use of their own clinical tools, these analysts were refraining from appropriating their competitors' methodologies and techniques.

A brief history of *IJP* is in order before delving into these writings by American analysts. The journal of the International Psychoanalytic Association was founded in 1920 by Ernest Jones (who served as its first editor) under the guidelines of Freud himself. Jones, a Welsh-born neurologist, analyst and Freud's first biographer, served as the president of the British Psychoanalytic Society and president of the International Psychoanalytic Association from 1920 to 1930. In these roles, he greatly influenced the English-speaking psychoanalytic establishment, its organizations and approaches. He helped establish the American Psychoanalytic Association in 1911 and was its secretary for the first two years of its existence. Jones was wary of American analysts because of their cultural approaches. He tried to stay ahead of Samuel Tannenbaum, a Hungarian-born psychoanalyst in New York who expressed his wish in 1918 to publish a psychoanalytic journal in English (Steiner, 1994, p. 886), so *IJP* was published in London and not in North

America. Jones saw the Americans as his cultural rivals, and he feared leaving psychoanalysis in American hands. He believed they had a tendency to "defuse," domesticate and anesthetize psychoanalysis and its impact, and to "marginalize new ideas" by "robbing psychoanalytic terms of their intrinsic meanings" in the name of "resistance to dogma," "freedom of thought," a "widening of vision," a "readjustment of perspective" and the like (Jones 1920, p. 4). The competition between London and America was motivated both by Jones's previous experience in America at the beginning of the century and by his fear of the enormous but rather superficial diffusion of psychoanalysis well beyond the close circle of specialists in North America. For these reasons Jones struggled to keep the *IJP* in the Old World (Steiner 1994).

In the 1940s, *IJP* became the flagship journal of psychoanalysis, and the fact that it was published in London (where most of Freud's writings were being translated into English) made London the center of the "psychoanalytic empire." While Jones held negative views about American psychoanalysis, he needed American subscribers, and so he appointed a number of American friends to the *IJP*'s executive board (Jones 1919 in Paskauskas 1993). Today's *IJP*, a bimonthly, publishes psychoanalytic articles on methodology, theory, technique, the history of psychoanalysis, clinical contributions, research on life-cycle development, education and professional issues, psychoanalytic psychotherapy and interdisciplinary research (tying psychoanalysis to subjects such as literature, the social sciences, linguistics, philosophy and the arts). Also published in it are key papers presented at conferences of the International Psychoanalytic Association, book reviews, posthumous articles and correspondence between professionals (recently including correspondence from Internet forums). Despite its complex history and its inclination toward British psychoanalysis, this is the only regularly published psychoanalytic journal that accepts contributions from writers around the world. As such, it will be used here to examine developments in the field of American psychoanalysis, as reflected in the international arena.

Bridges over the ocean: Ego psychology and object relations

In the 1960s, as already mentioned, the international arena allowed a broader and more flexible discussion of schizophrenia by American psychoanalysts. Discussions of the research and therapeutic work being conducted both in the United States and Britain allowed for a unique exchange of ideas and perspectives. American analysts who published in the *IJP* were invested in bridging the gap between the two psychoanalytic bodies of knowledge – object relations (from London) and ego psychology (from America, mainly New York). Bridging these two schools that grew out of Freud's paradigm produced a theory that emphasized a more relational approach – both interpersonally and intra-psychically – and focused less on mental defects or poor object internalizations and more on drives and conflicts. This approach, which was marginal in *JAPA*, occupied a

58   *Psychoanalysis, psychopharmacology*

central place in American articles published in *IJP* and opened the door for a renewed interest in analytic praxis with schizophrenic patients.

The referencing of American analysts to Melanie Klein, when they wrote about schizophrenia, seemed only natural when Klein's object-relations theory was as concerned with the early psychotic states as it was with the origin for later schizophrenic states. Klein's theories and techniques were not easily received by the American psychoanalytic community, partly due to their complexity and partly due to the American preference for concrete and pragmatic solutions. Even so, the many references by American analysts to Klein and the object-relations approach to schizophrenia indicated the attempt to strengthen psychoanalysis from within, and to bridge the gap between Anna Freud, ego psychology and America on the one hand, and Melanie Klein, object-relations theories and England on the other.

In this integrative vein, Hans Loewald (1960), an American analyst of German descent who stressed the importance of the mother-infant dyad in forming a baby's mind, showed that the picture of schizophrenia was more complex than it seemed, and that object relations indeed affected the construction of the ego. If schizophrenia was seen as a flaw in the construction of the ego, and if the ego was constructed as part of the early relationship between the mother and the infant, then object relations played an important etiological role and transferential relationships with the analyst, which revived early object relations, could bring about change in the development of the ego. Like Loewald and unlike the ego psychologists who published in *JAPA*, Morris Katan (1960), a Dutch analyst who worked in the United States primarily with individuals with psychosis, argued that even in the purest forms of psychosis, there are nonpsychotic parts of the personality that remain untouched by the significant regression experienced by the person as a whole. This view that the ego is a complex, composite structure, with strong, weak, psychotic and nonpsychotic parts, was in essence an argument against the more general claim heard in the *JAPA* that the schizophrenic's ego is defective. Unlike this latter claim the view offered by Katan supported the inclusion of schizophrenic patients in the therapeutic efforts of psychoanalysis.

Like Loewald and Katan, Margaret Mahler (1960) also chose to publish in the *IJP*. Mahler, who theorized that childhood development is rooted in early relationships, connected the early relationship of mother and infant to pathologies later in life, both as considered by ego psychology as well as by object relations. Other attempts by American analysts in the *IJP* to bridge ego psychology and object relations emerged in articles about specific psychotic symptoms such as hallucinations and delusions, perceived as part of the defensive effort of the ego and not the result of faulty brain functioning or defects in the ego (Havens 1962; Frosch 1967). Thus, psychotic symptoms were viewed as meaningful and analyzable.

Harold Searles (1963), already mentioned as one of the very few analysts who published clinical cases studies of schizophrenic patients in *JAPA*, additionally contributed many articles on schizophrenia to *IJP* during the 1960s.

His conception of schizophrenia – combining Melanie Klein's emphasis on the internal, unconscious world (which most Americans largely rejected) with the Sullivanian notion of underscoring a patient's interpersonal experience – further indicated an attempt to bridge theories divided not only by the Atlantic, but also by psychoanalytic allegiances formed in the United Kingdom by Melanie Klein and her followers on the one hand and Anna Freud and her acolytes on the other. While working with schizophrenic patients, Searles recognized that even the most deep-seated and chronic symptoms should not be considered "the tragic human debris left behind by the awesome glacial holocaust, which this illness surely is" (Searles 1963, p. 249). In the course of therapy, Searles argued, the analyst "can come to reveal – an aspect which is both rich in meaning and alive . . . with unquenched and unquenchable energy" (p. 249). Searles assumed that even the most psychotic patients had sane aspects to their personality and argued that Klein and her successors contributed more than anyone else to understanding psychotic transference (pp. 253–257). Alongside this approbation, however, Searles contended that Klein's followers (such as Wilfred Bion and Herbert Rosenfeld) did not sufficiently account for early influences of a patient's family of origin or the presence of a symbiotic parent who did not allow for the child to individuate and view himself as separate and different from the parent. As opposed to Bion's claim that the psychotic patient hates reality, Searles suggested that these patients hate the reality that they know – a reality colored by the symbiosis with the parent that is false and misleading. Unlike the British analysts he was in conversation with, Searles saw the schizophrenic's hatred of reality not as destructive but as a creative experience (p. 265): through the destruction of the twisted symbiotic reality, he believed, the patient sought to emerge and be born as an individual (p. 268).

Other such integration between ego psychology and object relations was offered by Donald Rinsley (1968), a prominent analyst at the Menninger Clinic in Topeka who claimed that the ego weakness inherent in schizophrenia indicated losing touch with internalized objects. Similarly, Arnold Modell (1963), a renowned analyst in Boston, emphasized the need for psychoanalytic integration of internal biological predispositions with the patient's relationship with his or her mother, and claimed that maternal failure is largely responsible for developmental arrests in the ego.

The bridge formed between American and British analysts, when combined with the need to strengthen the analytic approach towards schizophrenia, resulted in the theoretical notion that object relations significantly impact the construction and development of the ego, as well as the integrity of its functioning. In schizophrenia, it was suggested, the original relationship between mother and infant does not allow for a healthy process of separation-individuation of the child from the mother, and as such the child never develops a separate and unique identity of his own. Psychotic symptoms are conceived, not as a result of a defect in the ego, but as the ego's desperate attempt to save, repair and integrate itself due to the pressure of the drives and the intense conflicts that threaten to fragment it.

A return to unitary theory

Along with these endeavors at "trans-Atlantic" integration, American psychoanalysts further sought to establish their hold on schizophrenic clientele during the 1960s by returning to Freud's unitary theory. The groundbreaking work of Jacob Arlow and Charles Brenner (1969), prominent analysts at the Psychoanalytic Institute in New York, which offered among other innovations a revised psychoanalytic theory of the psychoses, was published in *IJP* during this era. As has been shown, analysts began treating psychotic patients following Freud's proposition that psychosis is a similar phenomenon to other normal experiences such as dreaming, falling in love and so forth. Arlow and Brenner claimed that unlike Freud's theory of schizophrenia, which excluded these patients from the purview of psychoanalytic treatment, their revision was based on clinical findings and provided the rationale for psychoanalytic therapy of the psychoses. The wealth of their clinical observations dictated that psychotic patients do not show libidinal withdrawal, but instead exhibit extreme adhesion to their objects. Psychotic transference can be fleeting and unstable, and the patient can fight them aggressively, but Arlow and Brenner had no doubt that psychotic patients do establish transference to their analysts. The significant difference between the neuroses and psychoses, according to this model, is only in the severity of these processes, but the processes themselves (fixation, trauma, conflict, regression, etc.) are the same qualitatively for both neurosis and psychosis.

As previously explained, the predominant themes in articles by American analysts in the *IJP* were of a clinical nature and promulgated the return to and emphasis on clinical work. Therapeutic encounters with schizophrenic patients led these analysts to reformulate a phenomenological picture of mental health and illness that deconstructed previously binary oppositions, such as psychotic-neurotic, schizophrenic-healthy and primitive-developed. The beginning of such a dialectical approach further advocated the notion of the psychotic as not completely psychotic, but rather as having sane parts to his or her personality. Similarly, this approach represented the notion that, while the schizophrenic's ego and superego are relatively primitive, some of their ego structures and functions are preserved, including the ability to create transferential relationships. This dialectical continuum presents a more complex view of the schizophrenic and establishes the possibility of implementing analytic praxis with schizophrenic patients.

Boyer's studies

Supporting this theoretical position, which endorsed the efficacy of the psychoanalytic treatment for schizophrenic patients, Bryce Boyer (1961), a prominent California analyst and codirector of the Center for Advanced Study of the Psychoses, presented his own results of classical analyses of psychotic patients. He conducted an experiment over the course of 13 years, during which his patients received either a full regimen of analytic treatment or analytically oriented psychotherapy (chosen because of a lack of time and funds for the full analytic experience). Psychoanalytic sessions were conducted four times a week, with an occasional fifth and even sixth as necessary. The fact that Boyer describes his work as an "experiment" with an "aim" and "methodology" is evidence of the way in which American analysts learned to tie their work to "science" to defend it during their jurisdictional struggles. That said, Boyer's "experiment" was not based on research methods practiced by the hard sciences or in the laboratory studies of ego psychology. Rather, Boyer explored psychoanalytic treatment by studying the treatment experience itself. Thus, the results of his research revealed that in 13 instances of analytic treatment with schizophrenic patients (including patients who were diagnosed with long-term mental illnesses), there were marked therapeutic successes: after 500 to 1,200 hours of analysis, any significant signs of psychosis disappeared, and improvements in character structure and social functioning were evident. Boyer admitted to the difficulty of fully validating his findings due to the small number of subjects and the inability to compare his treatment with other treatments conducted by other analysts (with other personality traits). However, these factors are not case specific to Boyer's work; they are often cited as lending limited generalizability to most studies on the effectiveness of psychoanalytic treatment or, for that matter, of psychotherapies in general. Boyer's purpose was not only to maintain the uniqueness of psychoanalysis as a method of treatment among the various modalities of psychotherapy, but also to maintain its unique research method (which also differs from those used in other disciplines).

Highlighting the unique contributions of psychoanalysis

Thus, while American analysts publishing in *JAPA* tried to gain leverage over somatic psychiatry by strengthening the medical and scientific roots of psychoanalysis, American analysts publishing in the international arena sought to strengthen the legitimacy of psychoanalysis by underscoring and highlighting its uniqueness and offering different methods of study and research, a different mode of therapy and a unique conceptualization of the relationship between the schizophrenic patient and the therapist. Analysts' actual clinical work with schizophrenic patients, their investment in internally strengthening their theoretical, clinical and scientific foundations and their creation of bridges between different schools of psychoanalysis rather than with their competitors allowed them to maintain a dialectical tension in their perception of their patients (in whom they saw both psychosis and neurosis, the primitive and the mature, the irrational and the rational) and themselves. They differentiated themselves from the "scientific" and medical psychiatrists who worked with "sick" patients and avoided the hazard of undermining the distinctness of the psychoanalytic method by offering themselves as "surrogate mothers" who raised "symbiotic children." In this way, psychoanalysis could maintain its uniqueness as a theory, a therapeutic practice and a research method, compared to both psychiatry and other supportive psychotherapies that were popularized during this period and threatened the position of psychoanalytic work with schizophrenic patients.

62 *Psychoanalysis, psychopharmacology*

American analysts publishing in *IJP* during the 1960s were also engaged in the work of establishing borders against encroaching somatic psychiatry by expressing their dissatisfaction with medical and somatic psychiatric treatment of schizophrenic patients. At best, they argued, drugs are worthwhile in supporting psychoanalytic therapy; at worst, they insisted, such methods of treatment were dangerous and destructive to the patient. These analysts presented evidence of deterioration and harm caused by somatic treatments such as ECT, insulin shock and neuroleptic drugs. ECT was reported to cause memory loss, and the sedatives often administered to psychotics were described as creating a "narcissistic serenity" and a false reality state in the individual and also causing harmful side effects, such as obesity, fatigue and moodiness. With such reliance upon somatic treatments, Searles argued, one should not be surprised, for example, if a patient who was hospitalized for over 10 years in closed wards appeared apathetic to treatment or if one who was treated with 140 insulin shocks and electroconvulsive treatments showed acute confusion (Searles 1962). Those patients who were not helped by somatic treatments or who refused to accept them were described as gaining most from analysis, which dealt with the "real" reality of the patient – his difficulties with object relations addressed in that kind of treatment.

Vouching for the competitors and resisting

Although the majority of American analysts publishing in *IJP* attempted to preserve the uniqueness of psychoanalysis in its encounter with schizophrenia, a minority wanted to forgo the treatment of schizophrenic patients and praised the new alternative of community psychiatry. Psychoanalysis was presented in these articles as a method that could best address other issues such as lack of marital adjustment or satisfaction, problems at work or school, sexual perversions, irrational fears or feelings, guilt, anger, lack of joy, emptiness and self-destructive behaviors (Pleune 1965). These analysts could imagine only a peripheral role in the treatment plan for schizophrenia, since analysis could contribute very little to the treatment of acute patients in state hospitals, and treatment would be better conducted by nurses, occupational therapists and psychiatrists. Community care, combined with the use of neuroleptic drugs, was presented by these analysts as a viable alternative to psychoanalysis. This positive view of community psychiatry was challenged in an article on psychiatry of the poor, by Gustav Bychowski (1970), an analyst who studied with Carl Jung in the Burghölzli Clinic and with Freud in Vienna. Bychowski, one of the pioneers of psychotherapy for psychosis in the United States, argued that what led to the development of community psychiatry was an interest in the mental health of large population groups. He argued that the submovement within psychoanalysis to incorporate family and group therapy led to the abandonment of dual relationships, which are the basis of the psychoanalytic encounter.

Another minority American view in *IJP* was an attempt to accommodate psychoanalysis to the neosomatic trend in psychiatry. Here hybrid theories combined psychoanalytic and medical terminologies to create a new discourse. The most extreme example is an article by Mortimer Ostow (1961), in which he

Psychoanalysis, psychopharmacology 63

attempted to quantify the libido and measured it on a scale ranging from 0 to 10. In states of melancholy or catatonia, he argued, the ego libido is at 0, and in states of mania and early schizophrenia, it is at 10. Ostow claimed that the libido was located within brain structures – the "basal ganglia (perhaps especially the globus pallidus)" (p. 491). Arguing that the libido was organic in nature and could be quantified and measured empirically, Ostow claimed that psychoanalysis was in a position to discuss drugs (the new and attractive arsenal of somatic psychiatry) and thus contribute to the understanding of their operations. He claimed, "Reserpine and the phenothiazine tranquillizers reduce ego-libido level while the hydrazine energizers increase it" (p. 494). The attempt to rationalize the use of drugs that had become available for mental illness demonstrates the difficulty of analysts in ignoring the new and rising power of somatic psychiatry. Some American analysts attempted to remain relevant in the field, if not by dictating the mode of treatment of schizophrenic patients, then at least by providing the analytical theories to explain the effects of the drugs that "cured" patients.

Since schizophrenia was seen by such analysts as a somatic illness, there was a strong backlash against British psychoanalytic theories (particularly Klein and her followers) which, it was claimed, "ignored" these factors. Though such analysts agreed that psychoanalysis and psychotherapy in general were helpful and effective, they provided the caveat that this was only in addition to psychopharmacological treatment (Reg 1962). In this vein an article was written by Kurt Eissler (1969) in a special issue of *IJP*, published in honor of its 50th anniversary, as part of a broader discussion of psychoanalysis as a science and method of treatment. Eissler, a Viennese analyst who emigrated to Chicago after the annexation of Austria by Nazi Germany, presented psychoanalysis as not having a bright future in the wake of new drug treatments. He claimed that the therapeutic effects of medications on schizophrenia were greater than those wrought by psychoanalysis (at least in the acute phase), and he predicted that the medical and psychological professions would rightfully continue in this direction due to medication's relatively smoother and more rapid return of the patient to the pre-disordered condition. Eissler also predicted that psychoanalysis would become useful for small and select groups of people whose issues and diagnoses did not lend themselves to pharmacological treatment (a prediction that came true).

Unlike Eissler, other American psychoanalysts publishing in *IJP* were more disconcerted with the rising power of medications and the marginalization of the "talking cure," and in many articles they alluded to the specific complication this kind of treatment could have when used with schizophrenic patients. Searles (1962), for example, described the schizophrenic's wish "not to be" and his wish to become inanimate and not human. He also added the tendency among patients with schizophrenia to relate to the nonhuman as human. Given these tendencies, in a world where concrete objects (like pills) and machines (like those used for ECT) take the place of people, schizophrenic patients may experience a wish fulfillment of the most destructive type. Thus, the drug technologies of somatic psychiatry, which treat the patient as a "faulty machine" rather than as

64 *Psychoanalysis, psychopharmacology*

a complex human being, contribute to the patient's pathological tendency to minimize his own humanity.

Summary

The neosomatic revolution in psychiatry was initiated when antipsychotic medications began to be used with schizophrenic patients, who were then discharged from overcrowded state asylums into the care of community psychiatry. It was the finest hour of somatic psychiatry and community care, and psychoanalysis in its jurisdictional struggles reacted to these shifts and changes with its own theoretical formulation of schizophrenia and its praxis with these patients. American psychoanalysis, unlike psychoanalysis in other places in the world, and especially in Europe, was medicalized, and thus was struggling for jurisdictions against somatic psychiatry. During these struggles American psychoanalysts developed different theories of schizophrenia and ideas about practice, with some psychoanalysts actually doing practical analytical work with schizophrenic patients, especially in private hospitals.

Both the theorists and those who practiced psychoanalysis with schizophrenics are represented in the articles that have been discussed here. Those publishing in *JAPA* were much more concerned with trying to match or compete with the neosomatic trends in psychiatry as they were writing on schizophrenia, while American analysts who published in *IJP* were invested less in boundary work with their neighbor professions and more in their own unique theory and technique as it served them when treating schizophrenic patients. These two strands of psychoanalysis created a very different view of schizophrenia and its treatment. American analysts publishing in the American journal were mostly influenced by American ego psychology, which formulated an approach to schizophrenia (not unlike somatic psychiatry) of defective organ functioning (i.e., the ego) and appropriated for itself tools from a "medical" toolbox, such as classifications, empirical studies, etiological formulations of the schizophrenic situation and psychoanalytic explanations of the effects of neuroleptic drugs. The danger in this approach, which attempted to keep psychoanalysis relevant in the field of schizophrenia through the use of a medical model, was that the unique research and treatment methods of psychoanalysis were abandoned. The adjustment of analytic theory to include "defective organ functioning" led to therapies so far afield from classic psychoanalytic theory that it was difficult to distinguish between psychoanalysis and other forms of psychotherapy that were simply supportive in nature. These efforts resulted in the creation of a hybrid discourse, combining the abstract language of psychoanalysis with medical jargon of somatic psychiatry. This new hybrid rhetoric within psychoanalysis reflected a collapse of a dialogue between the disciplines of the mind and the disciplines of the brain, those of the psych and those of the soma, and seems to be a result of the idiosyncratic needs of psychoanalysis in the particular situation of its jurisdictional struggle with somatic psychiatry.

The second, clinical-based strand of American psychoanalysis, found mostly in the *IJP*, explained the psychotic and neurotic states as differing only quantitatively.

Instead of touting their superiority in the struggle for professional jurisdiction, analysts turned their attention to sharpening the therapeutic and treatment tools unique to their trade. Their research method was the analytical one, their laboratory the analyst's room and the only manipulation was the psychoanalytic treatment. In attempting to distance themselves from medicine, these analysts criticized somatic treatments in general and pharmacotherapy in particular. They also differentiated psychoanalysis from other forms of psychotherapy, whose main aim was to cure, as they showed an ethical commitment to the deep understanding of the complexity of the schizophrenic state.

Seemingly, it was through the attempt to resolve the internal schisms within psychoanalysis by strengthening ties among the various approaches, especially that of object relations from the United Kingdom and ego psychology from the United States, that a more elaborated psychoanalytic theory of schizophrenia developed and that more attempts at treating these patients were made. By emphasizing its separateness from medicine and highlighting its unique methods of research and practice in the field of schizophrenia, psychoanalysis proved itself more committed to both the understanding of this phenomenon and the treating of it.

As Freud had feared, the attempt to fit psychoanalysis into the neosomatic paradigm blurred the uniqueness of psychoanalysis and risked turning it from a unique mode of research and practice into a simple therapeutic technique to be used by psychiatry. But the danger in this alternative was not only that psychoanalysis would lose its uniqueness, but that schizophrenic patients would lose the opportunity to be treated by a method that focused on their complexity rather than on their pathology. If psychoanalysis were to lose its jurisdictional struggle with somatic psychiatry, schizophrenic patients would revert to being treated according to their own destructive wishes as broken objects that could only be mechanically fixed.

References

Abbott, A., 1988. *The system of professions. An essay on the division of expert labor.* Chicago, IL: University of Chicago Press.

Arlow, J. A., and Brenner, C., 1969. The psychopathology of the psychoses: A proposed revision. *International Journal of Psychoanalysis*, 50, pp. 5–14.

Bergmann, M. S., 1963. The place of Paul Federn's ego psychology in psychoanalytic metapsychology. *Journal of the American Psychoanalytic Association*, 11, pp. 97–116.

Book Notices, 1970. *Journal of the American Psychoanalytic Association*, 18, pp. 736–738.

Boyer, L. B., 1961. Provisional evaluation of psycho-analysis with few parameters employed in the treatment of schizophrenia. *International Journal of Psychoanalysis*, 42, pp. 389–403.

Bychowski, G., 1970. Psychoanalytic reflections on the psychiatry of the poor. *International Journal of Psychoanalysis*, 51, pp. 503–509.

Deri, F., and Brunswick, D., 1964. Freud's letter to Ernst Simmel. *Journal of the American Psychoanalytic Association*, 12, pp. 93–109.

66 *Psychoanalysis, psychopharmacology*

Eissler, K. R., 1969. Irreverent remarks about the present and the future of psychoanalysis. *International Journal of Psychoanalysis*, 50, pp. 461–471.

Fisher, C., 1965. Psychoanalytic implications of recent research on sleep and dreaming – Part II: Implications for psychoanalytic theory. *Journal of the American Psychoanalytic Association*, 13, pp. 271–303.

Freeman, T., 1969. *Psychopathology of the psychoses.* New York: International Universities Press.

Freud, S., 1914. On narcissism. In: *The standard edition of the complete psychological works of Sigmund Freud*, Volume 14. London: Hogarth Press. pp. 67–102.

Freud, S., 1938. An outline of psycho-analysis. In: *The standard edition of the complete psychological works of Sigmund Freud*, Volume 23. London: Hogarth Press. pp. 139–208.

Freud, S., 1950. Project for a scientific psychology. In: *The standard edition of the complete psychological works of Sigmund Freud*, Volume 1. London: Hogarth Press. pp. 281–391. (Original work published 1895).

Fries, M. E., 1961. Some factors in the development and significance of early object relationships. *Journal of the American Psychoanalytic Association*, 9, pp. 669–683.

Frosch, J., 1967. Delusional fixity, sense of conviction and the psychotic conflict. *International Journal of Psychoanalysis*, 48, pp. 475–495.

Frosch, J., 1987. Journal of the American Psychoanalytic Association: A retrospective (1953–1972). *Journal of the American Psychoanalytic Association*, 35, pp. 303–336.

Gitelson, M., 1964. On the identity crisis in American psychoanalysis. *Journal of the American Psychoanalytic Association*, 12, pp. 451–476.

Gosliner, B. J., 1960. Psychosomatic diseases in children and adolescents. *Journal of the American Psychoanalytic Association*, 8, pp. 152–158.

Greenacre, P., 1960. Regression and fixation – Consideration concerning the development of the ego. *Journal of the American Psychoanalytic Association*, 8, pp. 703–723.

Hale, N. G., 1995. *The rise and crisis of psychoanalysis in the United States. Freud and the Americans 1917–1985.* New York: Oxford University Press.

Havnes, L. L., 1962. The placement and movement of hallucinations in space: Phenomenology and theory. *International Journal of Psychoanalysis*, 43, pp. 426–435.

Joint Commission on Mental Illness and Health, 1961. *Action for mental health.* New York: Basic Books.

Jones, E., 1920. Editorial. *International Journal of Psychoanalysis*, 1, pp. 2–5.

Kaplan, M., 1956, March 11. Analyst hits use of calming drugs. *The New York Times.*

Katan, M., 1960. Dream and psychosis: Their relationship to hallucinatory processes. *International Journal of Psychoanalysis*, 41, pp. 341–351.

Kennedy, J. F., 1963, February 5. 50 – Special message to the congress on mental illness and mental retardation[online]. Available at: <http://www.presidency.ucsb.edu/ws/?pid=9546> [Accessed October 13, 2014].

Kernberg, O., 1965. Notes on countertransference. *Journal of the American Psychoanalytic Association*, 13, pp. 38–56.

Lehmann, H. E., 1954. Chlorpromazine: New inhibiting agent for psychomotor excitement and manic states. *Archives of Neurology and Psychiatry*, 71, pp. 227–237.

Lidz, T., Fleck, S., and Cornelison, A., 1965. *Schizophrenia and the family.* New York: International Universities Press.

Lidz, T., and Lidz, R. 1949. The family environment of schizophrenic patients. *American Journal of Psychiatry*, 106, pp. 332–345

Lipton, S. D., 1961. Aggression and symptom formation. *Journal of the American Psychoanalytic Association*, 9, pp. 585–592.

Loewald, H. W., 1960. On the therapeutic action of psycho-analysis. *International Journal of Psychoanalysis*, 41, pp. 16–33.

Loewenstein, R. M., 1967. Defensive organization and autonomous ego function. *Journal of the American Psychoanalytic Association*, 15, pp. 795–908.

Mahler, M. S., 1960. Symposium on psychotic object relationships – Perceptual de-differentiation and psychotic "object relationship." *International Journal of Psychoanalysis*, 41, pp. 548–553.

Mahler, M.S., Furer, M. (1968). On human symbiosis and vicissitudes of individuation. Vol I: Infantile psychosis. New York: International University Press.

Modell, A. H., 1963. Primitive object relationships and the predisposition to schizophrenia. *International Journal of Psychoanalysis*, 44, pp. 282–292.

Nierenberg, H. H., 1963. Symptom formation. *Journal of the American Psychoanalytic Association*, 11, pp. 161–172.

Ostow, M., 1961. The clinical estimation of ego libido content. *International Journal of Psychoanalysis*, 41, pp. 486–496.

Ostow, M., 1962. *Drugs in psychoanalysis and psychotherapy.* New York: Basic Books.

Pleune, F. G., 1965. All dis-ease is not disease: A consideration of psychoanalysis, psychotherapy and psychosocial engineering. *International Journal of Psychoanalysis*, 46, pp. 358–366.

Reg, J. H., 1962. Psychotherapy with schizophrenics. *International Journal of Psychoanalysis*, 43, pp. 471–476.

Rinsley, D. B., 1968. Economic aspects of object relations. *International Journal of Psychoanalysis*, 49, pp. 38–48.

Ross, N., 1960. An examination of nosology according to psychoanalytic concepts. *Journal of the American Psychoanalytic Association*, 8, pp. 535–551.

Searles, H. F., 1962. The differentiation between concrete and metaphorical thinking in the recovering schizophrenic patient. *Journal of the American Psychoanalytic Association*, 10, pp. 22–49.

Searles, H. F., 1963. Transference psychosis in the psychotherapy of chronic schizophrenia. *International Journal of Psychoanalysis*, 44, pp. 249–281.

Settlage, C. F., 1964. Psychoanalytic theory in relation to the nosology of childhood psychic disorders. *Journal of the American Psychoanalytic Association*, 12, pp. 776–801.

Silverman, L. H., 1967. An experimental approach to the study of dynamic propositions in psychoanalysis. The relationship between the aggressive drive and ego regression – Initial studies. *Journal of the American Psychoanalytic Association*, 15, pp. 376–403.

Silverman, L. H., 1970. Further experimental studies of dynamic propositions in psychoanalysis – On the function and meaning of regressive thinking. *Journal of the American Psychoanalytic Association*, 18, pp. 102–123.

Socarides, C. W., 1960. Theoretical and clinical aspects of overt male homosexuality. *Journal of the American Psychoanalytic Association*, 8, pp. 552–566.

Steiner, R., 1994. 'The Tower of Babel' or 'After Babel in Contemporary Psychoanalysis'? Some historical and theoretical notes on the linguistic and cultural strategies implied by the foundation of the International Journal of Psycho-Analysis, and on its relevance today. *International Journal of Psychoanalysis*, 75, pp. 883–901.

68 *Psychoanalysis, psychopharmacology*

Wallerstein, R. S., 1966. The current state of psychotherapy: Theory, practice, research. *Journal of the American Psychoanalytic Association*, 14, pp. 183–225.

Wallerstein, R. S., 1967. A development and metapsychology of the defense organization of the ego. *Journal of the American Psychoanalytic Association*, 15, pp. 130–149.

Whitaker, R., 2002. *Mad in America – Bad science, bad medicine and the enduring mistreatment of the mentally ill.* New York: Basic Books.

4   The "dopamine hypothesis" and evidence of genetic factors in schizophrenia (1971–1980)

> *... we must recollect that all our provisional ideas in psychology will presumably some day be based on an organic substructure. ... We are taking this probability into account in replacing the special chemical substances by special psychical forces.*
>
> (Sigmund Freud, "On Narcissism" 1914, p. 78)

> *If the psychoanalytic movement itself takes refuge in what I regard essentially as a phenothiazine-and-genetics flight from this problem, then the long dark night of the soul will have been ushered in ...*
>
> (Harold Searles, "On Countertransference" 1979, p. 227)

When American experts in psychiatry were asked about the major accomplishments in their field from 1970 to 1980, there was a consensus in their responses. Most agreed that the greatest accomplishments within the field of schizophrenia were "the dopamine hypothesis" and the confirmation of a genetic component in schizophrenia based on twins research (Strauss, Yager and Strauss 1984). These two developments marked the second stage in the neosomatic revolution in American psychiatry within the field of schizophrenia, and psychoanalysis in the United States continued to establish itself in that field during the 1970s, in response to the growing influence of the neosomatic trend in psychiatry.

The dopamine and genetic connections in schizophrenia

If the first stage of the somatic revolution in psychiatry within the field of schizophrenia began with introducing neuroleptic medications, then the second stage detailed these medications' modus operandi and created a hypothesis regarding brain pathology in schizophrenia. Solomon Snyder (1976), who was then a researcher in psychiatry and today is a neuroscientist at Johns Hopkins University (where the neuroscience department is also named after him), was the first to suggest the "dopamine hypothesis" of schizophrenia. Snyder based his studies on pharmacological findings accumulated in the previous decade, when

70 The "dopamine hypothesis"

antipsychotic medications began to be widely used. In a groundbreaking article, Snyder reported that certain medications blocked dopaminergic receptors in the human brain, alleviating many schizophrenic symptoms. The four pieces of evidence leading to the dopamine hypothesis were:

1 High dosages of amphetamines caused psychotic states in normal subjects, similar to those observed in schizophrenia. Snyder claimed that in this context, amphetamine-induced psychosis was the best medical model available for schizophrenia at the time.
2 Amphetamines exacerbated schizophrenic symptoms in patients who were in remission.
3 Dopamine antagonists that reduced the dopaminergic activity and, in particular, phenothiazines (i.e., antipsychotic medications) alleviated certain schizophrenic symptoms.
4 The higher the affinity or interaction between a specific phenothiazine and a dopaminergic receptor (the neurotransmitter's action on the receptor can be compared to putting a key in a lock), the higher was the potency – that is, the efficacy of the medication in alleviating schizophrenic symptoms.

These facts led Snyder (1976) to hypothesize that increased secretion of dopamine or increased activity in the dopaminergic receptor, and especially in the D2 receptor, mediated some of the schizophrenic symptoms.

The dopamine hypothesis, tested in many studies conducted during the following decade, attempted to find the link between the increased dopaminergic activity and schizophrenic symptoms (Seeman et al. 1976). These studies, which were further developed throughout the 1980s and 1990s, claimed to have found that dopamine activity in different areas of the brain was connected to different symptoms. It was argued that excess dopaminergic activity in the mesolimbic system was related to positive symptoms (i.e., delusions and hallucinations), while reduced dopaminergic activity in the mesocortical areas was found to be related to negative symptoms (i.e., a decline in motivation, initiative and cognitive functions). These conditions were described as hyperdopaminergic and hypodopaminergic, and were the rational for the development of more "precise" medications (Davis et al. 1986).

The results of these studies gave the impression that even though schizophrenia was a complex neurological disorder that could not be explained solely by dopamine levels, it should be studied by focusing on the brain's neurological activity, and that treatment should be accordingly focused on the synaptic level. David Healy (2002), an Irish psychiatrist who was a fierce critic of the relationship between the pharmaceutical companies and university hospitals (where most of these studies took place), claimed that the dopamine hypothesis was promoted for the purpose of marketing the drugs the pharmaceutical companies were selling.

The "dopamine hypothesis" 71

Somatic psychiatry not only strengthened its position in its jurisdictional struggles in the treatment of schizophrenia via the dopamine hypothesis; it also provided evidence supporting the hypothesis of schizophrenia's genetic etiology. The most prominent figure among the genetic hypothesis proponents in the United States, Seymour Kety, who began exploring the field as early as 1961, published his seminal studies in the 1970s (Kety, Rosenthal, Wender, and Schulsinger 1976; Kety, Rosenthal, and Wender 1978). Although twins studies were initiated in Denmark during the 1950s and showed higher rates of schizophrenia among monozygotic twins than dizygotic twins, Kety did not settle for these data. He elected for the adoption methodology used by psychologists to assess the genetic component in intelligence. Conducting his research with psychologist David Rosenthal from the National Institute of Mental Health (NIMH) and psychiatrist Paul Wender from Saint Elizabeth's Hospital in Washington, D.C., Kety showed that genetics was a dominant component in the etiology of schizophrenia, but he did not fully contradict the zeitgeist promoted by R. D. Laing and Theodor Lidz, who argued that the cause for schizophrenia was not in the individual but the result of familial and interpersonal toxic environments. Kety did not ignore the complexity of the disorder, arguing that schizophrenia was a syndrome (a cluster of symptoms, with various manifestations and possibly many causes). Although during the 1970s only four responses directly addressing the dopamine hypothesis and Kety's studies were published in the *Journal of the American Psychoanalytic Association* (*JAPA*), American psychoanalysts' formulation of schizophrenia during that time was clearly influenced by these additional findings supporting the neosomatic revolution in psychiatry in the field of schizophrenia.

The pages that follow discuss the development of psychoanalytic theory and practice in the field of schizophrenia, while referencing three seminal events that occurred in somatic psychiatry in an approximately 30-year period (1954–1980): the introduction of neuroleptic medications, the dopamine hypothesis that posited brain pathology in schizophrenia and the hypothesis that schizophrenia had a genetic component. In addition to the two journals that were highly respected by the psychoanalytic community in the 1960s (*JAPA* and the *International Journal of Psychoanalysis*, or *IJP*), during the 1970s two new journals relevant to the study of psychoanalysis and schizophrenia appeared: the *Journal of the American Academy for Psychoanalysis and Dynamic Psychiatry* and the psychiatric journal *Schizophrenia Bulletin*. This chapter studies the published literature on schizophrenia, written by American psychoanalysts in these four journals during the 1970s, for the purpose of developing this discussion and drawing conclusions about the response of these analysts to somatic psychiatry's new accomplishments in the field of schizophrenia. The number of articles on schizophrenia published by psychoanalysts in the 1970s in *JAPA*, the mainstream American journal of psychoanalysis, was about half of what it had been in the previous decade. Even when they did tackle the topic, analysts in the American Psychoanalytic Association showed an increasing inclination to arm themselves with the "weapons" of

72 The "dopamine hypothesis"

their competitors – somatic psychiatrists. Freud "the scientist" was once again resurrected with both his hopes for future biological insights about the mind and his inclination to exclude schizophrenic patients from the jurisdiction of psychoanalysis. Indeed, the hybrid rhetoric from the previous decade returned, mixing the abstract psychoanalytic discourse of ideas with the more concrete, materialistic, somatic terms. Thus, articles written on schizophrenia by psychoanalysts and published in psychoanalytic journals were mainly preoccupied with detailing different brain structures, discussing the functions of neurotransmitters in the nervous system and studying the influence of drugs on various receptors.

The split in psychoanalysis: Somatic psychoanalysis and psychological psychoanalysis

A decade after the introduction of neuroleptic drugs and the deinstitutionalization of the mentally ill, and just before the seminal publication of the dopamine hypothesis, *JAPA* reported on a program funded by NIMH, the institutional offspring of the mental hygiene movement. In the midst of the many accomplishments of somatic psychiatry, the program studied the use of psychotherapy in schizophrenia (Gunderson 1974). The program, led by the well-known analyst Robert Wallerstein, was created for three reasons: (1) discontent about available treatments for schizophrenia, which emphasized mainly pharmacological interventions; (2) a perceived need to examine the conclusion, unlikely but ubiquitous, that intensive psychotherapy (i.e., psychoanalytic treatment) added little to the treatment of schizophrenic patients and (3) the intention of paving the way for seasoned clinicians to use their expertise for relevant and influential future studies on therapy. One of the conclusions reached by the panel discussing that program was that psychoanalysis had not invested enough in studying the two central and influential movements of the previous two decades – namely, psychopharmacology and community psychiatry – which gradually won jurisdiction as they drove psychoanalysis away from the field. Thus, in the 1970s, psychoanalysts continued to operate in the long shadow of the somatic revolution, with some trying to accommodate themselves to a medical approach and others championing the superiority of the talking cure. Psychoanalysts who attempted to reengage with the field of schizophrenia formed two new versions of psychoanalysis – namely, somatic psychoanalysis and psychological psychoanalysis. Somatic psychoanalysis, although never so-named by its proponents, presented Freud as a somatic scientist. As early as 1895, Freud had abandoned the "project for scientific psychology," his attempt to come up with a psychology firmly based on neurophysiology. However, many psychoanalysts writing in *JAPA* in the 1970s on the topic of schizophrenia did not believe they should follow his lead, since such neglect would equal resisting the spirit of scientific investigation. And even though Freud dedicated most of his work to psychological observations, he was portrayed by these analysts as consistently aware of the role of hereditary factors and the contributions of chemical and organic factors in the etiology of mental illness.

The *"dopamine hypothesis"* 73

One clear example of this new somatic psychoanalysis was an article by Gret Heilbrunn (1979), a psychiatrist from Washington University in Seattle and the most outspoken proponent of the new trend. To justify psychoanalysis's "old-new" approach, Heilbrunn repeatedly quoted Freud, the undeniable authority of psychoanalysis (and sometimes took him out of context), as a firm believer in the cardinal place biology would have in the future understanding and treatment of the psyche and its disorders. A variety of his quotes in articles published in *JAPA* strengthened the connection between psychoanalysis and somatic medicine. A few examples of these quotes follow:

> Even when investigation shows that the primary exciting cause of a phenomenon is psychical, deeper research will one day trace the path further and discover an organic basis for the mental event. But if at the moment we cannot see beyond the mental, that is no reason for denying its existence.
>
> (Freud 1900, pp. 41–42)

> . . . we must recollect that all our provisional ideas in psychology will presumably some day be based on an organic substructure.
>
> (Freud 1914, p. 78)

> Biology is truly a land of unlimited possibilities. We may expect it to give us the most surprising information and we cannot guess what answers it will return in a few dozen years to the questions we have put to it. They may be of a kind, which will blow away the whole of our artificial structure of hypotheses.
>
> (Freud 1920, p. 60)

> In view of the intimate connection between the things that we distinguish as physical and mental, we may look forward to a day when paths of knowledge and, let us hope, of influence will be opened up, leading from organic biology and chemistry to the field of neurotic phenomena. That day still seems a distant one, and for the present these illnesses are inaccessible to us from the direction of medicine.
>
> (Freud 1926, p. 231)

> The future may teach us how to exercise a direct influence, by means of particular chemical substances, upon the amounts of energy and their distribution in the apparatus of the mind. It may be that there are other undreamt-of possibilities of therapy.
>
> (Freud 1938, p. 182)

74 The "dopamine hypothesis"

This somatic trend within psychoanalysis proved to go hand in hand with handing over schizophrenic patients to the treatment of somatic psychiatry, and here too, Freud was used as the authority, who categorically warned analysts concerning "the radical inaccessibility of the psychoses to analytic treatment" (Freud 1933 in Heilbrunn 1979).

Aside from claiming the somatic authority from Freud himself, other articles in *JAPA* in this same somatic vein explored anatomic parallels to mental states, based on animal and human studies. To judge from their writings these analysts clearly preferred biological/organic/somatic discourse to the psychological. It was not uncommon to find discourse like this in the psychoanalytic journals of the day: "Chlorpromazine blocks the postsynaptic dopaminergic receptor sites and thus reduces the production of psychotogenic 6-hydroxydopamine which would otherwise be formed due to the dearth of dopamine-beta-hydroxylase, the enzyme normally responsible for the conversion of dopamine to NE" (Heilbrunn 1979, p. 620). Although there was no evidence of the rhetorical hybrid language of the previous decade (e.g., that phenothiazines acted on the *ego*, or that these drugs were influencing *libidinal* levels), the alternative to this jumble of concepts was a purely biological discourse, which seemed odd in a psychoanalytical journal. Furthermore, despite somatic psychoanalysts' paying lip service to the claim that psychotherapy, as opposed to somatic therapy, should remain a part of the psychiatrist's toolbox, they clearly considered pharmacological interventions more important, especially when discussing schizophrenic patients. Heilbrunn (1979) even speculated that "there is every reason to expect the eventual manufacture of drugs that allow the chemical comprehension and manipulation of specific emotions, of personality traits, and of defensive attitudes," and said, "only the future can tell whether or not such pharmaca can decisively influence neurotogenic conflict, and whether existing conflicts can be mitigated molecularly" (p. 621).

While the declared purpose of such articles was bridging physiological and biological processes with basic psychoanalytic notions, it seems as though these bridges were being used to allow analysts to cross over to the side of the victorious profession, somatic psychiatry. Such articles constituted the majority of texts by psychoanalysts on the topic of schizophrenia, reflecting psychoanalysis's somatic trend. The other type of psychological discourse, based on Freud's concepts of drives, conflicts, anxiety, defenses, transference and so forth, was only marginally represented in *JAPA*'s offerings. When such articles found their way to publication, they ostensibly reflected a nostalgic longing for Freud's unitary theory of schizophrenia, and for the psychoanalytic treatments in hospitals prior to the invention of community psychiatry.

John Kafka (1976), a psychiatrist and psychoanalyst working at Chestnut Lodge, quoted Jay Haley, a family therapist who said that if the first psychiatric revolution took psychotic patients out of the attic and into the hospital, the second one took patients out of the hospital and back into the attic (Kafka 1976, p. 713). Since the goal of the treatment became discharging patients back into the community in the shortest amount of time, even psychoanalysts who endorsed psychoanalysis as a viable treatment for schizophrenia agreed that drugs would be the most effective means to reach this goal. Still, analysts expressed their discontent with this goal (Hershey 1978) and were nostalgic for an era when the discussion did not revolve around "schizophrenia," the disorder, but rather, in the spirit of Adolph Meyer, it immersed itself in the schizophrenic individual who might have been born with a normal psyche and only responded to conflict with schizophrenic decompensation (Hartocollis 1976). The idea that with psychoanalytic therapy patients with schizophrenia would benefit in a significant way, and not just simply be made docile enough to be released to the community, reminded analysts of the forgotten advantages of psychiatric hospitals, especially the ones that were psychoanalytically oriented (Book Notice 1971).

The split in psychological psychoanalysis:
Specific vs. unitary theory

In addition to the split between somatic and psychological psychoanalysis, there was also a divide in the psychological psychoanalytic approach to schizophrenia: analysts who adhered to the deficit model of schizophrenia (the specific theory) suggested an adaptation of psychoanalytic treatment tailored specifically to schizophrenic individuals. In contrast, those who held the defense model (the unitary theory) offered classical analytic treatment for schizophrenia with as few parameters as possible.

As noted, the deficit model of schizophrenia, born out of Freud's specific theory, posited a flaw in the ego, caused by congenital, hereditary or metabolic factors, which damaged the formation of initial object relations that, in conjunction with lack of "good enough" mothering and traumatic events, caused the illness. This approach led to treatment designed to repair inner-object representations and construct object constancy, with technical recommendations directed at creating and maintaining rapport, while striving to preserve communication and identification with a caring therapist. In contrast, the defense model, based on Freud's unitary theory, proposed that the loss of mental representations and the distorted ego in schizophrenia were caused by defenses that strove to rid the individual of unbearable affect, terrifying instincts and painful reality. This model called for analysis of impulses and defenses, in addition to providing interpretations of internalized, conflicting and contradictory internal-object relations.

The theory held by clinicians treating schizophrenia affects their treatment technique more than it does in any other mental disorder. Those who believe schizophrenia results from defensive processes view treatment based on the deficit theory as damaging, as it prevents the resolution of psychological conflicts, thus hindering potential ego growth. The defense model/unitary approach assumes that psychotic patients use the primitive defense mechanism of splitting as their core measure of defense, and that appropriate and consistent interpretation

76 The "dopamine hypothesis"

of such defenses, in the context of therapeutic transference, will eventually repair the split and bring forth the use of more mature defenses, such as repression. Therefore, for example, understanding symptoms as the product of early conflicts, which evoke primitive defenses, was presented as the remitting agent in the case of a schizophrenic girl who was observed until adulthood (Sperling 1971). Similarly, a schizophrenic reaction in a young boy (Benson and Pryor 1973) or hallucinations stemming from unprocessed mourning over the death of his brother (Pollock 1972) were both successfully treated with psychoanalysis based on the defense model.

In the face of such claims for therapeutic successes, analysts supporting the opposing deficit model argued that the conflict theory (defense model or unitary theory) lacked validity, and that therapeutic techniques derived from it were ineffective. Interventions stemming from the unitary theory dictate the use of classic analytic technique, which has been described in the literature as dangerous for schizophrenia, because empirical experience has shown that the classical approach increases regression. According to proponents of the deficit theory, during the initial stages of the psychotic regression, the goal of treatment should be creating rapport with the patient, ensuring that the terrified patient receives adequate nutrition and basic health standards. Deficit theory proponents want to minimize the regression and offer the patient a connection, because they perceive the relationship, and not the psychoanalytic interpretation, as the healing agent for the flawed ego. Even after the patient has recovered from the psychosis, these analysts suggest to target the influence and complications brought into the patient's life due to the psychotic episode itself (Gunderson 1974).

As mentioned, both models found in the articles published in *JAPA* offered a psychological psychoanalytic explanation of schizophrenic states, and both offered psychological interventions for work with such patients; however, each, depending on its theory, indicated a very different intervention. While one offered a psychoanalytic approach with as few parameters as possible, the other offered a more supportive treatment, which could easily be confused with other supportive therapies.

A counterculture approach to schizophrenia

In the beginning of the 1970s a new journal emerged in the American psychoanalytic arena, which was particularly active in the field of schizophrenia: the *Journal of the American Academy for Psychoanalysis and Dynamic Psychiatry* (*Journal of the Academy*). The Academy itself, founded in 1956 by a group of psychoanalysts who resigned from the American Psychoanalytic Association, was known for its interest and investment in the treatment of schizophrenic patients, especially in the spirit of Harry Stack Sullivan. The Academy was dedicated to expanding the concept of psychoanalysis beyond that presented by the American Psychoanalytic Association, which was considered a rigid and conservative organization. The pioneers who formed the Academy were Sullivan and Frieda Fromm-Reichmann, in addition to Clara Thompson, an American analyst greatly influenced by Sandor Fereneczi (the renowned Hungarian analyst); Sandor Rado, also Hungarian, who founded the Psychoanalytic Institute at Columbia University; and Franz Alexander, a Hungarian analyst who emigrated to Chicago and was the first to hold an academic position in a university as a psychoanalyst. These analysts were idealists and rebels who declared war on the American Psychoanalytic Association (Hale 1995). While the Association was fighting for jurisdictions in nonmedical disciplines and battling analysts who were not medical doctors, the main thrust of the Academy was debating the place of psychoanalysis within medicine and criticizing psychoanalytic training trends and the American Psychoanalytic Association at large.

Analysts in the Academy emphasized dynamic insight into human behavior, based on scientific findings, without the orthodoxy's rigidity, which was perceived as unequivocally accepting of Freud's original findings. As noted by Silvano Arieti, editor of its first issue published in 1973, the Academy's journal was dedicated to "the psychoanalytic exploration of man in its broadest possible sense, without adherence to the tenets of any one school, a journal open to whoever has a contribution to make in this ever-expanding field" (Arieti 1973a, p. 1). Indeed, in its first decade, the *Journal of the Academy* reflected a distinct interest in schizophrenia. However, within its eclectic voices, the reader was hard-pressed to find a clear theoretical or practical psychoanalytic tendency aside from rebelliousness.

Indeed, in its earliest articles, the *Journal of the Academy* seemed to represent the same intellectual ambiance as the "counterculture" that was its contemporary. On the one hand, analysts in the Academy turned against the "psychoanalytic culture" that had established ego psychology, and on the other, they protested against the broader "psychiatric/somatic/medical culture" and published anti-psychiatric papers. Resistance to psychiatric treatment methods, the diagnosis methods psychiatry offered and its legal right to impose involuntary treatment was present since the beginning of the 19th century. However, the phrase "anti-psychiatry" was coined by David Cooper only in 1967 (Cooper 1967/2001), and the anti-psychiatry movement flourished mainly during the 1960s and 1970s. R. D. Laing (1960), a British psychiatrist and psychoanalyst, was renowned for his interest in schizophrenia and his critical analysis of familial politics, and the American psychiatrist Theodore Lidz (1965) was known for his contribution to the study of schizophrenic patients' families. Both conceptualized schizophrenia as an injury caused by familial malfunction or as an individual's healthy attempt to cope with a sick society. In the same spirit, Thomas Szasz (1960) claimed that mental illnesses were a myth, and the use of the concept "mental illness," he argued, was society's way of policing and controlling deviation from social norms. Similarly, Michel Foucault (1965/1988) posited that ideas such as "sanity" and "insanity" were social constructs, reflecting mainly the power the "sane" had

78 *The "dopamine hypothesis"*

over the "insane." Erving Goffman's (1961) main interest was institutionalized oppression, as it was for Gilles Deleuze and Felix Guattari, who wrote the famous *Anti-Oedipus: Capitalism and Schizophrenia* (1973/1983). All of these writers criticized the belligerent and oppressive place of psychiatry and psychoanalysis in society.

Many sociological issues fueled the growth of the larger counterculture movement in America, which opposed the Vietnam War, racial discrimination, sexual conservatism and more; mainly it rebelled against traditional forms of authority. In this very spirit the Academy's culture was mainly counter to psychiatric authority and its argument that schizophrenia was a disease or a somatic defect. The Academy was also counter to orthodox psychoanalytic authority and its focus on the psyche of the individual, while ignoring his social world. The *Journal of the Academy* was an unofficial representative of the counterculture, emphasizing the paramount role of society in the construction of an individual as "healthy" or "mentally ill" (Davidson 1979). Articles published by analysts in the *Journal of the Academy* frequently referred to the possible connection between schizophrenia and the many changes witnessed in American society: the Vietnam War (Liebert 1974), immigration and urbanization (Schecter 1974), divorce, juvenile delinquency and drug abuse (Gibson 1974). Society was often portrayed in the *Journal of the Academy* as sick and manufacturing sickness. Individuals within the society were depicted as having to choose between mass madness and their own madness. Societal impact on the development of schizophrenia was also mentioned in the context of the American myth of self-reliance and individualism, as lauded in the writings of such as Henry David Thoreau and Ralph Waldo Emerson (Spiegel 1973). The myth, leading to solitude, was described as a social value that, in its harsh shuttering of the illusion of merging and unity, might cause psychosis (Satran 1978).

Another societal characteristic perceived as a potential cause of psychosis was related to society's rejection of homosexuality and schizophrenia. The emphasis on the societal component of mental illness implied that the plight of homosexuals stemmed first and foremost from having to live in a heterosexual society, and that this risk factor might instigate the outbreak of schizophrenia (Levy 1979). What appears to be a "blaming society" trend was at times radicalized, and society was portrayed as a "dangerous and hostile jungle" (Gralnick 1979). In this context, the spirit of Freud's seduction theory, which located the source of trauma in the mistreatment of children and which he abandoned early in the development of his psychoanalytic theory, as he realized the significance of childhood sexuality and phantasies, was reintroduced into psychoanalytic discourse.

Placing the leading cause of schizophrenia as external and distancing the discussion from the intra-psychic realm, on the one hand, and the somatic (genetic and brain malfunctioning) realm, on the other, seemed to undermine the conceptual meaning of illness and health. Parting with the medical conceptualization of schizophrenia manifested not only in objecting to the use of concepts such as "illness" and "health;" it also brought forth the argument that those who perceive the psychotic process as solely a disease reject the possibilities it offers. Arguing that schizophrenic states are in fact an opportunity for growth, some analysts in the Academy called for a different treatment (Shainberg 1973). Sedatives, for example, would be carefully and hesitantly administered if the process were perceived as potentially beneficial: "To dull the pain might in fact hurt the patient more than help him. This is a violation of our basic Hippocratic oath. Using the paradigm I am suggesting our goal would be to encourage the person in his struggles rather than dulling his process" (Shainberg 1973, p. 284). In the *Journal of the Academy*, psychosis was portrayed as an opportunity to express repressed emotions in people harmed by society, those who suffered incest and complex traumas such as the Holocaust, the dropping of the atomic bomb on Hiroshima and the Vietnam War (Lifton 1976). Because of the supposition that schizophrenia was caused by social and environmental circumstances, the schizophrenic person was perceived as a survivor. Any survival condition might result in avoidance, stagnation and petrifaction; however, it might also stimulate confrontation, heightened sensitivity and rejuvenation. In this context, psychosis was not understood as a disease but as an opportunity for development and growth.

The conceptualization of psychosis or schizophrenic states, not as an illness in the medical sense, but as a potential for change, growth and development, marked the departure of the Academy from the medical model of illness. Few would have recommended the psychotic state for the purpose of development due to the pain and risk it entails. However, to view a psychosis as "nothing but an unfortunate illness, or to define the goals of psychotherapy with severely disturbed patients simply as getting over their craziness" was understood as doing "great violence to the inner experience of the individual and to the developmental struggle in which she or he is engaged" (Keniston 1973, p. 31). Thus, within the *Journal of the Academy*, schizophrenia was presented as a developmental struggle, and this served a more general argument that, since psychoanalysis did not deal with diseases, it did not fit the medical model. It was argued that, on a superficial level, psychoanalysis in the United States could be seen as part of the medical field, since most psychoanalysts were also medical doctors. They treated patients who suffered from illnesses such as neuroses or psychosomatic disorders, and these were diagnosed via established medical techniques. However, in the view of analysts publishing in the Academy, psychiatric disorders were not diseases but rather behavioral disturbances, devoid of organic or somatic pathology (Redlich 1974; Guntrip 1973). Freud and "The question of lay analysis" were also recruited to prove that the medical aspect was not essential for the analyst. The decision to tie analysis to the medical profession was perceived as valid in analysis's early stages in the United States, but during the 1970s, when psychoanalysis has already expanded and gained prestige, it was argued that this position must change, and psychoanalysis should not be considered as a medical subspecialty, but rather as a new method for "growth" and "development."

80 The "dopamine hypothesis"

Dissidents in the academy

Critics of the anti-psychiatry approach within the Academy emerged as well, albeit marginally. There was some criticism of psychiatrists who wrote about the "death of the family" or considered marriage as "a trap," recommending alternative, communal lifestyles and childrearing practices (Ryckoff 1975). Laing, for example, was presented as the one who has created a myth in which "the character named Family (Capitalism) wears the black hat, and the character called Schizophrenic Child wears the white one" (Ryckoff 1975, p. 127). Criticizing this trend, the author added:

> Unlike the movies, however, in this scenario the good guys do not always win . . . my own thought and experience has left me with the conviction that the human condition is inherently dichotomous and full of conflict, that we struggle *toward* unity, and that by and large we end up with reconciliation, a less exciting but useful outcome.
>
> (p. 128)

As stated, the most distinctive characteristic of the Academy was its eclecticism. And so, alongside the dominant voice of social/nurture influences in the development of schizophrenia, articles that supported Kety's findings emerged as well, pointing to a genetic component central to schizophrenia. In one such article, the child was perceived as born with a genetic defect and, therefore, even the best of environments would be experienced by the child as not "good enough" (Kestenbaum 1980). Attachment-focused studies and infant observation supported such hypotheses. Even "good enough" mothers were presented as unable to live up to the added challenges of raising such "defective" children, who are flooded with emotions they cannot comprehend; children who cannot differentiate between anger and fear, sadness and frustration, and who need tremendous assistance in recognizing and managing their subjective emotions and in correcting emotional distortion (Symonds 1973). Parents in these articles were viewed, not as those who created the illness, but rather as victims of their child's inborn disorder. Life with a schizophrenic child was portrayed as potential "hell" for the parent, and those parents described in early psychoanalytic texts as the cause of the child's condition were now depicted as the burnt-out victims of living with a seriously disturbed child (Symonds 1973, p. 175). In the same spirit, Silvano Arieti (1977) reported, for example, that in 75% of cases observed in psychodynamic therapies of schizophrenic patients, the mother does not fit the image of the "schizophrenogenic mother" and the patients neither come from a disturbed milieu nor disclose unusual psychodynamic history. Arieti, who gave much importance to genetics in the causality of schizophrenia, posited that lack of adequate attachment and object constancy were not the fault of the child or the mother. He suggested circumventing the trap of "blame psychology" and with it the problematic concepts such as the "schizophrenic mother" or "refrigerator parents." Despite the emphasis on genetics in these articles, implying incorporation of the psychiatric research findings, almost all of the articles published in the *Journal of the Academy* stressed the combination of genetics and the environment that contributed to the etiology of schizophrenia. Nature versus nurture discussions were frequent, and it was argued that "to speak of the relative contribution of genetic and environmental factors in the individual case is as reasonable as speaking of the relative contribution of the sperm and the egg to the production of a fetus. They are both necessary" (Cancro 1975, p. 356). Not all individuals have the potential to become schizophrenic, and the disposition is hereditary, but the idiosyncratic pattern of traits that create such vulnerability in a specific setting could be more adaptive in another setting.

Alongside the "counter" voices in the Academy that put a strong emphasis on the social factors in schizophrenia, the seminal studies in somatic psychiatry discussing the physiological factors in schizophrenia and especially highlighting genetics were incorporated into the psychoanalytic etiological explanation of schizophrenia. Because genetics could not be considered the sole cause of schizophrenia, the environment would determine whether an individual with such a disposition would indeed develop schizophrenia. Thus, another focus in the *Journal* was the nature of genetic vulnerability. These discussions shifted from familiar psychoanalytic concepts, such as impulses, conflicts and defenses, to discussions of emotions and cognitions.

Since the theoretical understanding of schizophrenia held by psychoanalysts in the Academy was unique, so were the Academy's clinical recommendation. Most discussions called for caution in prescribing high doses of medications that might harm patients' health and deter them from possibly using the psychosis for growth (Gibson 1974). Repeatedly, analysts warned that "magic drugs" that eliminate illnesses or "miracle pills" that fix the distortions in patients' lives are nothing but an illusion (Heath 1974). Neuroleptic medications were perceived as not sufficiently specific, and studies allegedly supporting the hypothesis that pharmacological interventions were more effective than psychoanalytic psychotherapy were challenged by claims that they were based on results from inexperienced therapists trained in a classically Freudian approach, which was argued as being inappropriate for the treatment of schizophrenia (Schecter 1974).

Those who believed schizophrenia could be treated with psychoanalytic psychotherapy noted that the diagnosis itself sometimes caused prognostic hopelessness and therapeutic nihilism, but they were divided in two camps when it came to treatment. The first approach, influenced mostly by Mahler's object-relations theory and child observations, believed that the schizophrenic patient needed "re-parenting" due to the symbiotic familial patterns of his or her upbringing. Therapeutically, this approach recommended a symbiotic stage of treatment, within which the patient would gradually grow and develop separation and individuation capacities. The second approach, influenced by cognitive perspectives in psychoanalysis, claimed that the patient was born with a genetic vulnerability and was trapped in primitive thinking patterns and defective symbolic functioning that caused a distorted understanding of the world and its objects, which the patient perceived as partial. According to this approach, the patient needed

82 *The "dopamine hypothesis"*

to be "re-educated" and given access to knowledge and insight regarding his or her condition. This approach, too, emphasized the therapeutic relationship, since it perceived cognition as interpersonally developed (Crowly 1980). Both approaches viewed treatment as contributing to the expansion of the patient's degrees of freedom. However, the first approach, born in private hospitals and represented by Searles's work, posited that the patient should be allowed to regress into symbiosis; the second approach, born in public and academic treatment settings and represented by Arieti, posited that the patient should be treated as an adult who can learn how to regain control over his or her pathology and thus increase the level of autonomy and agency. During the 1960s, Searles's approach was the leading one in the *International Journal of Psychoanalysis*, but Arieti's was notably dominant in the *Journal of the Academy*.

The psychoanalytic counterculture presented in the *Journal of the Academy* perceived treatment as an agent of "growth" and "development" and not as an instrument of "cure" or "health," and psychoanalysis was seen as an approach to strengthen the patient's autonomy, individualism and creativity, and as means for reigniting the desire to gain control over his or her life. As noted, the Academy went against the new trend in psychiatry, as well as mainstream psychoanalysis. Arieti, who won a National Book Award for his 1974 edition of *Interpretation of Schizophrenia*, argued that one could not directly reach the unconscious and, therefore, as a therapist he chose to connect to the more integrated aspects of the ego, even if the price was neglecting the more primitive components of the psyche, such as phantasies. Arieti compared the treatment goal in schizophrenia to guiding the pseudo-poet, the patient, in his or her return to reality by using secondary processes (that is, the more rational, conscious thought processes as opposed to the unconscious, primary thought processes). This treatment was an alternative to the psychoanalytic encouragement of regression (as in the writings of Searles, for example) that was criticized in the Academy, and the somatic treatment that created dependency on medications. Both these treatments were depicted as infantilizing the schizophrenic patient, instead of encouraging his or her efforts at autonomy and growth (Shainberg 1973). Suffering was understood as a motivational factor for change and, unlike the view of the medical model, did not necessarily indicate a disorder (Redlich 1974). In this context it was also advised that a lower dose of medication should be used in order to not sedate the patient and instead allow the process of growth to reach its fullest potential (Gibson 1974). The shock treatment that created quiet and compliant, "orally dependent" patients was criticized as misunderstanding the nature of mental illness (Shave 1974). Instead of viewing the analyst-patient relationship as a mother-child relationship, most authors writing in the *Journal of the Academy* argued that the therapeutic relationship should not encourage regression to a more childish, dependent, compliant functioning, but should be conceived as a relationship between equal parties who would contribute to moving the patient from primitive cognition to higher, mutual, co-constructed cognitive functioning.

The "dopamine hypothesis" 83

Apparently, the articles that highlighted strengthening the patient's independence also stemmed from the new reality established after the era of deinstitutionalization. After the widespread discharge of patients from hospitals back to the community, schizophrenic patients were not provided with suitable conditions for regression-based psychoanalytic treatments. Since most patients were discharged to day programs, only private hospitals enabled psychoanalytic treatment in which the patient could be allowed to "regress to symbiosis" with an analyst. Allowing psychoanalysis to function within private practice and day treatment centers, alongside community and pharmacological treatments, required psychoanalytic treatment that promoted not "regression in the service of progress" but rather "progress in the service of progress"; not "dependency in the service of independency" but rather "independency in the service of independency"; not an investigation of the inner world of phantasies to strengthen the grip on reality, but rather strengthening the grip on reality for the purpose of promoting more effective functioning within it.

Though these analysts presented an attempt to fortify the integrative aspects of the patient, they did not ignore the inherent difficulty of working analytically with schizophrenic patients. They argued that analysts who work with such patients were coping with powerful countertransference reactions and required sustainable resources of compassion, diligence, patience and persistence (Ehrenberg 1974). This notion demonstrated the commitment of the analyst to working with schizophrenic patients. However, it also hinted at the strain of the therapeutic encounter with such patients. This strain, alongside changes occurring within psychoanalysis, was one of the reasons that psychoanalysts distanced themselves from these patients.

As mentioned, Sullivan's statement that "we are all much more simply human than otherwise" hovered above the Academy's publications, and during the 1970s a vibrant ethical discussion took place, influenced by philosophers such as Martin Buber, about the concept of "otherness." Arieti (1973b), who was influenced by these ideas, argued that by connecting to schizophrenia's "otherness" one can connect to the most humane, potent and universal parts of oneself. In his written response to his book award he stated that the judges who granted him the award probably understood that the study of schizophrenia transcended the investigation of the condition itself:

> No other condition in human pathology permits us to delve so deeply into what is specific to human nature. Although the main objective of the therapist of the schizophrenic is to relieve suffering, he will have to deal with a panorama of the human condition, which includes the problems of truth and illusion, bizarreness and creativity, grandiosity and self-abnegation, loneliness and capacity for communion, interminable suspiciousness and absolute faith, motivated self-destruction and unmotivated crime, blaming and self-accusation, surrender to love and hate and imperviousness to these feelings.
>
> (Arieti 1975, p. 234)

84 The "dopamine hypothesis"

The deliberation over finding similarities between the schizophrenic state and other human conditions, such as the reaction to loss of loved ones (Shave 1974), the reaction to traumatic events like the Holocaust, Hiroshima or the Vietnam War (Lifton 1976), as well as mystical experiences of trance (Nafatlin 1975) and creative processes (Barnett 1979), illustrated the determination to see the schizophrenic individual, although an "other," neither as a complete stranger nor outside of the range of human experiences.

American analysts in the international arena: Researching the root of Freud's split theory of schizophrenia

While this was the tone in the Academy, American analysts publishing in the international arena were attempting, too, to rework their theories of schizophrenia to adapt to the genetics findings of somatic psychiatry. Kety's research concerning the genetics of schizophrenia required analysts to rethink the "defective" heredity of the schizophrenic patient. In the international arena, the 1970s were marked by searching Freud's theory of the "deficit" in schizophrenia, and the old historic split between the "deficit" theory and the theory of the "conflict" were widely discussed. Critical reading of Freud's writings and expanding on some of his undeveloped ideas brought either a more established support for one side of the split, while maintaining some acceptance of the other side, or an attempt to synthesize both sides and create a new theory of schizophrenia. Such new theories leaned not only on various psychoanalytic theoretical bases, but also on clinical experience with schizophrenic patients and empirical research in the field. Though the declared purpose of these synthetic endeavors was to develop a contemporary psychoanalytic theory "worthy of schizophrenia," one can argue that, in the context of the blow psychoanalysis suffered in the previous decade, another goal was to prove that psychoanalysis was "worthy of schizophrenia," or in other words, that as professionals psychoanalysts could contribute to the understanding of this disorder and its treatment. The numerous theoretical developments during these years illustrate the level of intellectual investment on the part of American psychoanalysts in this topic. Some of this significant work was done by Nathaniel London (1973a, 1973b), from the New England Psychoanalytic Society, who studied Freud's two theories of schizophrenia; Ping-Nie Pao (1973, 1977), an analyst who managed the psychotherapy department of Chestnut Lodge and was known for his work with hospitalized schizophrenic patients; Gerald Aronson (1977), a Los Angeles-based psychoanalyst who was a member of a research group that studied psychoanalysis and its encounter with schizophrenia; James Grotstein (1977a, 1977b), also from Los Angeles, a psychiatrist and psychoanalyst who based much of his theory on the writing of analysts such as Wilfred Bion, Jacques Lacan and Ignacio Matte-Blanco; as well as Thomas Ogden (1980), an analyst from San Francisco known for referencing British theories of psychotic disorders. Contributions by Grotstein and Ogden best represent the depth of psychoanalytic inquiry and the intellectual undertaking of American psychoanalysts to unite theory and practice in psychoanalysis within the field of schizophrenia.

James Grotstein (1977a, 1977b) published two papers in *IJP* titled "The Psychoanalytic Concept of Schizophrenia: I. The Dilemma" and "The Psychoanalytic Concept of Schizophrenia: II. Reconciliation," which suggested a rewriting of the psychoanalytic theory of schizophrenia. Grotstein argued for integrating psychoanalytic metapsychology with the newer psychoanalytic contributions, such as in ego psychology, object relations, narcissism and infantile development in particular, and with the rapidly expanding body of knowledge in the behavioral sciences generally. In the first article, he presented the dilemma (deficit or conflict theories) through a review of psychoanalytic theories, and in the second paper, he brought forth a reconciliation of the dilemma in an attempt to match the theory to the clinical data on schizophrenia, for the purpose of rectifying, reintegrating, re-exploring and reconciling the theory with a considerable body of behavioral scientific data. The two theories of schizophrenia – conflict (Freud's unitary theory) and the defective ego (Freud's specific theory) – were presented as a split left from Freud's legacy. Grotstein, in the spirit of reconciliation, suggested bridging the gap between these two psychoanalytic theories by using the concept of "threshold apparatus." The "threshold apparatus" (or frontier, or barrier) is considered to be the psychoanalytic prototype of the newborn's ability to defuse impulses and tension caused by external stimuli. This ability is developed as a result of the presence of neutralizing object representations – that is, memory traces of significant others. It is suggested that, in schizophrenia, this frontier is flawed, and primitive defense mechanisms such as splitting, magical omnipotence, denial, idealization and projective identification function as psychological parallels to that blocking frontier or neutralizing barrier, which facilitate the ignoring, delaying or elimination of awareness of intrusive or painful reality. If the schizophrenic patient is born with a flawed threshold apparatus, his or her omnipotent denial and projective identification would intensify to prevent external stimuli from flooding the patient. Because these are not particularly effective defense mechanisms, the patient then experiences increased psychic stress and more conflicts. Thus, Grotstein did not choose between deficit and conflict, between ego defect and dynamic struggles. Instead, he argued that the defect in the ego could be conceptualized as a heightened sensitivity to emotional conflicts.

Although he does not directly refer to Kety's findings on genetic vulnerability, Grotstein quoted researchers who found that schizophrenic children had a deficit or delay in the integration of perceptive processes and further suggested that infants "at risk" for schizophrenia show a dichotomy of premature sensitivity and premature closure. Since the primitive stimulus barrier fails to defend them from overstimulation, there is an overreaction of the defensive equipment available, and premature closure is one such defense. In these cases a schizophrenic personality develops alongside the normal personality, and it becomes the core characteristic of what Grotstein called "real schizophrenics," those who could be described as having an ego defect. Grotstein also made an important distinction between schizophrenia and psychosis (which is very often overlooked, as these concepts are used

86 The "dopamine hypothesis"

interchangeably): schizophrenia begins to reveal itself as ongoing bizarreness of thoughts and cognition, as well as other aspects of behavior, and can "silently" exist in the normal psyche as "nonpsychotic schizophrenia." Psychosis, in contrast, can present itself in the context of schizophrenia or outside of it. Psychosis, Grotstein argued, consists of a lack of ego-boundary organization and mental representations, poor reality testing and a state in which the "wall of the psychic space" has collapsed (Grotstein 1977b, p. 433). Grotstein argued that psychosis has some points in common with schizophrenia, especially in terms of bizarre behaviors, and they both have a psychosomatic nature. However, the schizophrenic personality develops from a defective neurophysiological personality, related to the failure of the stimulus-barrier apparatus and defective integration of sensory information. Psychosis, in contrast, involves biochemical alterations in the neural systems.

Although Grotstein, too, is using the somatic discourse of the time, it seems that he used his understanding of the physiological mechanisms in schizophrenia to actually reinforce the psychoanalytic jurisdiction when it comes to treatment. He criticized his competitors in the jurisdictional struggle – somatic psychiatry – saying that the antipsychotic medications aimed at changing the abnormal chemistry of the brain were missing the real goal, which is the alteration of the personality structure, itself the product of distorted development. Phenothiazines might potentially treat the biochemical changes present in schizophrenic psychosis, he argued, but only psychoanalytic treatment could change the schizophrenic structure that is at the core of the phenomenon of psychosis.

Grotstein's integrative approach was an attempt to integrate neurobehavioral and biological data with the psychoanalytic metapsychology of schizophrenia to reach an ultimate conceptualization. In his effort to fortify psychoanalysis within the field of schizophrenia he united not only the soma and the psyche, but also the splits within psychoanalysis itself, between the deficit theory and the conflict theory. "Schizophrenia deserves a worthy psychoanalytic theory" (Grotstein 1977b, p. 450), he wrote, suggesting that the two theories could be reconciled through a unifying theory that emphasized the relationships among narcissism, infantile psychosis and infant development. This integration of the splits, as reflected in Grotstein's discourse, not only enriched the understanding of schizophrenia, but also contributed to the unification of psychoanalytic schools, thus strengthening psychoanalysis as it faced the rising status of somatic treatments of schizophrenia.

Much like Grotstein, Thomas Ogden (1980), in his article "On the Nature of Schizophrenic Conflict," also made an attempt to integrate the split within the psychoanalytic theory of schizophrenia. His psychoanalytic formula suggested that schizophrenia is a form of psychopathology involving both a meaningful conflict (as in the conflict theory) and meaningless states (as in the deficit theory). According to Ogden, the schizophrenic conflict is nothing else but a conflict between wishes to maintain a psychological state in which meaning can exist, and wishes to destroy meaning, thought and the capacity to think and to create experience. Ogden suggested that, unlike the neurotic conflict, the schizophrenic conflict does not involve tension between two contradictory sets of meaning, but rather a tension between meaning, on the one hand, and an attack on meaning, on the other. He mentioned other writers who emphasized states of "unthinking" or "non-experiencing" in schizophrenia; however, contrary to such writers, he proposed that these states are phases in the process of resolving the schizophrenic conflict, and are not terminal or final states.

Ogden, who believed in the efficacy of psychoanalytic therapy with patients suffering from schizophrenia, proposed four stages in the process of resolving the schizophrenic conflict: "non-experience," "projection identification," "psychotic experience" and "symbolic thought." Each stage is contingent on the developmental achievements established in the previous stage. Ogden presented these stages by describing an analytic treatment of a schizophrenic patient who he saw even during periods of acute psychosis and hospitalizations.

In his articles, Ogden, like Grotstein, contributed to an area in which somatic psychiatry had not shown much development, and that is the differentiation between psychosis and schizophrenia. He viewed psychosis as a form of psychological disorganization that could occur in any personality structure under certain conditions, causing blurring of ego boundaries, disturbance to the ego functions – especially integration and reality testing – and increased primary thinking processes. In contrast, schizophrenia refers to a personality structure that has a specific type of organization and development. Ogden, even more sharply than Grotstein, argued that somatic psychiatry might be able to treat psychosis but cannot treat schizophrenia and, furthermore, may impede the ability to recover from schizophrenia when it is treated as a psychosis that should be eliminated.

Ogden emphasized the gap between his psychoanalytic approach and somatic psychiatry. While the latter attempted to cancel the period of acute psychosis and symptomology via drug treatments, he viewed the state of psychosis as an essential stage in the conflict resolution process of schizophrenia. Without explicitly naming the disagreement, Ogden stated that sometimes, when patients are hospitalized, some treatment teams, together with family members, exert pressure on the patient to take antipsychotic medication at a time when the patient is trying to desperately live his or her perceptions, experiences and thoughts, even if they are primitive. Ogden posited that it is actually the unmedicated patient who appears to be vibrant and accessible in treatment, even if that person is acutely psychotic. The danger, which is used to legitimize somatic psychiatry's arguments against psychoanalytic treatments, is that during this period of growth the patient might try to and even succeed in committing suicide or harming others. But, Ogden argued, in this stage there is a fine line between suffocating the patient's potential for experience and the risk of the patient being flooded and becoming violent or suicidal in order to end the experience.

Ogden presented psychoanalysis as more willing to take risks in the name of growth and development than somatic psychiatry. He presented somatic psychiatry as silencing and numbing at its best, damaging the patient's potential to experience and fully live life, and, at its worst, as collaborating with the psychotic apparatus, which aims to stop the thinking. According to Ogden, if the patient is allowed to go through the third dangerous stage, the next stage in the process of resolving the psychotic conflict would allow the patient to reach symbolic

88 *The "dopamine hypothesis"*

thinking capacities. This would reduce the auditory hallucinations, paranoid and grandiose delusions and states of confusion. Psychoanalysis is presented as a braver and more effective treatment method than psychiatry's somatic treatments, and somatic psychiatry and its pharmacological interventions are depicted as harmful for the possibility of conflict resolution.

The risk assumed by psychoanalysts when pursuing such tasks became a focal point in the greater discussion of American psychoanalysts in the international arena – in particular on psychoanalysis disengaging from schizophrenic patients. Aside from "blaming" the successes of the neosomatic revolution in psychiatry for the disconnect of psychoanalysis from these patients, analysts were searching their own souls and suggesting that it was the mere difficulty that analytic work with schizophrenia created, due to the countertransference quality, that could be the potential reason for analysts' choice to turn their backs on such treatments. This countertransference could have been containable in the context of the psychiatric hospital, but was too much when analysts have to manage it on their own. The supposedly humanistic act of discharging patients from hospitals is portrayed as exchanging the "containing walls" of the hospitals for medications (Shoenberg 1977). The hospital walls, named "The Brick Mother" by the British psychiatrist and psychoanalyst Henri Rey (1994), could provide the function of a containing mother, and thus help the analyst to make meaning of the tormenting psychotic experiences endured by the psychotic patient. The use of drugs to eliminate symptoms was perceived to be an escape and a regression (Katan 1979), and, rather than being a novel invention of psychiatry, it was sarcastically argued that the fact that drugs could control unwanted moods was as old as gin and whisky (James 1975, p. 111). The call for continuous access to analytic treatment for schizophrenic patients was grounded in the confidence that analysis could provide a worthy alternative to somatic psychiatry's "mass drugging." This confidence stemmed from the recognition that in the therapeutic encounter, the analyst does not face "a mad mob" s/he needs to silence, but rather connects to the unique individual. Robert Stoller's book, *Splitting: A Case of Female Masculinity* (1973), reviewed in *IJP*, provided an example of the ability of an analyst to maintain a unique view of one schizophrenic patient (Vanggaard 1975). In its 400 pages, the book told the story of Stoller's analytic treatment of a woman diagnosed with schizophrenia, including the various inpatient hospitalizations she had, at times as an involuntary patient, notwithstanding her own perspective of her experiences. This book demonstrated the difference between somatic psychiatry's view and treatment of patients with schizophrenia, and that of psychoanalysis, and it obviously stressed psychoanalysis's uniqueness and superiority over other methods.

Psychoanalysis "light" for psychiatrists: Contributions from the *Schizophrenia Bulletin*

During the 1970s another journal was added to the discourse on schizophrenia. *Schizophrenia Bulletin*, sponsored by NIMH, first appeared in December 1969, initially as an experiment, and since 1974 has been published quarterly. NIMH's goal in sponsoring the *Bulletin* was to support psychological, behavioral and neurological research to reduce the hardship caused by mental illness and behavioral disturbances. NIMH funded psychoanalytic trainings and schizophrenia studies in previous decades. However, from the end of the 1970s onward, it directed most of its resources to the study of core sciences, behavioral science and the use of new discoveries in neuroscience, molecular genetics and brain imagery techniques, while attempting to translate that new knowledge into clinical research questions. Since the Social Security Amendment of 1956, NIMH has provided the funds and the frame for a combined committee on child mental health and community mental health centers. Additional constitutional amendments in 1975 prompted NIMH to increase its support of community mental health centers.

The *Bulletin* itself offers a review of recent developments and empirically based hypotheses in the field of schizophrenia etiology and treatment. The editors stated that they support a wide and thorough perspective, and therefore give space to papers focused on the molecular basis of schizophrenia and on social and cultural factors that cause the illness. Each issue is edited by a guest editor and is focused on a specific theme. The *Bulletin* features writings by American and international contributors and is distributed internationally. First person accounts of life with schizophrenia are regularly included in this publication. The *Bulletin* offers various opinions regarding brain research, clinical discourse and the environmental and genetic factors in schizophrenia, and features artwork by artists suffering from mental illness on every issue's cover.

Because of the shifting interest of the U.S. government, NIMH's investment in schizophrenia diminished in favor of an emphasis on addictions, suicide, eating disorders, panic disorders, depression and minorities. Its former interest and investment in psychoanalysis has also shifted, and the NIMH is supporting mainly research in basic sciences, brain sciences, neuroscience, genetics and psychopharmacological treatment. As a result, in 2004 the NIMH stopped its support of the *Bulletin*, and it was transferred to Oxford University Press, a private company, and the Maryland State Center for Psychiatric Research.

The aim of analyzing the articles published in the *Bulletin* is to uncover psychoanalysts' attitudes toward schizophrenia when they wrote for psychiatrists working within the field of schizophrenia. The result of this specific exploration of articles published in the *Bulletin* during the 1970s revealed a limited involvement of psychoanalysis in the field. Only seven articles considered psychoanalysis, and of these only three expanded on psychoanalytic treatments for schizophrenia, and even these papers presented a "light" version of psychoanalysis. In contrast to the American psychoanalysts' endeavor in the international arena to develop a psychoanalytic theory of schizophrenia and techniques to use in working with patients, the *Bulletin* gave little space to psychoanalytic theories of schizophrenia and barely studied schizophrenia's etiology or phenomenology from a psychoanalytic viewpoint. The *Bulletin* was mostly concerned with its treatment, in all

90 *The "dopamine hypothesis"*

stages and settings, from the moment of hospitalization until the release into private practice.

These articles suggest that in the shadow of the rising power of neosomatic and community psychiatry, a new kind of psychoanalysis was established, designed for psychiatrists and "speaking" their language. Unlike the psychoanalytically rich and sophisticated discussions on the theory and treatment of schizophrenia flourishing among American psychoanalysts in the international arena, analysts in the *Bulletin* were more medically oriented. Their emphasis was on observable behaviors, and they rarely lent themselves to an in-depth analysis of the historical question posed by Menninger: "What is behind the symptom?" In the same spirit, the therapeutic recommendations were more oriented toward medicine and nursing than psychoanalysis. For instance, when he presents a psychoanalytic understanding of the schizophrenic dynamic, Clarence Schultz (1975), an analyst from the Washington Psychoanalytic Institute, as an example, based his explanation of schizophrenic symptoms on the normal development model. But even then, the schizophrenic state is equated to the infantile state, without allowing room for variance and complexity: omnipotence and egocentricity are equated to the infant's self-centered and narcissistic position, which results in poor reality testing; delusions and hallucinations are equated to the infant's primitive thinking and hallucinatroy wish fulfillment when a need is not met; schizophrenic splitting is similar to those seen in early infancy, when the baby splits experiences into "good," "bad," and so forth. According to Schulz, other schizophrenic characteristics, such as preverbal speech or early verbal speech, lack of sphincter muscle control, distractibility, all-embracing identification with others, denial, inability to process loss, experience of boundlessness and so forth, are all characteristics of normal infant development as well (pp. 51–58). Sometimes it seems that Schulz's delivery of psychoanalysis to the psychiatric reader was simple or even simplistic, easily digestible and "user friendly" to psychiatric residents in hospitals. Although he presented a "light" version of psychoanalysis, Schulz still found it superior to neosomatic treatments. As for medications, his recommendation was to minimize dosages and avoid routine use. Even when they were used, Schulz suggested that they should not interfere with psychotherapy and therefore should not be sedating. He also addressed day treatment and community treatment, which were relatively new concepts in his time and far less commonly mentioned, if at all, in analytic journals.

While Schulz's approach addressed mostly the behavioral aspects and symptomatology of schizophrenia in theory and in practice, the *Bulletin* also published Gaetano Benedetti, who represented a different approach. Benedetti was an Italian analyst based in Switzerland who was among the founders of the International Society for the Psychological Treatments of the Schizophrenias and Other Psychoses (ISPS). Benedetti (1980) claimed that schizophrenia challenged psychiatry. He disputed one of the seminal findings of somatic psychiatry in those years – the genetic factor – and argued that a child's mental health is extensively dependent on the adopting family's mental health. Much like the attempts of American psychoanalysts in the international arena to unify the split between the different theories and treatment approaches in schizophrenia, Benedetti tried

The "dopamine hypothesis" 91

to integrate the nature-nurture poles and offered that the very same process of integration was also the curing factor in schizophrenia, suggesting that his psychoanalytic approach would be called "psycho-synthesis." He posited that it was actually the therapeutic entrance into the psychotic realm, and not its description by an external observer, that was curative in the work with such patients. In striving to emphasize the importance of the inner psychotic world, Benedetti argued that schizophrenia is not only an internalization of the family's irrationality, as Theodore Lidz claimed in his family research, nor is it limited to internalization of society's irrationality, as claimed by Franco Basaglia, who led the dismantling of psychiatric hospitals in Italy. Benedetti asserted that schizophrenia is in fact an internalization of the irrationality of existence as such. He identified a core paradox of psychotherapy for psychosis, claiming that psychotherapy uses the same dynamic in its communication with patients as the one that leads to schizophrenic pathology. Just as their patients are holding to a delusion, so too do their therapists, who are holding a "delusional grip on reality." Their clinical strains, their expectations, their giving of hierarchical privileges to "normality," their tendency to use cognitive authority with patients and their need that patients adhere to their own views should all be given up. He claimed that the therapist's entrance into the patient's psychotic world, to the world of death, is more important than the structuring of the past, as is customary in psychoanalytic treatment of the neuroses. Interpretations designed to allow the therapist an entrance into the psychotic world of the patient meant that this very world was of value to the therapist. Confronting the hypothetical claim that such treatment can benefit only a minority of psychotic patients, Benedetti argued that this treatment's contribution to society lay elsewhere. He suggested that this kind of in-depth psychoanalytic psychotherapy with psychotic patients develops unique sensitivities in the treating psychiatrist, enabling the therapist to enhance his or her mastery of other psychotherapeutic tasks and thus benefit all facets of psychiatry. Working intensively with fewer patients (as the treatment of schizophrenic patients calls for 6 to 8 hours per week) can teach the therapist about the essence of schizophrenia much more than theoretical data derived from numerous cases of patients in psychiatric facilities. According to Benedetti, the most important contribution of psychoanalysis with schizophrenic patients lies beyond the narrow psychiatric interest of schizophrenia and is embedded in knowing what it means to be human.

Summary

The formulation of the dopamine hypothesis in the mid-1970s and the consolidation of evidence for the genetic component in the etiology of schizophrenia during those same years constituted the second stage of the neosomatic revolution in psychiatry, and psychoanalysis in the United States continued to reconstruct itself in the field of schizophrenia in response to the accomplishments of this revolution. While in the previous decade psychiatry offered antipsychotic drugs, during the 1970s it added a neurological phenomenology and genetic

92 The "dopamine hypothesis"

etiology of schizophrenia. In this jurisdictional struggle American analysts within the mainstream American Psychoanalytic Association were far less interested in schizophrenia and schizophrenic patients, and when they were discussing schizophrenia they were highly influenced by their rivals' discourse.

Freud "the scientist" was resurrected by these psychoanalysts, along with his hope for future biological findings that would replace the psychological ones. The hybrid language of the previous decade became purely biological, and analysts were concerned not with the unconscious drives and defenses, but instead with brain structures, neurotransmitters in the nervous system and the effect of drugs on various receptors. In contrast, the American Academy for Psychoanalysis and Dynamic Psychiatry, established by analysts who resigned from the American Psychoanalytic Association, showed great interest in schizophrenia. Despite the counterculture bias that characterized the *Journal of the Academy*, its eclecticism allowed it to develop and publish various theoretical ideas about schizophrenia. Its articles accepted and internalized genetic findings, and therefore shifted from the strict "ego defect" hypothesis to a more subtle suggestion that schizophrenic patients are born with a genetic "vulnerability." However, this also raised criticism, and others in the Academy argued that, given enough stressors, anyone might develop schizophrenia. Because of the eclectic nature of the Academy's discourse, analysts were also grappling with the other side of the nature-nurture debate. A notable emphasis was given to environmental influence in general and, in the wake of the counterculture, also to the "sick" society as a cause of schizophrenia. The "counter" attitude was also apparent in criticism of somatic medical treatments (i.e., drugs) and classic psychoanalysis, both of which were seen as promoting regression and infantilization in schizophrenic patients.

During this decade, in the international arena a very different type of American psychoanalysis was evolving in the field of schizophrenia. This form of psychoanalysis registered the neosomatic trend, but, instead of imitating its discourse or giving up the discussion of schizophrenia altogether, it worked from within the profession to strengthen its foundation by attempting to heal the splits between the main theories of schizophrenia. In the face of the "injury" it sustained in its jurisdictional struggle, this kind of psychoanalysis meticulously studied the history of schizophrenia within psychoanalysis, discussed contemporary theoretical developments and deepened analytic and therapeutic understanding of this disorder. American analysts publishing in the international arena during this decade declared that they were seeking to create a psychoanalytic discourse worthy of schizophrenia. This kind of a "worthy discourse" was to be psychoanalysis's best weapon in its jurisdictional struggle with somatic psychiatry. Not only did it develop theoretical understanding of the illness itself and of the human mind more generally, but it kept psychoanalysis relevant and viable in the field of mental health.

When examining psychoanalysis's place among psychiatry in the field of schizophrenia during the 1970s, its limits in both scope and depth become apparent. It was rarely present, and when it appeared psychoanalysis adopted a "light" version of itself, focusing on behaviors and forsaking the in-depth exploration of the complexities and richness of the inner world. Psychiatry, abandoning psychoanalysis, became increasingly descriptive of the surface, a trend that will be further discussed in the next chapter, especially with the publication of the DSM-III.

References

Arieti, S., 1973a. Editorial. *Journal of the American Academy for Psychoanalysis and Dynamic Psychiatry*, 1, pp. 1–2.

Arieti, S., 1973b. Schizophrenic art and its relationship to modern art. *Journal of the American Academy for Psychoanalysis and Dynamic Psychiatry*, 1, pp. 333–365.

Arieti, S., 1974. *Interpretation of schizophrenia*. New York: Basic Books.

Arieti, S., 1975. Response. *Journal of the American Academy for Psychoanalysis and Dynamic Psychiatry*, 3, p. 234.

Arieti, S., 1977. Cognitive components in human conflict and unconscious motivation. *Journal of the American Academy for Psychoanalysis and Dynamic Psychiatry*, 5, pp. 5–16.

Arnson, G., 1977. Defence and deficit models: Their influence on therapy of schizophrenia. *International Journal of Psychoanalysis*, 58, pp. 11–15.

Barnett, J., 1979. Review of *Creativity: The magic synthesis*, by Silvano Arieti. *Journal of the American Academy of Psychoanalysis*, 7, pp. 135–136.

Benedetti, G., 1980. Individual psychotherapy of schizophrenia. *Schizophrenia Bulletin*, 6, 633–638.

Benson, R. M., and Pryor, D. B., 1973. "When friends fall out": Developmental interference with the function of some imaginary companions. *Journal of the American Psychoanalytic Association*, 21, pp. 457–473.

Book Notice, 1971. *Journal of the American Psychoanalytic Association*, 19, pp. 180–182.

Cancro, R., 1975. Genetics, dualism, and schizophrenia. *Journal of the American Academy for Psychoanalysis and Dynamic Psychiatry*, 3, pp. 353–360.

Cooper, D., 1967/2001. *Psychiatry and anti-psychiatry*. London, UK: Tavistock Press.

Crowly, R. M., 1980. Cognitive elements in Sullivan's theory and practice. *Journal of the American Academy of Psychoanalysis and Dynamic Psychiatry*, 8, pp. 115–126.

Davidson, L., 1979. Catholic patients – Modifications of technique for a subculture based on sublimation. *Journal of the American Academy of Psychoanalysis and Dynamic Psychiatry*, 7, pp. 601–609.

Davis, K. L., Bonnie, M. F., Davis, M., Mohs, R. C., Horvath, T. B., and Davidson, M., 1986. Dopaminergic dysregulation in schizophrenia: A target for new drugs. *Drug Development Research*, 9(1), pp. 71–83.

Deleuze, G., and Guattari, F., 1983. *Anti-Oedipus: Capitalism and schizophrenia*. Minneapolis: University of Minnesota.

Ehrenwald, J., 1974. The telepathy hypothesis and schizophrenia. *Journal of the American Academy of Psychoanalysis and Dynamic Psychiatry*, 2, pp. 159–169.

Foucault, M., 1965/1988. *Madness and civilization: A history of insanity in the age or reason*. New York: Vintage Books.

Freud, S., 1900. The interpretation of dreams. In: *The standard edition of the complete psychological works of Sigmund Freud*, Volume 4. London: Hogarth Press, pp. ix–627.

94   The "dopamine hypothesis"

Freud, S., 1914. On narcissism. In: *The standard edition of the complete psychological works of Sigmund Freud*, Volume 14. London: Hogarth Press. pp. 67–102.

Freud, S., 1920. Beyond the pleasure principle. In: *The standard edition of the complete psychological works of Sigmund Freud*, Volume 18. London: Hogarth Press. pp. 1–64.

Freud, S., 1926. The question of lay analysis. In: *The standard edition of the complete psychological works of Sigmund Freud*, Volume 20. London: Hogarth Press. pp. 177–258.

Freud, S., 1938. An outline of psychoanalysis. In: *The standard edition of the complete psychological works of Sigmund Freud*, Volume 23. London: Hogarth Press. pp. 139–208.

Gibson, R. W., 1974. The intensive psychotherapy of hospitalized adolescents. *Journal of the American Academy of Psychoanalysis and Dynamic Psychiatry*, 2, pp. 187–200.

Goffman, E., 1961. *Asylums: An essay on the social situation of mental patients and other inmates*. Garden City, NY: Anchor Books.

Gralnick, A., 1979. In-patient psychoanalytic psychotherapy of adolescents. *Journal of the American Academy for Psychoanalysis and Dynamic Psychiatry*, 7, pp. 437–445.

Grotstein, J. S., 1977a. The psychoanalytic concept of schizophrenia: I. The dilemma. *International Journal of Psychoanalysis*, 58, pp. 403–425.

Grotstein, J. S., 1977b. The psychoanalytic concept of schizophrenia: II. Reconciliation. *International Journal of Psychoanalysis*, 58, pp. 427–452.

Gunderson, J. G., 1974. The influence of theoretical model of schizophrenia on treatment practice. *Journal of the American Psychoanalytic Association*, 22, pp. 182–199.

Guntrip, H., 1973. Science, psychodynamic reality, and autistic thinking. *Journal of the American Academy for Psychoanalysis and Dynamic Psychiatry*, 1, pp. 3–22.

Hale, N. G., 1995. *The rise and crisis of psychoanalysis in the United States. Freud and the Americans 1917–1985*. New York: Oxford University Press.

Hartocollis, P. 1976. Review of *Schizophrenia and the need-fear dilemma*, by D. L. Burnham, A. I. Gladstone and R. W. Gibson. *Journal of the American Psychoanalytic Association*, 24, pp. 714–721.

Healy, D., 2002. *The creation of psychopharmacology*. Cambridge, MA: Harvard University Press.

Heath, R. G., 1974. Application of Sandor Rado's adaptational psychodynamic formulations to brain physiology. *Journal of the American Academy of Psychoanalysis and Dynamic Psychiatry*, 2, pp. 19–25.

Heilbrunn, G., 1979. Biological correlates of psychoanalytic concepts. *Journal of the American Psychoanalytic Association*, 27, pp. 597–625.

Hershey, D. W., 1978. Time experience and certain type of mourning. *Journal of the American Psychoanalytic Association*, 26, pp. 109–130.

James, M., 1975. Autism and childhood psychosis. *International Journal of Psychoanalysis*, 56, pp. 106–111.

Kafka, J. S., 1976. The origin and treatment of schizophrenic disorders. *Journal of the American Psychoanalytic Association*, 24, pp. 706–714.

Katan, M., 1979. Further exploration of the schizophrenic regression to the undifferentiated state – a study of the "assessment of the unconscious". *International Journal of Psychoanalysis*, 60, pp. 145–174.

Keniston, K., 1973. Developmental aspects of psychological disturbances. *Journal of the American Academy for Psychoanalysis and Dynamic Psychiatry*, 1, pp. 23–38.

The *"dopamine hypothesis"* 95

Kestenbaum, C. J., 1980. The origins of affect – Normal and pathological. *Journal of the American Academy of Psychoanalysis and Dynamic Psychiatry*, 8, pp. 497–520.

Kety, S. S., Rosenthal, D., and Wender, P., 1978. Genetic relationships within the schizophrenia spectrum: Evidence from adoption studies. In: R. L. Spitzer and D. F. Klein, eds., *Critical issues in psychiatric diagnosis*. New York: Raven Press. pp. 213–223.

Kety. S. S., Rosenthal, D., Wender, P. H., and Schulsinger, F., 1976. Studies based on a total sample of adopted individuals and their relatives: Why they were necessary, what they demonstrated and failed to demonstrate. *Schizophrenia Bulletin*, 2, pp. 413–428.

Laing, R. D., 1960. *The divided self: An existential study in sanity and madness*. London, UK: Tavistock Press.

Levy, N. J., 1979. The middle-aged male homosexual. *Journal of the American Academy of Psychoanalysis and Dynamic Psychiatry*, 7, pp. 405–418.

Lidz, T., Fleck, S., and Cornelison, A., 1965. *Schizophrenia and the family*. New York: International Universities Press.

Liebert, R. S., 1974. Review of *Home from the war*, by Robert J. Lifton. *Journal of the American Academy of Psychoanalysis and Dynamic Psychiatry*, 2, pp. 171–173.

Lifton, R. J., 1976. From analysis to formation. *Journal of the American Academy for Psychoanalysis and Dynamic Psychiatry*, 4, pp. 63–94.

London, N. J., 1973a. An essay on psychoanalytic theory: Two theories of schizophrenia. Part I: Review and critical assessment of the development of the two theories. *International Journal of Psychoanalysis*, 54, pp. 169–178.

London, N. J., 1973b. An essay on psychoanalytic theory: Two theories of schizophrenia. Part II: Discussion and restatement of the specific theory of schizophrenia. *International Journal of Psychoanalysis*, 54, pp. 179–193.

Naftalin, M., 1975. Watch your language. *Journal of the American Academy of Psychoanalysis and Dynamic Psychiatry*, 3, pp. 307–319.

Ogden, T. H., 1980. On the nature of schizophrenic conflict. *International Journal of Psychoanalysis*, 6, pp. 513–533.

Pao, P., 1973. Notes on Freud's theory of schizophrenia. *International Journal of Psychoanalysis*, 54, pp. 469–476.

Pao, P., 1977. On the formation of schizophrenic symptoms. *International Journal of Psychoanalysis*, 58, pp. 389–401.

Pollock, G. H., 1972. Bertha Pappenheim's pathological mourning: Possible effects of childhood sibling loss. *Journal of the American Psychoanalytic Association*, 20, pp. 476–493.

Redlich, F., 1974. Psychoanalysis and the medical model. *Journal of the American Academy for Psychoanalysis and Dynamic Psychiatry*, 2, pp. 147–157.

Rey, H., 1994. *Universals of psychoanalysis in the treatment of psychotic and borderline states*. London, UK: Free Association Books.

Ryckoff, I. M., 1975. The transforming self: New dimensions in psychoanalytic process. *Journal of the American Academy of Psychoanalysis and Dynamic Psychiatry*, 3, pp. 125–128.

Satran, G., 1978. Notes on loneliness. *Journal of the American Academy for Psychoanalysis and Dynamic Psychiatry*, 6, pp. 281–300.

Schecter, D. E., 1974. Review of *Interpretation of schizophrenia*, 2nd ed., by Silvano Arieti. *Journal of the American Academy for Psychoanalysis and Dynamic Psychiatry*, 2, pp. 383–387.

96 The "dopamine hypothesis"

Schulz, C. G., 1975. An individualized psychotherapeutic approach with the schizophrenic patient. *Schizophrenia Bulletin*, 13, pp. 46–69.

Searles, H., 1979. *Countertransference and related subjects*. New York: International Universities Press.

Seeman, P., Chau-Wong, L. M., and Wong, K., 1976. Antipsychotic drugs doses and neuroleptic/dopamine receptors. *Nature*, 261, pp. 717–719.

Shainberg, D., 1973. The dilemma and the challenge of being schizophrenic. *Journal of the American Academy for Psychoanalysis and Dynamic Psychiatry*, 1, pp. 271–287.

Shave, D. W., 1974. Depression as a manifestation of unconscious guilt. *Journal of the American Academy of Psychoanalysis and Dynamic Psychiatry*, 2, pp. 309–327.

Shoenberg, P., 1977. Models of madness, models of medicine. *International Journal of Psychoanalysis*, 58, p. 252.

Snyder, S. H., 1976. The dopamine hypothesis of schizophrenia: Focus on dopamine receptor. *American Journal of Psychiatry*, 133, pp. 197–202.

Sperling, M., 1971. Spider phobias and spider fantasies – A clinical contribution to the study of symbol and symptom choice. *Journal of the American Psychoanalytic Association*, 19, pp. 472–498.

Spiegel, R., 1973. Gray areas between the schizophrenias and the depressions. *Journal of the American Academy of Psychoanalysis and Dynamic Psychiatry*, 1, pp. 179–192.

Strauss, G. D., Yager, J., and Strauss, G. E., 1984. The cutting edge in psychiatry. *American Journal of Psychiatry*, 141(1), pp. 38–43.

Symonds, M., 1973. Parents of schizophrenic children. *Journal of the American Academy of Psychoanalysis and Dynamic Psychiatry*, 1, pp. 171–178.

Szasz, T. S., 1960. The myth of mental illness. *American Psychologist*, 15, pp. 113–118.

Vanggaard, T., 1975. Splitting. A case of female masculinity. *International Journal of Psychoanalysis*, 56, pp. 492–497.

5 The emperor's new clothes
DSM-III and the abandonment of psychodynamics in favor of the biomedical model (1980–1990)

Whether we like it or not the issue of defining the boundaries of mental and medical disorders cannot be ignored. Increasingly there is a pressure for the medical profession and psychiatry in particular to define its areas of prime responsibility.

(Spitzer, Endicott and Robin in Healy 1997, pp. 233–234)

A new disease afflicting psychiatry, but not psychiatry alone . . . a disease without a name, whose presenting symptom is a retreat from patients . . . rationalized, culturally supported and approved by many eminent psychiatrists . . . the flight from the one teacher who can continue to teach us for as long as we live, namely, the intransigent patient.

(Laurence Kubie 1971, p. 64)

The formative event during the 1980s in the history of American psychiatry was the publication of the third edition of the *Diagnostic and Statistical Manual of Mental Disorders* (DSM-III). This manual ushered in the third stage of the neosomatic revolution in psychiatry, which in its turn shaped American psychoanalysis's discourse in the field of schizophrenia. Writers from diverse disciplines agree that psychiatry underwent a revolution in the beginning of the 1980s and that the DSM-III was its primary artifact. This paradigmatic change expressed itself in a renewed interest in diagnostic theories, as was customary in the medical model, and was the most significant aspect of the re-medicalization of American psychiatry. Through World War II and up to the 1970s, the more popular model in psychiatry was psychosocial, which was very gradually replaced with a biopsychosocial model. Since the publication of DSM-III in 1980, the model has morphed, as postulated by Steven Sharfstein (2005), a Maryland-based psychiatrist and a past American Psychiatric Association president, into a "bio-bio-bio" model. Some writers describe the paradigm shift in psychiatry as a move "from Freud to Kraepelin" and from psychoanalysis to descriptive psychiatry.

Attack on the psychodynamic model

As already noted, the psychosocial model (which psychoanalysis, or psychodynamics, belongs to) is based on certain assumptions:

98   *The emperor's new clothes*

1   The boundary between mental illness and mental health is fluid, and "normal" people might become mentally ill if exposed to severe enough trauma.
2   Mental illnesses are located on a spectrum of severity, from neurotic disorders on the mild end, through borderline states, to psychosis on the severe end.
3   A combination of a toxic environment and emotional conflict produces mental illness.
4   The mechanisms that facilitate mental illness in the individual are psychologically mediated.

The most eloquent spokesperson of the psychodynamic model that developed in the United States was not Freud (who did not necessarily view mental illness as locatable on a spectrum), but rather the American psychiatrist Karl Menninger, who disputed descriptive psychiatry and supported a psychosocial theory of psychopathology. He viewed all illnesses as stemming from a failure to adjust, ranging from a mild failure that would be manifested in neurosis to a severe one that might result in psychosis. Menninger's most quoted phrase in this context is: "What is behind the symptom?" (Meninger 1963), which is the motto that expresses the essence of dynamic psychiatry's approach. Understanding the meaning of symptoms, treating the psychogenic origin and not manipulating symptoms directly with medications, suggestibility and so forth are all key to the practice of dynamic psychiatry.

The psychodynamic and psychosocial models, particularly in the field of schizophrenia, were the targets of an overall attack on American psychiatry at the end of the 1960s. Psychiatrists who adopted the neosomatic approach attacked from within, while academic and social critics from outside the psychiatric profession claimed that if the psychosocial conceptualization was valid, then schizophrenia and other "disorders" were social, political and legal entities and not illnesses, and as such did not belong in the jurisdiction of psychiatry. Gerald Grob (1987), a renowned historian of American psychiatry, argued that the psychodynamic model generated the demand for the DSM-III within psychiatry. This model greatly expanded the boundaries of psychiatry, as it rejected the traditional medical division between mental health and mental illness. DSM-III was conceived to clear up this "confusion" and provide clear, categorical definitions in place of what was seen as an increased blurring of the lines between normal and abnormal behaviors. The *Manual* offered clear categories instead of overlapping dimensions, and it provided a list of unambiguous and observable symptoms instead of vague, hidden etiological mechanisms.

The history of the DSM

Before World War II, the major motivation for developing a classification of mental disorders was the need to collect statistical information about mental health in the United States. While the 1840 census recorded only the frequency of "idiocy/insanity," in the 1880 census, seven categories of mental health were distinguished: mania, melancholia, monomania, paresis, dementia, dipsomania and epilepsy. In 1917, the American Medico-Psychological Association, together with the National Commission on Mental Hygiene, formulated a plan for gathering uniform statistics across mental hospitals. The American Psychiatric Association subsequently collaborated with the New York Academy of Medicine to develop a nationally acceptable psychiatric nomenclature. This nomenclature was designed primarily for diagnosing patients in hospitals with severe psychiatric and neurological disorders. In 1921, the American Medico-Psychological Association changed its name to the American Psychiatric Association. After World War II, a much broader nomenclature was developed by the U.S. Army to better incorporate the outpatient presentations of servicemen and veterans (e.g., psychophysiological, personality and acute disorders). Concurrently, the World Health Organization (WHO) published the sixth edition of *International Classification of Diseases* (ICD-6), which for the first time included a section for mental disorders. ICD-6 included 10 categories for psychoses and psychoneuroses and seven categories for disorders of character, behavior and intelligence. The first edition of the DSM was developed by the American Psychiatric Association Committee on Nomenclature and Statistics in 1952. DSM-I contained a glossary of descriptions of the diagnostic categories and was the first official manual of mental disorders to focus on clinical utility. The use of the term "reaction" throughout DSM-I reflected the influence of Adolf Meyer's psychobiological view that mental disorders represented reactions of the personality to psychological, social and biological factors.

In part because of the lack of widespread acceptance of the mental disorder taxonomy, DSM-II was developed. It was similar to DSM-I but eliminated the term "reaction." During the 1960s, the anti-psychiatry movement presented challenges to the concept of mental illness itself, and these critics were viewed as attacking the efficacy of psychiatric diagnosis. During this period of upheaval, the DSM-I was revised and published in 1968 as the DSM-II. Although the term "reaction," associated with dynamic psychiatry, was dropped, the term "neurosis," associated with psychoanalysis, was retained. Both versions of the DSM included biological perspectives and concepts from Kraepelin's famous system of classification, and both reflected the predominant view of psychodynamic psychiatry. Disorders were viewed as reflections of broad, underlying conflicts or maladaptive reactions to life problems. The psychoanalytic distinction between neurosis and psychosis was kept in DSM-II, but the psychodynamic model that did not emphasize a clear boundary between normality and abnormality still predominated. In 1974 psychiatrists began criticizing DSM-II as an unreliable diagnostic tool (Spitzer and Fleiss 1974). They found that psychiatrists were rarely in agreement about DSM-II categories when diagnosing patients with similar problems.

Development of DSM-III

The DSM-III task force was led by Robert Spitzer, the most vociferous critic of the DSM-II. A psychiatrist from Columbia University, Spitzer went through

100 *The emperor's new clothes*

psychoanalytic training but claimed that psychoanalysis was "too abstract and theoretical" and that he did not see how it was helping his patients (Spiegel 2005). His task force was considered by sociologists to be an "invisible college," composed of geographically diverse professionals who, nevertheless, shared Kraepelin's perspective and wanted to advance the biomedical approach in psychiatry. The geographical center of that theoretical model was Washington University in Saint Louis, Missouri, where Kraepelin was always preferred over Freud. According to the Kraepelinian approach, if psychiatry were to be considered a medical science, it had to develop epidemiological schema for the classification of illnesses, or, in other words, a nosology of mental illnesses. Kraepelin's three basic postulates, which were central to the call for a move from a psychodynamic to a biomedical perspective through the application of the DSM-III, were (Mayes and Horwitz 2005):

1   Mental disorders are best understood through analogies to physical disorders.
2   Classification requires careful observation of symptoms and should not be generated from conclusions based on unproven causal theories.
3   Empirical research would eventually demonstrate the organic and biochemical origin of mental disorders.

The reasons for this paradigmatic shift are examined in a vast body of secondary literature on the DSM-III. The literature reflects a consensus view arguing that psychiatry needed to prove, in the face of internal and external attacks, that it was a legitimate medical and scientific field, and therefore deserved recognition from governmental bodies and insurance companies, which have funded a substantial portion of psychiatric treatments since the beginning of the 1970s. Psychoanalysis, together with the larger field of psychodynamics, was forced out of the DSM-III, which was designed according to a biomedical theoretical model. This shift affected patients with schizophrenia more than any other group of patients and contributed to the already developing rupture between psychoanalysis and the mentally ill. With the rise of the biomedical model, patients with schizophrenia who were discharged from hospitals due to the movement of deinstitutionalization were receiving mainly pharmacological treatments, while psychoanalysis was cynically said to be treating only the YAVIS – young, attractive, verbal, intelligent and successful patients.

The shift from the psychodynamic to the biomedical model in psychiatry, with the publication of the DSM-III, solved two problems for the third-party payer – whether a private insurance company or governmental program such as Medicare and Medicaid. The first problem was that the spectrum perspective offered by the psychodynamic model did not allow for a clear definition of sickness, and, therefore, a clear determination of who did or did not deserve medical coverage. The second problem was the liability for third-party payers, who would be responsible for paying for long-term psychotherapy that was not "scientifically" proven to be effective, or for years of "expensive psychoanalysis" for people who were "not sick" but "only" trying to improve their quality of life.

Much of the secondary literature on the topic of the DSM-III identifies the direct hit it made to psychoanalysis with the removal of "neuroses" from the manual – the bread and butter of psychoanalysis. However, psychoanalysis suffered further blows, also in the field of schizophrenia, with psychiatry's shift in its interest from the inner psychic world of the patient to the observable symptoms posited as generated by the brain, the organ of the mind. During the 1970s, psychoanalysts hardly responded to the ongoing development of the DSM-III's infrastructure in their writing about schizophrenia. The few who wrote about the new manual argued that it was reductionist, limited and simplistic. It was ironically claimed, in the context of this paradigm shift, that by increasingly focusing on the brain psychiatrists were quite literally losing their minds (Reiser 1988). Though only the minority of Spitzer's task force were connected directly to the fields of psychopharmacology or biology, the biological link to the DSM-III stemmed from one of the neo-Kraepelinian assumptions mentioned above: that the core symptoms of mental illness were the result of brain dysfunction.

DSM-III as a game changer

The publication of DSM-III, the crossroad that marked American psychiatry's divorce from psychoanalysis, was considered to be a political, rather than scientific, accomplishment of psychiatry, since it offered no professional innovations (Faust and Miner 1986). One reason for the DSM-III's development was the need for further medicalization of psychiatry, and some claimed that it was a result of increased governmental involvement in mental illness research and policy making (Hall 1993). Others argued that it resulted from the insurance companies' growing pressure on psychiatrists to prove the effectiveness of their practices, and many critically claimed that the DSM-III was developed to satisfy the marketing needs of the pharmaceutical companies (Mayes and Horwitz 2005). Because each of these reasons further pushed psychiatry toward somatization, the publication of the DSM-III constituted the third stage of the neosomatic revolution in American psychiatry. As will be shown in this chapter, this stage, too, contributed to psychoanalysis's construction of its theory of schizophrenia and its praxis with these patients. As in the previous chapters of this book, the primary sources examined here appeared in three major publications covering the fields of psychiatry and psychoanalysis: the *Journal of the American Psychiatric Association* (*JAPA*), the *International Journal of Psychoanalysis* (*IJP*) and the *Journal of the American Academy for Psychoanalysis and Dynamic Psychiatry* (*Journal of the Academy*).

In the 1980s, it seemed that analysts publishing in *JAPA* were less interested in schizophrenia. Very few psychoanalytic articles addressing the problem of schizophrenia were published during these years – fewer than in the two previous decades already reviewed. When schizophrenia was addressed, the discussion was centered on either defining psychoanalysis's boundaries with biological psychiatry or identifying schizophrenia on the far end of borderline disorders, the new "baby" of psychoanalysis. In other words, schizophrenia was placed outside

102 *The emperor's new clothes*

the borders of psychoanalysis and as part of somatic psychiatry's jurisdiction, but schizophrenia also became the marker of the boundaries of psychoanalysis's jurisdiction that claimed as its most severe pathology the borderline disorders.

One of the three main responses of psychoanalysis to the DSM-III was recognizing that it constituted a break from psychoanalysis, which led to criticism of the manual on the one hand and offerings of alternative diagnostic tools based on psychoanalysis on the other. The difference between psychiatry and psychoanalysis was depicted as one related to nosology, data collection methods and treatment outcome understanding. While psychiatric nosology was presented as searching for similarities between an individual patient and a group of patients, psychoanalysis was characterized as seeking to identify what makes an individual in a group different from others. In the same vein, while analytic data collection was presented as striving to learn about the meaning of behaviors by means of empathy, intuition or insight, psychiatric data collection, in the spirit of DSM-III, was characterized as learning about the patient through observation only. Moreover, while psychoanalysis was presented as seeing satisfactory treatment progress even without significant changes in symptoms and at times seeing the elimination of symptoms and quick changes as a sign of defensive avoidance and not real progress, psychiatry was interested in an observable change in symptoms (Simons 1987).

Given these contradictions between psychiatry and psychoanalysis, analysts in the 1980s began to think of alternatives to the DSM-III, and some even called for more involvement of analysts in designing its future versions. Without declaring it to be an alternative to the psychiatric diagnostic system, psychoanalysts were offering an investigation of their own literature for a suggested diagnostic system while claiming scientific validity. Ping-Nie Pao's suggestion to use a developmental framework that would take into consideration inner psychic structures and construct taxonomical categories based on analytic data was discussed (Schwartz 1984). The need for such diagnostic tools among psychoanalysts stemmed from DSM-III's neglect to include in its definition patients' information about their inner psychic organization, ego strengths, vitality and possibility for exploration of future options and risks.

Leopold Bellak's system of personality assessment was also reviewed (Kantrowitz 1986). Bellak, a famous ego psychologist, designed a methodology for assessing ego functions, which was clearly based on psychoanalytic theory and lent itself to measurements and replication. He argued that this suggested diagnostic alternative would be able to differentiate between normal people, neurotics and schizophrenics. This system is called ego function assessment (EFA), and it estimates 12 ego functions to be used for diagnosis, prognosis, treatment planning and research.

The discussion of Kernberg's suggested diagnostic system and his development of the psychoanalytic interview as a diagnostic technique (Wallerstein 1986) could also be viewed as an "analytic alternative" in the context of psychoanalysts' attempts in the 1980s to provide a different option to the psychiatric-based diagnosis. The diagnostic categories suggested by Kernberg are related to pathologies of the ego and superego, pathologies of internalized object relations and pathology in development as a product of libidinal and aggressive drives. These are further classified at a high, moderate and low level of functioning. Not only are Kernberg's diagnoses outlined with psychoanalytic concepts, but, according to him, psychoanalytic interventions can serve as diagnostic tools, and the distinction between psychotic organization and borderline organization could be based on the patient's response to the analyst's interpretations of her/his material. Although Kernberg himself supported what he saw as the scientific achievement of the DSM-III, he mostly argued that the manual might damage the psychoanalytic diagnostic tradition and showed how the DSM-III operated to shrink the scope of schizophrenic disorders and artificially increase the class of the more popular affective disorders.

In addition to the above reaction to psychiatry's attempt to exclude them from the field of diagnosis, analysts publishing in *JAPA* also reacted more specifically to their further marginalization from the field of schizophrenia and tried to strengthen their hold on the field. A review of Bertram Karon and Gary Vandenbos's book, *Psychotherapy of Schizophrenia: The Treatment of Choice*, presented the authors' conclusion that the research indicating that medication and not psychotherapy was the treatment of choice for schizophrenia had used a flawed methodology (Appelbaum 1985). Although they agreed that psychoanalytic psychotherapy required a longer period of time when applied to schizophrenic patients, they noted that it contributed more than any other treatment to reducing hospitalizations and to the patient's ability to live independently after discharge. The writers also emphasized that the cost of treatment was 20% lower among patients treated with psychotherapy (as compared to psychopharmacology alone) during the first 20 months of treatment and 43% lower in the two-year range, because of the decreased number of hospitalizations.

Since they recognized that descriptive and somatic psychiatry also threatened to exclude psychoanalysis from the treatment of schizophrenia, psychoanalysts saw the need to prove the benefits of analytic treatment. That said, they also acknowledged the difficulty inherent in demonstrating its efficacy by using a scientific framework. Alongside their emphasis on the need to continue basing their conclusions on case studies of long-term treatments, based on traditional psychodynamic principles, analysts also argued that such research could not easily prove validity and reliability, and thus, findings could not be generalized (Oldham 1988). Psychoanalytic concepts, much like metapsychological concepts, were perceived as abstract, and analysts recognized the challenge in developing clear and consistent concepts that could be measured in observable behaviors – those offered by DSM-III. While appreciating this difficulty, analysts also acknowledged the inescapable task of creating operational concepts so that studies could be replicated and psychoanalysis could be part of evidenced-based medical discourse.

Psychoanalysts examine their role in the narrowing of their jurisdiction

While some psychoanalysts called for a departure from psychiatry, as it became increasingly descriptive and somatic, and criticized its research and therapeutic methods, which they said could not be reconciled with psychoanalytic theory, others who were interested in schizophrenia attempted to find their way back to psychiatry. Many articles related to schizophrenia written by psychoanalysts in the 1980s were concerned with the role psychoanalysts themselves played in narrowing the field's jurisdiction, and with the role they should be taking in instilling psychoanalytic approaches in psychiatrists. Thus, for example, one review of psychiatry textbooks from a biopsychological perspective stated that the Kraepelinian descriptions constituting the inspiration for DSM-III could not convey the schizophrenic experience of a personal and familial catastrophe, could not portray schizophrenia as a considerable regression and did not depict it as a meaningful human experience (Shapiro 1983). Analysts were called to bring to institutionalized psychiatry an emphasis on empathic listening, informed by developmental theories (p. 342). Such an orientation not only provided another perspective to biology, but also offered a framework of insight into the meaning of therapeutic interventions. Psychoanalysis was illustrated as a roadmap to all the therapeutic decisions, including when and how to use medications. The review argued that DSM-III enabled students to distance themselves from the painful reality of working with psychotic patients and ignored the needs of students treating such patients. Finally, the review proposed that, above all, the most important texts to thoroughly explore were the patients themselves (p. 343).

Analysts in *JAPA* made additional attempts to study ways in which they were responsible for their own demise in the field of mental illness. One such attempt was by Stuart Asch and Eric Marcus (1988) of Weill-Cornell Medical College. These researchers evaluated psychoanalysis's place in medical students' curricula at 12 American medical programs by examining the top 18 recommended psychiatric texts. This examination revealed that in premed and medical-prep programs, the subjects that dominated the curriculum were physics and biology. Although since the 1960s there had been a notable interest in other aspects of psychiatry, such as doctor-patient relationships, ethics and the use of the arts in the practice of medicine, it was argued that the descriptive DSM-III became a sort of bible of psychiatry and as a result, "students tend to stop their thinking where the descriptions stop" (p. 1037). Even if some of the recommended books for medical students did incorporate psychoanalytical terms, some students completely ignored them, and when it came to a discussion of schizophrenia, most texts did not suggest that symptoms might have meaning stemming from early childhood experiences. Texts focused on neuroses allowed more room for psychoanalytic treatment, but when schizophrenia was discussed, pharmacology was highlighted as the treatment of choice (p. 1046).

Asch and Marcus (1988) also reflected on the possible contribution of psychoanalysts to their weakening role in psychiatry. Focusing on functional neurotic patients whom they saw in their private practices, psychoanalysts realized that they had isolated themselves from the hospital systems, which provided a home to academic departments (p. 1049). This tendency distanced older psychoanalysts from the younger generation of medical practitioners and potential psychoanalysts who were unlikely to enter the profession. Another explanation was that young analysts who wished to progress in their careers in psychoanalytic institutes tended to choose roles that were valued by psychoanalytic institutes, such as teaching candidates in training, serving on the institute's committees and so forth. Since the goal of a psychoanalytic institute was "first and foremost to tend its own garden first" (p. 1050), Asch and Marcus argued that these institutes were overlooking the young people in medical schools from whom future candidates would come. Asch and Marcus also argued that there were financial reasons for psychoanalysts' abandonment of medical schools. Psychoanalytic training, they claimed, was expensive: the high tuition in psychoanalytic institutes and the payments for training analysis and supervisions meant that psychoanalysts of all levels of training had to increase their income, making teaching in medical schools, which was almost like volunteering, undesirable (p. 1050). However, even if psychoanalytic institutes would politically and economically encourage their members and candidates to work in hospitals and train the next generation of psychiatrists, there would still be tremendous obstacles to teaching psychoanalysis to medical students. Asch and Marcus (1988) argued that medical students had difficulties with abstract, philosophical thinking and were perplexed when confronting such ideas. They confused dynamics with etiology (how something happened and why something happened), could not tell universal fantasies from illnesses and confused the concrete with the metaphorical, the unconscious with the conscious, normal development with pathology. A renewed examination of the question "is medicine the most appropriate profession for psychoanalytic training" brought up the notion that though psychoanalysis could be taught in medical schools, great care would have to be taken in choosing the relevant concepts for medical students, identifying a pedagogy that would simplify those concepts and recognizing what was suitable for understanding nosology categories within general medicine (p. 1054). Thus, even when they recommended that psychoanalysis return to psychiatric hospitals and medical schools and be in touch with hospitalized patients (ones with major psychotic illnesses), Asch and Marcus suggested exactly what Freud and Jones were dreading: that in America, in the name of pragmatism and broad-mindedness, psychoanalysis would be swallowed up by medicine and lose its courageous and rigorous nature. Freud (1926) wished that analysis would stay a "'depth-psychology', a theory of the mental unconscious. . . . indispensable to all the sciences which are concerned with the evolution of human civilization and its major institutions such as art, religion and the social order" (p. 248), and not just the simplified, "psychiatrically friendly" type of theory and technique that Asch and Marcus suggested for introduction to somewhat challenged medical students.

During the 1980s, and possibly due to the publication of the DSM-III and the further distancing of psychiatry from psychoanalysis, other psychoanalysts repeatedly debated the place of their profession in medical school. Theodore Shapiro (1989), the editor of *JAPA* at the time, argued in a particularly provocative editorial that psychoanalysis had to reinvent itself now that it was "not the only show in town." Alongside questions such as "should the couch be replaced with brain imaging" (p. 4) and concerns that young psychiatrists might not take

106 *The emperor's new clothes*

an interest in psychoanalysis now that new technologies could, in essence, turn the brain on and off, Shapiro insisted that psychoanalysis was still important, claiming, for example, that even if one could see which areas of the brain light up when one hates, "we cannot yet biologically distinguish how hatred of a parent is distinguished from dislike of broccoli . . ." (p. 5). According to Shapiro, analysts needed a stronger presence in medical centers. However, unlike Asch and Marcus, he did not offer to simplify the psychoanalytic language, but instead urged the creation of "enthusiasm with which we all joined in trying to understand the mind psychoanalytically" (p. 5). This enthusiasm could be created if psychoanalysts offer "cogent and good arguments face-to-face with our candidates-to-be." Again, as opposed to Asch and Marcus, Shapiro offered to use a language that "will make students perk up their ears and remark that the most coherent explanation of their patient's behavior – the one that makes them say, 'aha' – is psychoanalytic" (p. 5). Shapiro's conclusion that there was not a contest between physiology and psychology suggested that even if psychosis did have a biological physiological basis, psychoanalysis could still be relevant and contribute to the field. Thus, even with schizophrenic patients, which most analysts seemed to give up in favor of their more neurotic patients, there was a meaning behind the symptom. The psychoanalytic mode, Shapiro suggests, could allow us to learn what schizophrenic patients think, and an adequate history taken in this mode may tell more of the story than the "dopalytic activity" would tell (p. 5).

Psychoanalysts turn to borderline patients

Contrary to the above claims, some psychoanalysts consistently argued in their writing that since schizophrenia was a biological disorder, the real jurisdictional struggle that psychoanalysis should be invested in was the one concerning borderline patients. Critical voices began to challenge the contemporary dominant voice within psychoanalysis, which posited a developmental timeline of internalized object relations and ego functions, as well as specific stages of fixation that create specific psychopathologies such as schizophrenia or borderline disorder. Two psychoanalysts from Columbia University, Michael Stone (1986), a forensic psychiatrist who was invested in borderline disorders, and Martin Willick (1983), an enthusiastic supporter of the neurobiological approach to schizophrenia, both argued that schizophrenia, unlike borderline disorders, was the result of abnormal genetics and not of environmental or developmental circumstances. This approach represented an attempt to prove that psychoanalysts could spout the trendy discourse of psychiatry while handing over schizophrenic patients to the treatment of somatic psychiatry and keeping the borderline population in their own jurisdiction. Willick (1983), for instance, challenged the use of psychoanalytic concepts for etiological and pathogenic factors in severe mental illness and used data from biological research in clinical psychiatry, providing support to the claim that schizophrenia was a physical illness. Though he stated that his goal was not to provide evidence for the central role of genetics or biology in the long-lived nature versus nurture debate, Willick proposed that contemporary psychiatric studies indicated that the two forms of adult psychosis, schizophrenia and bipolar disorder, were illnesses with significant genetic/biological components. In 1983 Willick conducted a review in which not one of the theoreticians who wrote about schizophrenia from a psychoanalytic perspective escaped his scrutiny. He criticized Freud's conceptualization of narcissistic paranoia and autoeroticism in schizophrenia; denounced Karl Abraham, an analyst from Berlin associated with Freud, who was the first to indicate the role of the depriving mother in the etiology of psychoses; rebuked Melanie Klein and her understanding of psychosis as a failure to emerge from the schizo-paranoid position; disapproved of Hannah Segal, Klein's follower, who placed psychotic fixation in early infancy, and disagreed with Winnicott, who argued that schizophrenics did not have a "good enough" mother. He rejected Hartman, Kris and Lowenstein of the American ego psychology movement, who emphasized the lack of separation between self-representations and an undifferentiated primary state, Mahler and Jacobson, who each in her turn presented schizophrenia as a regression to a state of merger between self and object, and Fromm-Reichmann, Searles, Ping Nie Pao and the generation of the Washington School of Psychiatry and Chestnut Lodge, where schizophrenia was conceptualized as resulting from early disturbances in the mother-child relationship. Even Kernberg, who suggested a correlation between the developmental stage of fixation and the severity of the disorder, erred when it came to schizophrenia, according to Willick.

All these analysts, who explored the environmental role in the development of schizophrenia, were criticized by Willick (1983), who tied the defect theory, which he supported, to biological explanations. He saw schizophrenia as a developmentally rooted deficit and not a behavioral syndrome motivated by conflict. Instead of using the psychoanalytic discourse, Willick (1990b) referred in his discussion of schizophrenia to brain imaging findings of alleged biochemical abnormalities in schizophrenia, to the role of atypical antipsychotic medications and to molecular biology in the study of genetics and chromosomal abnormalities. This tendency, together with the demoted role he assigns to psychoanalysis in the field of schizophrenia, seem to suggest that, as far as Willick is concerned, it is somatic psychiatry that has the solutions to the problem of schizophrenia. Even when Willick (1990b) declared that psychoanalysis had valuable insights to offer, since "no matter what organic impairments and biochemical abnormalities are present in the psychoses, they still manifest themselves through the patient's mind and the alterations of his self-experience" (p. 1078), his general approach to schizophrenia was mostly biological, an approach not uncommon among analysts during the 1980s. Many texts published in *JAPA* contain an abundance of biological concepts, and a clear demand is voiced, insisting on reclaiming the neurophysiological endeavor as an enriching and legitimate aspect of the psychoanalytic exploration. But analysts' attempts to once again use Freud's discourse of the "project" rendered them merely as advocates of the somatic trend in the understanding and treatment of schizophrenic patients. Such conduct, even if it enabled psychoanalysts to remain in the field of schizophrenia, obliterated the very essence of psychoanalysis – its unique conceptual explanation of

108 *The emperor's new clothes*

the schizophrenic state of mind and the option to treat these patients with the psychoanalytic method.

Analysts' conceptualization of schizophrenia as a biological illness whose treatment belonged in the jurisdiction of somatic psychiatry served two main goals: keeping psychoanalysis's status within psychiatry by using psychiatry's somatic discourse and keeping borderline patients within the jurisdiction of psychoanalysis. Historically, borderline disorders were placed between the neuroses and the psychoses on the spectrum of mental illnesses. However, an interesting finding related to the DSM-III shows that one of the changes occurring with the shift from DSM-II to DSM-III was the splitting of "latent schizophrenia" diagnosis into two separate diagnoses: Schizotypal Personality Disorder and Borderline Personality Disorder, both considered to be severe disorders with schizophrenic characteristics that do not amount to severe schizophrenia. Most of the articles addressing schizophrenia that were published during the 1980s in *JAPA* were actually concerned with borderline disorders. The increased interest in borderline disorder at the expense of schizophrenia was also evidenced by the funding of an international conference on the issue of borderline disorder (and of books published following the conference) by the Menninger Fund and the National Institute of Mental Health (Kafka 1981), two organizations that were known for their financial support of schizophrenia studies. Psychoanalysts' move from focusing on schizophrenia to centering their efforts on borderline disorders was also reflected in Robert Wallerstein's candid statement that borderline and narcissistic patients are the "paradigmatic patients of our time" (Wallerstein, 1986), and in Willick's (1990a) declaration that since the 1960s the interest in psychoses was replaced with an interest in borderline and narcissistic states.

Distancing psychoanalysis from medicine

In addition to those analysts who endeavored to keep the field of severe mental illness, including schizophrenia, in their jurisdiction and, alternatively, those analysts who accepted the assumption that it was a "biological illness," other voices emerged, affiliating themselves with professional allies outside of psychiatry. These analysts attempted to distance psychoanalysis from medicine, claiming that the former was interpretative, hermeneutic and, unlike the natural sciences, more similar to history in its methodology (Olinick 1984). They argued that the fundamental science of psychoanalysis was not chemistry or biology, but rather philology. Anthropology was also suggested as an alternative to the elusive explanations biology and physiology offered to explain psychosis, and they argued that in primitive cultures, true schizophrenia is absent until such cultures are exposed to oppressive outside cultural processes. Religion, mythology and literature were presented as more efficient than natural sciences in studying the primitive human core as it is manifested in psychosis (Satinover 1986).

In general, the focus on boundary work, found in texts of analysts who published in *JAPA*, prevented them from reaching theoretical, technical and practical depths with schizophrenic patients. The only "schizophrenics" addressed in their writing throughout that decade were not their own schizophrenic patients but rather famous schizophrenic patients or popular "psychotic" individuals. Examples included Freud's Anna O (Orr-Andrawes 1987) and "The Wolf-man" (Rogow 1985), Jung's Sabina Spielrein (Silverman 1985), Zelda Fitzgerald (Waites 1986), Friedrich Hölderlin (Niederland 1986) and John Hinckley, Jr., the man who attempted to assassinate Ronald Reagan (Volkan 1987). Articles exploring the inner psychic world of ordinary, contemporary patients were completely absent, a fact that raised the question of whether these analysts even treated this kind of patients.

In contrast to these articles, analysts publishing in the *Journal of the Academy of Psychoanalysis and Dynamic Psychiatry* (*Journal of the Academy*) during the 1980s did not directly criticize the publication of the DSM-III as a defining moment in psychiatry. However, implicit criticism about psychiatry's changing nature, as it pushed psychodynamic perspectives away in favor of a phenomenological/somatic perspective, did come up in relation to schizophrenia. For example, an article by Silvano Arieti (1981), the editor of the *Journal of the Academy* and the president of the Academy during these years, opened the decade with criticism of psychiatry's attempts to prove itself "scientific" and its exclusion of psychoanalysis from the field of schizophrenia. Without pointing fingers at medicine at large or psychiatry in particular, Arieti argued that the scientific method of quantification and statistics might be very effective when applied in certain limited domains; however, when used to examine the life of a person, the uniqueness and individuality were lost, creating depersonalization. Arieti quoted the famous German pathologist Rudolph Virchow (1821–1902), who once said, "I have dissected many corpses in my life, but I have never come upon a soul or a psyche" (p. 173), as he rejected the possibility that the medical model was applicable to psychiatry. Arieti was careful not to use anti-psychiatry discourse, which was partially responsible for triggering the demand that psychoanalysis become medical/scientific/biological. He argued that psychoanalysis could not accept either of two assertions: that of anti-psychiatry, which claimed that mental illnesses did not exist and were just "myths" or "human situations," and that of psychiatry, which claimed that mental illness was nothing but functional disturbances stemming from "molecular pathology."

Confronting psychiatry in his strong psychoanalytic stance, Arieti resembled Freud, who argued for a bridge between the psyche and the soma, the mind and the body, and who identified them as two separate entities mysteriously interacting. Arieti viewed assertions that a person is a chemical or physical entity rather than a psychological one as an expression of psychoanalytic nihilism, along with the idea that humans were just like the rest of the cosmos and not unique and extraordinary beings. He proposed that dualism is, in fact, a rescue for the human spirit. In the face of the biological trend in psychiatry, and as part of the effort to maintain psychoanalysis's relevancy in the field of schizophrenia, he offered dualism and mutual influence, not reducing one to the dimensions of the other, but considering the interaction between them in any human situation. Arieti was clearly voicing the wish to return not only to psychoanalytic perspectives, but also

110 *The emperor's new clothes*

to dynamic psychiatry and to Adolf Meyer's perspectives regarding the relationship between body and mind that characterized the Academy.

It seems that the general attitude that developed in American psychiatry from the 1960s through the 1980s was one of chasing the ghost out of the machine (to paraphrase the British philosopher Gilbert Ryle). During the 1980s the Academy, on the contrary, strove to put it back in without the reduction of the mental to the material, but also without awakening the "anti-psychiatry demon." This approach allowed even psychoanalysts who accepted the notion that hallucinations and delusions were indicative of an abnormal neurochemical activity in the brain to listen to the psychological content of these psychotic productions. These symptoms were treated much like dreams (which surely also have a neurochemical basis) as phenomena that could be understood and translated only through psychodynamic means. Psychiatrists who insisted that such insights were unnecessary and that all psychiatrists had to know was how to alleviate symptoms with pharmacological interventions were criticized by the Academy as being little more than technocrats.

Attempts by psychoanalysts publishing in the *Journal of the Academy* to create integration and bridge the mental and the somatic constituted part of their efforts to remain relevant when faced with the somaticists' determination to expel them out of the field of mental illness. Emotions were presented as a threshold phenomenon, a contact barrier between the mental and the somatic, and the debate about them was focused on the meeting of brain and periphery and mind and body. The contact barrier was first proposed by Freud in the 1920s, and in the debates between analysts and somaticists during the 1980s, it was specifically schizophrenia in which the contact barrier, the bridge between the physical and mental, was claimed to be the source of all difficulties. This defective barrier between the physical and the mental created diffused arousal, leading to a flooding of stimulations in the awareness, which in turn gave rise to various kinds of schizophrenic symptomatology. The fact that it was in schizophrenia, more than in any other psychiatric disorder, that the boundaries between the somatic and the psychic were marked as the source of the disorder located the phenomenon of schizophrenia on the borderland between somatic psychiatry and psychoanalysis.

Another boundary-related topic explored in the Academy, not only between the physical and psychic, but also between psychiatry and psychoanalysis, was the relationship between medical schools and analysts. Grotstein (1985) noted that in the past all psychiatry departments in medical schools were directed by analysts or by psychiatrists with strong ties to psychoanalysis. However, in the 1980s that changed dramatically, as the Asclepius approach to medicine that views humans holistically was replaced with the Hippocrates approach that strives for scientific precision. Analysts' preoccupation with the "machine" during this decade stemmed from the growing influence of the psychiatric and mental health movements that focused on the body, as well as new brain imaging technologies such as positron emission tomography (PET), computerized axial tomography (CAT) and magnetic resonance imaging (MRI). These imaging technologies found their way into psychoanalytic discourse as psychoanalysts were suggesting that the dysfunctions in schizophrenia were associated with brain atrophy and corpus callosum dysfunction (Grotstein 1985, p. 434). David Forrest (1988), a psychiatrist and psychoanalyst devoted to studying biological development in psychiatry and the "patient inside the machine," was intrigued by brain imaging technologies such as CT (computed tomography), NMR (nuclear magnetic resonance), BEAM (brain electrical activity mapping), RCBF (regional cerebral blood flow) and PET (positron emission tomography) scans, as they allowed a more "refined" study of schizophrenia (p. 492). Such focus implies not only that analysts were deserting "the ghost" in favor of "the machine," but also that the psychoanalytic gaze was replaced with a machine inspection, allegedly reflecting what was occurring within the "brain machine."

Psychoanalysts' attempts to partake in the neosomatic revolution were most apparent within the "movement for advancing unity in psychiatry," which tried to synthesize the two great intellectual traditions, psychoanalysis and neurobiology, declaring their position in a 1984 symposium in Pittsburg, titled ""Neurobiology and the Unconscious: Psychoanalysis Looks Toward the Future." The goal of this movement was "to avoid splitting the care of the patient into the partial domains of biotherapy that lacked the understanding of mental interrelations and purely psychological psychotherapy that was deficient in appreciating the embeddings of mental processes in brain function" (Forrest 1987, p. 331). The symposium was reviewed in *Journal of the Academy*, which even suggested a name for this new movement in psychoanalysis: "medical psychoanalysis" or "psychoanalytic medicine" (p. 353). An argument that was brought up during the symposium was that Freud turned to "pure" psychology, not because he doubted the brain as the platform of the mind, but rather because he felt that psychoanalysts who were medical doctors were too easily tempted to engage in neurological mechanisms instead of appreciating psychodynamic processes (p. 337). Additionally, extreme ideas were presented, such as that the new brain imaging technologies would be able to identify when doctors were thinking from a psychobiological point of view versus when they were thinking psychoanalytically, or that imaging techniques would be effective in studying object relations and uncovering the "neurology of mental representations" (p. 345). However, with these voices there were also others pointing to the difficulty of integrating psychoanalysis and neurology. Forrest (1991), for example, proposed that neurobiology and psychoanalysis would need a "Rosetta Stone" to decipher each other's language, and that psychoanalysis was very far from a point of meeting that would allow it to converse with neurobiology, especially on the issue of schizophrenia.

The battle between psychoanalysis and psychiatry in the field of schizophrenia was presented as a clash between a discipline that sees symptoms as meaningful and one that sees symptoms as meaningless biological events. Thus, Grotstein (1990) posited that the previous three decades constituted a renaissance in neurobiology, but its effect on psychoanalytic thought and on analysts who worked with psychosis in particular was too slow. Empirical studies, studies examining high risk for psychoses in children and "window to the brain" studies (using brain imaging techniques), combined with neuropsychological findings, offered

112 *The emperor's new clothes*

a significantly different profile of schizophrenia than that depicted by many psychoanalysts. Grotstein proposed that the most important finding provided by neurobiological data was that psychosis was a pathology devoid of psychodynamic meaning, but instilled with meaning by the therapist and the patient. He was careful, however, not to render his profession obsolete, stressing the importance of psychoanalytic treatment precisely in the realm of meaninglessness. The *Journal of the Academy* provided ample examples during this decade, conceptualizing the relationship of the schizophrenic patient with the analyst as the most essential agent of change. These examples include descriptions of long-term treatments, modification of therapeutic techniques and a willingness to work unconventionally within the alliance created with the schizophrenic patient. At times, extreme cases were presented, apparently in an attempt to highlight the uniqueness of psychoanalytic treatment, which manifests not only as meaning-making but also as making the analytic dyad meaningful. For example, the famous treatment of Marguerite Sechehaye, who fed her schizophrenic patient an apple as part of the "symbolic realization" processes she developed (Oelman 1981), was mentioned alongside Frieda Fromm-Reichmann's intervention that included lying in front of her patient in a fetal position (Barahal 1982). This trend can be explained by psychoanalysts' wish to prove their flexibility in coping with a tremendously difficult disorder that biological psychiatry claimed to treat so easily.

Despite the emphasis on the importance of psychoanalytic treatment, the question of supportive therapy came up during the decade even among psychoanalysts. About analysis, Jung said: "The cure is not something everyone can take, or an operation which when is contraindicated, can prove fatal" (Jung 1961, p. 141). Biological psychiatry's implicit call to "maintain" schizophrenic patients rather than cure them evoked similar thoughts among some analysts. In addressing the question of whether to try to cure schizophrenia or just offer "maintenance and support," some analysts offered to differentiate between those patients who could be helped and those who could not, while accepting the need to sometimes mourn the unpleasant verdict of reality (Kotin 1986).

Arguments pro and con: Treating schizophrenia with psychoanalysis

Alongside the repeated demonstrations of faith in the ability of psychoanalysis to offer viable therapeutic interventions with schizophrenia were critics who said that treatment came with risks. Arnold Rosen (1986), a psychiatrist and psychoanalyst from New York, reviewed Bryce Boyer's book on treating a schizophrenic patient by using classical psychoanalysis for 35 years. Rosen posed questions regarding the analyst's priorities and the weighing of chances of success with the risk of suicide in such treatments. Such debates often brought up a counterpoint, insinuating that psychotropic medications, which in the name of suicide prevention turned patients into "zombies," could not, in the end, completely prevent suicide (Garfield 1988). Psychoanalysts were, therefore, not only engaged in arguing the effectiveness of psychoanalytic treatments for schizophrenia, but also in confronting the competing treatment offered by somatic psychiatry, with the argument that it offered not a healing, but rather turned the patient into a "functional member of society." Somatic treatments were portrayed negatively, and a nostalgic attitude toward analytic treatments for schizophrenia were very common. In an article examining the treatment of psychotic Vietnam veterans, Harry Willmer (1982), a psychiatrist and analyst from Texas, described a hospital-based treatment unit that implemented individualized, psychodynamically informed psychotherapy. While in other hospitals schizophrenic patients were treated with high dosages of neuroleptics, especially Thorazine, which made them feel like "zombies," in Willmer's unit medications were reduced to a minimum, and most of the treatment focused on the patients' experiences from the war: the involvement in murder and massacres and the ensuing survivors' guilt and nightmares. Medications were viewed as obstacles to the integration of these experiences, and therefore, in that unit, sleep medications were not administered, as dreaming and sleeping were valued as meaningful. If a patient had nightmares, he would share them with the nurses, represent them in art and talk about them with his peers in "dream group." Medication dependency was presented as iatrogenic, resulting from pressure applied by the medical staff to the families to convince them that if patients were not forced to take medication, they would decompensate and require re-hospitalization (Easton 1984). The neuroleptic treatment based on the dopamine hypothesis and offered by somatic psychiatry was criticized, and based on findings from many studies, analysts questioned whether the abnormal dopaminergic mechanisms discovered in postmortem studies of schizophrenics were the result of the illness or were caused by the drug treatment (p. 578).

Even psychoanalysts who supported the creation of theoretical bridges with the neurobiological schools in psychiatry, such as Grotstein, objected to solely somatic treatments. Grotstein (1985) argued that although there was less and less doubt about the biological aspect of disturbances of the mind, psychopharmacology did not appear to be suitable for its treatment. Even if antipsychotic agents seem to be effective in alleviating psychoses, these medications increased the synaptic sensitivity and thus produce a vicious cycle in which the antipsychotic drug actually preserves the psychosis (p. 436). Those who acknowledged this paradox offered a combined treatment of psychoanalytic psychotherapy with small dosages of medication for short periods of time. Psychiatry was thus portrayed in some articles as highly limited in its understanding of schizophrenia's chemistry, and its chase after the "magic pill" remained evasive (Easton 1984). Arguments against somatic psychiatry and in favor of psychoanalysis further suggested that decompensation and regression that might lead to the readmission of schizophrenic patients were plausible even with pharmacological interventions, and in contrast, a viable change in behavior and substantial reduction in symptoms occurred precisely when medication dosages were actually lowered. A prolonged use of neuroleptics was presented as a potential obstacle for ego growth, because a certain level of tension is needed in recovery as well as in growth (p. 582). Another concern was that medications were often given by an inexperienced staff to reduce the team's anxiety. In this context, Ralph Kaufman, a Russian born analyst,

114　*The emperor's new clothes*

psychiatrist, American Psychoanalytic Association president and director of psychiatry at Mount Sinai Hospital in New York, stated: "The worst psychiatric hospitals have no suicides" (p. 582). Kaufman argued that if a psychiatric program is relying on the overuse of medications, "zombiefication of patients," 24-hour supervision and similar practices, it might indeed avoid suicide but would also prevent recovery and healing. While somatic psychiatry accused psychoanalysis of risking patients by allowing them to regress, psychoanalysts faulted somatic psychiatry for "drugging" schizophrenic patients, preventing true recovery and producing the "walking dead." Moreover, psychoanalysts argued that those taking antipsychotic medication might commit suicide if only to feel alive once again. In an article concerned with this type of scenario, David Garfield (1988), a psychiatrist and analyst from Massachusetts, wrote about a patient who refused to return to the hospital or to take medications. As a result of another admission, during which the patient felt humiliated and claimed to have "lost his sense of self-value" due to physical restrictions and forced medications, he became a "model patient:" he participated in all the groups, agreed to meet with his family and declared that he had realized that he was sick and needed medications, all the while resolving to commit suicide. Since the treatment team assumed that the patient gained insight and judgment regarding his illness (after all, he agreed to take medications and partake in the unit's activities), they discharged him. Alas, when the patient arrived at his home, he shot himself in the heart. This account by a supporter of analytic treatment demonstrated the failure of somatic psychiatric treatments to truly address the problem and their inability to deliver on their promise to be more effective than psychoanalytic treatments. Here, too, analysts in their struggles with somatic psychiatry's "magic pills" challenged the misleading conclusion from studies that somatic treatment was more effective than psychoanalysis. Instead, they argued, clinical studies and empirical studies showed that psychotherapy, when conducted by well-trained psychoanalysts, was in fact superior to both medications and combined treatments (Strahl 1983).

Understanding psychosis and treating schizophrenic psychoses by searching for meaning rather than by only alleviating symptoms was perceived as a way to reduce the tragic issue of the "revolving door" and to save patients from the torment of repeated psychotic crises. The struggles in which the analysts from the Academy engaged, in the name of psychoanalytic treatment of schizophrenia and against the allegedly appealing somatic treatments offered by psychiatry, not only attempted to erode the somatic movement's pretensions for cures and prevention of suicide, but also to present somatic treatments as damaging and inhibiting of growth.

When they were discussing why this damaging somatic treatment became so popular, analysts in the Academy cited economic inflation and recession that further emphasized cost-benefit considerations. They believed that the difficulty in proving psychoanalysis's treatment efficacy with "scientific methods" caused the policy makers to limit their investments to methods perceived as quick and cheap, namely, pharmacological treatments. That said, psychoanalysis was still presented by Ian Alger (1982), an analyst and psychiatrist and editor of the *Journal of the*

Academy, as a potential savior for psychiatry and its patients; namely, psychoanalysis could save patients from technocratic treatment providers that "managed" them, instead of meeting and respectfully interacting with them.

Psychoanalysts also recognized other forces jeopardizing the place of psychoanalytic psychotherapy in the treatment of schizophrenia during the rise of somatic psychiatry. Paul Chodoff (1984), a psychiatrist and analyst from Washington, D.C., argued that social processes reflected in the egoism of the "me generation" and narcissistic culture created unrealistic expectations of treatments. Such expectations obstructed the potential for understanding that nothing is perfect and accepting imperfect solutions without bitterness, vindictiveness or sarcasm. Chodoff argued that the hope raised by medications, which in the 1980s included Prozac (fluoxetine), and the desire to find a fast and easy solution were adverse to psychoanalytic treatment. Known as the "happy pill," Prozac is used today by approximately 23 million people in the United States, including children.

Nostalgia for the old days also showed up in articles written in the *Journal of the Academy,* with psychoanalysts frequently mentioning famous psychoanalytic examples of work with schizophrenic patients in psychiatric hospitals. Some of these articles, for example, covered Arieti's work at Pilgrim State Hospital, New York, where he discovered that those people who were held in the "back units" and believed to be hopeless cases actually improved dramatically with psychoanalytic treatment and were able to be discharged (Bemporad 1981); Sullivan's psychodynamic work with schizophrenic patients at the Sheppard and Enoch Pratt Hospital in Towson, Maryland (Brady 1984); the work of Edward Kempf, the first psychiatrist to present psychoanalysis as a treatment for psychoses in an American state hospital; Adolf Meyer's work in Worcester, Massachusetts, and at the Pathological Institute of the New York State Hospital system (today's New York State Psychiatric Institute) and William Alanson White's work with schizophrenic patients (Engel 1990). With these fond memories of the good work done at hospitals, analysts argued that psychoanalysis's departure from hospitals and medical schools was not only tied to psychiatry becoming more medical and "scientific," but also to psychoanalysis becoming a distinct discipline done in private practices and psychoanalytic institutes that treat neurotics. Milton Engel (1990), a psychiatrist from Washington, D.C., and a historian of medicine, posited that psychoanalysis could still return to the mental health hospitals where its initial development in America began. Similarly, it was proposed that psychoanalysis's insights could be used in treatment of schizophrenia also in community-based psychiatry, which, along with antipsychotic medications, was supposed to reduce schizophrenic patients' need for hospital admissions (Easton 1984).

Side by side with the ongoing discussion of the psychoanalysis-psychiatry relationship were calls for departing from medicine. David Forrest (1984) argued, for example, that psychoanalysis is much closer to art than to medicine. He presented the therapeutic hour as a work of art by the patient, with fantasy depicted as conscious art and symptom seen as unconscious art. The dream was perceived as an art piece and the treatment as the therapist's art. In this vein, Freud's statements

116 *The emperor's new clothes*

made in an interview with the journalist Giovanni Papini in 1934 were quoted, with the assertion that many think of him as a scientific figure, curing mental illnesses; but this was, in fact, an error. Gomez quoted Freud as saying:

> This is a terrible error that has prevailed for years and that I have been unable to set right. I am a scientist by necessity and not by vocation. I am really by nature an artist . . . My books in fact more resemble works of imagination than treatises on pathology. . . . I have been able to win my destiny in an indirect way, and have attained my dream: to remain a man of letters, though still in appearance a doctor.
>
> (Gomez 1986, p. 545)

In this realm, analyzing schizophrenia or psychoses outside of medicine was done by looking at literary characters, such as King Lear and Don Quixote, and schizophrenic artists, such as Schumann and Nijinsky (Fromm-Reichmann and Silver 1990).

Psychoanalysis on a tightrope – Between biology and hermeneutics

In this decade, as in previous decades, it was evident that American analysts' exploration of schizophrenia in the international arena was different from that in American journals. Unlike the majority of analysts publishing in American journals on schizophrenia, many of their colleagues who published in the *IJP* presented an attempt to distance themselves from challenges to psychoanalysis as a science. The alternative they offered claimed that psychoanalysis was a hermeneutics practice and should not be judged as a hard science. The main representative of American psychoanalysis who promoted this view was the New York psychologist and analyst Roy Schafer (1976). This development may have been related to attacks by Karl Popper (1959) on the notion of psychoanalysis as a science, which were intensified in this decade of the 1980s by Adolf Grünbaum's criticism (1984). Schafer addressed the criticism that psychoanalytic claims could not be verified and that it was not possible to infer theoretical structures from clinical observations. The hermeneutical approach he professed posited that psychoanalysis did not examine the reasons for a behavior but rather interpreted the behavior's meaning. He offered five theses:

1   Psychoanalytic metapsychology should be abandoned because it cannot be examined by clinical work, and it produces mechanistic and misleading insights.
2   Psychoanalysis should avoid dehumanizing terminology and only use humanistic terms.
3   Psychoanalysis does not explain behavior in causal terms; that is, psychoanalysis does not concern itself with the causal link between childhood events and neurotic symptoms.

The emperor's new clothes 117

4   Psychoanalysis focuses on meaning; that is, psychoanalytic theory calls for a systematic development of narratives organized on the psychosexual development axis, which function as organizers of the individual's experience.
5   There are always alternative explanations to human behavior, and psychoanalysis offers one of them.

Although hermeneutics freed psychoanalysis from the risks it faced when defined as a hard science similar to its competitor profession, somatic psychiatry, it did not solve psychoanalysis's endangered status in the field of mental health. A critic of the hermeneutical position was Roderick Anscombe (1981), a psychoanalyst from Massachusetts. Anscombe's discussion of Schafer's alternative theory of psychoanalysis showed its limitations in accounting for psychotic behavior. Schafer argued that, at some point, a person changes from a human organism to a human agent. He described a transition that occurs during infancy where the human being turns from a metabolic process bound by skin and provided with the appropriate orifices to a meaning-making human acting intentionally. Anscombe claimed that psychosis or schizophrenia cannot be accounted for in Schafer's hermeneutical alternative. He said, "personhood ends and with it most of the concepts germane to it, such as intending and choosing, as we move toward the unconscious phenomena which are not penetrable to these modes of thought" (Anscome 1981, p. 232). Anscombe wanted to ensure that those who could not be defined as "whole persons" were not shut out of psychoanalysis, and he reminded his readers that the psychoanalysis that Freud created always assumed a gap in personhood. He added,

> Accepting the view that we sometimes deal in therapy with someone other than an intact person does not mean that we have to abandon a humanist orientation or that we have to capitulate to a biological, mechanical, or causal view of the patient, or that we have to fall back irrevocably from a respect for their autonomy. When, in therapy, we come upon this gap in personhood, we may have to ignore it, or circumvent it, or label it, or translate it into full, rational, mentalistic constructs as if it had originally been thought that way: the orientation on which we decide is a tactical one and depends on the pragmatics of the therapy. However, as a guiding principle, when this loss of personhood occurs, we believe and act towards the future as though the patient retained within himself the *potential* to regain himself as a person.
>
> (p. 233)

The fear that the hermeneutic approach would "throw out the baby with the bath water" surfaced the suggestion to define psychoanalysis as autonomous from biology only from the onset of mentation. From this perspective, Michael Robbins (1983), a psychiatrist and psychoanalyst from Massachusetts, suggested that the initial stages of analytic work with "primitive" patients, a term that became synonymous with borderline and schizophrenic disorders, should be different from that with neurotic and normal patients. The connections between the "primitive"

118   *The emperor's new clothes*

stages of development, "primitive" disorders and neurophysiological explanations were an attempt to resolve what some analysts saw as an inability of the classical model of psychoanalysis, which is concerned with conflict-anxiety-defense, to explain such disorders as psychosis. The risk of psychoanalysts' abandoning the conflict theory in favor of the defect theory was in submitting the more primitive disorders to neurophysiological explanations. When Nathaniel London's observation that a deficiency state theory provided a better research strategy for those variables specific to schizophrenia, and when he tied this psychological deficiency to "evidence of deficiencies in information processing on a neurophysiological level" (London, 1985, p. 105), the link between so-called ego defects and biology when it came to schizophrenia, as opposed to the link between conflict and psychology when it came to the neuroses, became very clear. Schizophrenia was designated to the neurophysiological professions while the neuroses were seen as worthy of psychological explanations and psychoanalytic treatment.

In walking the tightrope between biology and hermeneutics, both invested in manifest behavior, American analysts publishing in the *IJP* seemed to be concerned with the descriptive fashion in psychiatry and the manufacture of diagnoses based on observable behavior. John Frosch (1983) directly criticized the DSM-III, ridiculing psychiatrists who used the prefix "pseudo" when deciding on DSM's diagnoses, which he said could be given only on the basis of observable symptoms. "Pseudo-neurotic schizophrenia" and "pseudo-psychotic schizophrenia" were only a few examples, since one could add "pseudo" to various diagnoses, he argued (p. 350). As a reaction to the threat to dynamic thinking posed by both the DSM-III and the hermeneutic suggestion of abandoning metapsychological thinking, American psychoanalysts in the international journal re-endorsed it. Dynamic thinking posited that there are unconscious forces that influence behavior, and it demanded a more critical and meticulous examination of clinical symptomatology than was offered by either the DSM-III or hermeneutics. Thus, Frosch (1983), for example, criticized narrow diagnoses and advocated returning to the psychodynamic model. He suggested diagnosing the basic anxiety in psychotic condition – that is, annihilation anxiety – and the defenses related to regression in conditions of losing separateness, such as projective identification, fragmentation, splits, massive denial and somatization. He recognized the diagnostic chaos that directed the DSM-III leaders to attempt to create order, specifically in the muddled field of severe mental illnesses: "schizophrenia," "ambulatory schizophrenia," "latent schizophrenia," "pseudo-neurotic schizophrenia" and more. With that said, he proposed not to neglect the psychoanalytic wisdom in the process of reorganization of psychiatric diagnoses (Frosch 1988).

American psychoanalysis turns to British object-relations theory

Some American psychoanalysts interested in schizophrenia and publishing in the *IJP* found an alternative to reductionist theories (both biological and

The emperor's new clothes 119

hermeneutics theories) in British object-relations theories. These theories, formulated during psychoanalytic work with severely disturbed patients, including hospitalized adults and autistic and psychotic children, became a psychoanalytic alternative to the American classic analytic thought, which is considered by many as inadequate for explaining severe disorders, especially psychotic states and schizophrenia. Drew Westen (1990), an analyst from Michigan, posited that although there were various object-relations theories, they tended to share some basic assumptions: there is a continuum of development that can be correlated with the continuum of pathology, the origin of severe pathology lies in the first three years of life, clinical data from pathological adults are necessary and largely sufficient for constructing and evaluating theories of object-relational pathology and development and so forth. The British and European influence on American psychoanalysts publishing in the international arena is indicated by repeated references to European analysts who showed special interest in psychoses. Melanie Klein, for example, was repeatedly cited, though she was marginalized by the majority of the American analytic community. Despite her great influence on understanding and working with the pre-Oedipal stages in psychoanalysis and her contribution to the growth of psychoanalytic treatment of schizophrenic patients, American analysts referred to Klein only when they discussed schizophrenia in *IJP*. Winnicott, another British analyst who was harshly criticized by New York psychoanalysts during the 1960s, was also frequently referenced in articles in *IJP*, along with Ronald Fairbairn, Wilfred Bion, Hanna Segal, Donald Meltzer, Jacques Lacan, Joyce McDougall, André Green and R.D. Laing, all prominent European analysts who worked with severe psychoses and published about it. It seems that American analysts were compelled to lean on their European colleagues who were not tied to psychiatry and, therefore, not influenced by psychiatric trends. Since the medicalization of American psychoanalysis tied it to psychiatry, and since the DSM-III was one more step in the divorce of the two, American analysts during the 1980s turned to their European colleagues for the theoretical and practical platforms for understanding psychoses and schizophrenia. These European theories provided an alternative to the biological explanations offered by psychoanalysts allying themselves with new trends in psychiatry, the hermeneutics theory that seemed to give up on the term "patient" altogether and the limitations of the American classical model, which could easily explain and treat the neuroses but was clearly lacking when it came to the more primitive states of mind.

The most prominent American analyst to implement and advance British object-relations theory was Thomas Ogden. Three of his articles (1983, 1985, 1989a), published in *IJP* during the 1980s, combined his familiarity with British theories with his vast clinical experience in treating schizophrenic patients. Ogden's ideas were portrayed by his fellow American colleagues as aligned with Kleinian analytic thought regarding treatment of schizophrenia and infant observations, but as being clearer than the primary European texts. A review of his book (King 1990) even sarcastically referred to Ogden's approach as "digestible for the American reader," described not as a "deep reader" but rather as a "busy

120   *The emperor's new clothes*

reader" (p. 733). In his book, *The Primitive Edge of Experience* (1989b), Ogden added to the Kleinian approach of positions (paranoid-schizoid and depressive positions) the autistic-contiguous position (or dimension of experience). He shed light on an earlier stage of pre-Oedipal development not offered by Klein, and with it a conceptualization of an earlier fixation which better matched severe disturbances, among them schizophrenia.

Using British theories developed on the basis of clinical work with young children, some of them severely disturbed, Ogden argued that understanding early forms of experience served to inform psychoanalysis about a universal dimension of human experience. These different modes of experience were presented by him as not inherently pathological. In fact, each mode provided a unique aspect to the dialectic of the whole human experience. Each mode of experience included certain defenses, certain aspects of object relations, a specific quality of anxiety, a level of subjectivity and so forth. Psychiatry had characterized some parts of the human experience as "sick," while the hermeneutic school of psychoanalysis might not address their developmental origin at all. But for Ogden, these parts of human experience were vital in the dialectic tension that preserved it. Ogden's proposal represented one of the solutions available for American analysts as they walked the thin line between two alternatives that ignored the intrapsychic realm – its complexity, its child parts, psychotic aspects and inevitable gaps. The biological approach focused on brain injuries characteristic of schizophrenia, and the hermeneutic approach removed from psychoanalytic discourse all the concepts that constructed the intra-psychic world with which psychoanalysis framed itself and its treatments. Ogden presented Klein and her followers as contributors to the comprehension of those early stages typical in schizophrenic mentation. Their approach was indirectly presented as contrary to the American approach, especially that of DSM-III, which focused on observable phenomena. Thus, American analysts appeared to be threatened not only by the hidden content of the fantasy world, but also by the mere existence of hidden processes, especially as they were expected to see (the observable symptoms) and be seen (as being able to diagnose adequately) during the decade of the DSM-III. Object-relations theories offered American psychoanalysts more than insight regarding pre-Oedipal stages, and as noted by Robert Emde (1988), a psychiatrist and psychoanalyst from Colorado, they allowed for a move from the all too constricting ego psychology, or one-person psychology, to a "we-go psychology" – that is, a two-person psychology. However, unlike the alternative offered by Sullivan and his American interpersonal school, which almost completely abandoned the intra-psychic world, and in contrast to Schafer's nearly behavioral ideas, this approach took into account external relations without renouncing the intra-psychic realm. Clearly, American psychoanalysts in the international arena look to the British and European psychoanalytic writers for theoretical ideas that would enable them to remain relevant in the field of severe mental illness, even as they were forced to integrate the discourse of somatic psychiatry.

An ongoing discussion of psychoanalytic treatments of schizophrenics took place throughout the decade, accompanied by distinct self-criticism when a treatment was unsuccessful due to the analyst's adherence to the classical model when attempting to understand the patient. Severely ill patients were understood to require an object-relations frame of thought, based on the early mother-infant relationship, and rely on the analyst's countertransference as means of gaining insight. Later in the treatment, when a patient has achieved some form of organization, the classic interpretations might be effective. Conceptualizing the two types of disorders, the neurotic and the psychotic, and the two models, the classic Oedipal model and the pre-Oedipal, object-relations model, provided platforms for a stage-based treatment for schizophrenia, as proposed by Kernberg. Kernberg (1986) brought back the psychoanalytic treatment of schizophrenia, now equipped with a theory suitable for pre-Oedipal stages. According to Kernberg, during the pre-Oedipal stages biological and physiological aspects were more important, and, therefore, pharmacological interventions were clinically indicated more often. Later on, when mentation developed, schizophrenic patients could benefit from classic psychoanalysis. By presenting a case of a schizophrenic patient, Kernberg clarified his proposed stages of treatment for the schizophrenic: the patient was admitted per his recommendation in the context of worsening delusions and hallucinations. The stages of treatment were reflected in the development of the analyst's relationship with her. First, medications that greatly reduced her affective distress were administered. The alleviation of her anxiety, rage and sensory stimulation attenuated the powerful activation of internalized, primitive object relations within the transference. Though this kind of rhetoric could be read as a return to hybrid discourse, especially when Kernberg suggested that "medications reduce the power of primitive object relations" (p. 156), it was evident that he used medications in the preparation stage of the analytic work. Kernberg identified the first therapeutic task in working with severely regressed psychotic patients – especially those who had lost their usual verbal capacities – as providing the security of an inpatient unit and establishing a meaningful connection. Meaningful connection cannot replace the analytic treatment but creates a foundation for the work. The goal of the second stage of treatment was to expand the patient's tolerance to ambiguity, merger and confusion, while contributing to the distinction between patient's and analyst's expressions. That is, once a connection has been made – one that is not framed in supportive terms that avoid the difficulties of a psychoanalytic interaction with a schizophrenic patient or that substitute for the analytic work itself – then the struggle of accepting the separateness from the analyst begins to be addressed. In advanced stages of the treatment with psychotic patients, when reality testing is restored and the therapist's care, concern and reflective functions are internalized, the concept of self-reflection starts to consolidate. This technical approach is derived from Winnicott's theory, and it proposes that the analytic therapist, who continues to interpret, even when faced with the schizophrenic patient's aggression, enables the island of self-reflective capacities to consolidate through the patient's identification with the therapist. Accepting the pre-mentation stages of the schizophrenic patient, those non-verbal stages in which the patient's physiology and biology are mostly present, requires the therapist to access knowledge about the

122   *The emperor's new clothes*

patient via countertransference. In other words, although biology plays a part in this model, it does not take over the treatment, and furthermore, as Kernberg argued, it is especially in these biological, wordless, meaningless points, when the regressed patient has no ability to tell his or her story, that the analyst is needed to recognize what is happening to the patient, by using countertransference and representing the patient's experience in words.

As noted, the analyst's physical availability and continuity are perceived as vital to the treatment of schizophrenics, and no less important is the analytic approach which enables the analyst to interpret the transference/countertransference relationship. Other American analysts in the international arena also brought up the importance of the initial connection with the therapist. These analysts viewed defense mechanisms, such as projection identification, as pathological, as well as part of the patient's attempt to establish meaningful connections with others. In psychotherapy with psychotics the remaining capacity to form a human connection is the key for future growth and a meaningful existence. This stance maintains the hopes of analysts regarding their ability to treat schizophrenic patients and allows the continuing theoretical hold of psychoanalysis in the field of schizophrenia, as well as in the realm of treatment of these patients. Because such treatments, at least in their initial stages, are perceived as highly demanding, the need for external management of the patient via hospitalizations is clear, and many of the cases presented in the literature were of hospitalized patients.

The Boston Psychotherapy Study: Another blow to psychoanalysis

Although psychoanalytic publications on schizophrenia in psychoanalytic journals were in decline, articles discussing psychoanalysis in the *Schizophrenia Bulletin* doubled in number in comparison to the previous decade. In 1984 an entire issue of the *Bulletin* was dedicated to the psychotherapy of schizophrenia, and the most prominent focus was on "The Boston Psychotherapy Study" (Stanton et al. 1984), a research project on psychotherapy with schizophrenics. This study, conducted in McLean Hospital, Boston University Hospital and the Boston Veterans' Hospital, all in Massachusetts, by researchers from the Harvard psychiatry department, was not the first of its kind. As already discussed, during the 1960s and the 1970s many studies examined the use of psychotherapy with schizophrenia, most of which were skeptical about the efficiency of this treatment. Moreover, these studies converted the question of "Is it ethical to withhold psychotherapy from schizophrenic patients?" to "Is it ethical to *provide* psychotherapy when its efficiency is not proven?"

One of the explicit goals of the Boston Psychotherapy Study Group was to correct the methodological problems that raised criticism of the original studies. The researchers used seasoned therapists and patients who were not too acute or chronic. In an almost oppositional stance, they used the *International Classification of Disease* (ICD), the diagnostic tool of the World Health Organization (WHO), and not the DSM-III, arguing that the move from DSM-II to DSM-III

The emperor's new clothes   123

reflected a trend of a more "narrow and specific definition" (Stanton et al. 1984, p. 526). The method and tools of this study were designed to assess the relative worth of exploratory, insight-oriented psychotherapy (EIO), also known as analytically oriented psychotherapy, in comparison to reality-adaptive supportive psychotherapy (RAS). EIO's goal was defined as self-understanding of the individual's thoughts and feelings, and how they influenced that person's life. Therapy sessions focused on the therapeutic relationship and other significant relationships in the patient's life, and on exploring emotions and conflicts. This therapy mode focused on searching for meaning, uncovering hidden and unconscious motivations and exploring the present and the past. The technique included support, strengthening of boundaries, clarifications, interpretations and catharsis. Positive and negative transference were allowed, as well as countertransference of conflicting emotions that the therapist usually did not display to the patient. The approach itself was an adaptation of Frieda Fromm-Reichmann's approach, which was based on psychoanalytic theories of treatment and psychopathology; however, unlike classical psychoanalysis, it did not attempt to interpret primary processes and did not encourage regressive transference, as promoted by Searles (Stanton et al. 1984).

RAS, the more common treatment offered to schizophrenic patients at the time, was aimed at symptom reduction via pharmacology and the strengthening of existing defenses. Sessions were focused on managing the patient – that person's complaints, interpersonal issues and present problems. The emphasis was on current awareness and not on hidden agendas, and on the present and the future, while the techniques were support, validation, clear boundaries, clarifications, directing the patient and suggesting manipulations of the environment and using community resources. Only positive transference was reinforced, and therapists actively avoided encouraging negative transference. In terms of countertransference, positive emotions were important and expressed, and negative emotions were to be "controlled." Although this was a psychological treatment, it was evident that the core goal was encouraging medication compliance, and, at times, the therapist would provide the patient with a coherent theory about the origin of the patient's illness, emphasizing the biological origin and the need for long-term pharmacological treatment (Stanton et al. 1984).

These descriptions of the differences between EIO and RAS treatments show that the EIO therapists used a psychoanalytic approach to etiology and treatment, while the RAS "supportive" therapy approach had a more biological/medical focus. Thus, one can argue that somatic psychiatry generated psychological treatments aimed at producing a more compliant patient who would accept the somatic treatment, while "learning" that his or her problem stemmed from a brain disease. Despite the fact that all the therapists in the study were well trained, had over 10 years of experience and were mostly working in psychiatric hospitals, there was a distinct difference between these mental health professionals. The "analytic" group was not serving the needs of somatic psychiatry, and perhaps the opposite was also true. The "supportive" group might have been supportive, but more than supporting the patient, they supported the somatic therapy by promoting compliance with the medications. The analytic therapists assumed

124 *The emperor's new clothes*

that developmental factors were the critical ones in the etiology and treatment of schizophrenia. They believed in the possibility of a meaningful change in the core of schizophrenic pathology, using indirect techniques based on exploring the transference relationship and its growth. The supportive therapists put much more emphasis on genetics in the etiology of schizophrenia, believing that these factors created unchangeable aspects in the pathology.

Although similar studies had been conducted in the past, aimed at determining which is more effective, dynamic treatment or medications, the main question of the researchers in the decade of the 1980s, though not explicitly declared, was this one: "Which psychotherapy is more effective in addition to the basic pharmacological treatment – or in support of it?" The researchers themselves, though presented as supportive of dynamic psychotherapy, seemed to be mostly driven by cost considerations. Despite EIO's positive effect on the patients' inner world and on core aspects of schizophrenic pathologies, RAS was presented as the preferable treatment, since patients showed better functioning, such as longer periods of time outside of the hospital and more stable employment. RAS was presented as a treatment that paid for itself quickly and reduced expenses related to the unproductiveness of schizophrenic patients. In other words, although the Boston group allegedly wanted to defend psychodynamic treatments and their value for the patient's insight, empowerment and agency, in the end they championed "functionality and productivity" as the most important values, at a time when cost-effectiveness appeared to be the ultimate test.

The Boston group's study was criticized by those who supported psychoanalytic treatments for schizophrenic patients. Facing the statistical results and empirical evidence it offered, these analysts brought their own data, collected through years of working psychoanalytically with schizophrenic patients. The conclusions of influential psychiatrists in the United States and Europe were recruited to refute the findings of the Boston group. These psychiatrists favored the psychodynamic approach and developed and implemented it with schizophrenic patients. Among them were the analysts at Chestnut Lodge in Maryland, at the Burghölzli clinic in Zurich, alongside Ernst Simmel from Berlin and Paul Federn from Vienna, who worked with psychoses and challenged the conclusion that they could not be helped by psychoanalysis. The history of jurisdiction battles between psychoanalysis and somatic psychiatry also came into play in this context. Gerald Klerman (1984), a psychiatrist appointed by President Jimmy Carter to chair the National Agency of Mental Health, claimed that the interpersonal paradigm that was developed in the Washington, D.C./Baltimore area was able to bravely withstand the competition with biological treatments such as insulin coma, electroconvulsive therapy and antipsychotic medications. He also mentioned the Boston study, noting that it did not provide a comparison between psychotherapy groups and placebo groups or psychotherapy in comparison to medications, but rather looked at whether psychotherapy adds anything to the psychopharmacotherapies. Klerman gave the victory to somatic psychiatry and its psychopharmacology, since according to him very few, if any, psychiatrists would dare to study the efficacy of psychotherapy without medications (p. 610). In a seminal paper published during the 1980s in the *Bulletin*,

The emperor's new clothes 125

Bertram Karon (1984), a psychiatrist and analyst known for promoting the psychodynamic approach for the treatment of schizophrenia, made the same point as he argued that the pharmacological marketing efforts scared the professionals in the field. Mental health professionals stopped treating schizophrenic patients without antipsychotic medications almost completely and were afraid to reduce the drug treatment once it began.

Karon proposed to reexamine the original question that was not raised at all by the Boston group, which was whether drugs should be used *at all*. This appeared to represent an attempt by dynamic psychiatry to raise the notion that psychotherapy was not an additional treatment but actually a stand-alone option that might be hindered by the use of medications. Antipsychotic medications were perceived as obscuring the affective system with which psychotherapy created change. Thus, reducing medication use must be an integral part of psychodynamic-oriented treatment, and the failure to do so impeded the long-term effectiveness of such treatments. Moreover, Karon argued that the drugs not only hindered psychotherapy's ability to heal but also cut off the possibility of spontaneous recovery that, according to Karon, occurred in 35% of cases.

Christian Müller (1984), a Swiss psychiatrist who, together with Gaetano Benedetti, established what eventually became the International Society for Psychological Treatments of Schizophrenia and the Psychoses (ISPS), wrote after the Boston Study that under the influence of Sullivan and Fromm-Reichmann he became "a brother in arms" of European therapists who tried to treat schizophrenic patients analytically. He asked – in the face of the Boston Study's conclusion that there is no advantage to the psychoanalytic approach to schizophrenia – what he should say about the enthusiasm of analysts during the 1950s and 1960s and about all the sacrifices he and his colleagues had made when they decided to treat these patients (p. 618). Müller emphasized that studies such as the Boston Study were focused on schizophrenic patients in general and therapists in general and were not concerned with the individual patient or the individual therapist. He brought up his own examples and statistics of working dynamically and reaching significant results, not only by the therapist's standards but also by objective measures of integration into sociocultural life, vocational stability, mental well-being and even remission of symptoms.

Private statistics, though contrary to the zeitgeist that demanded rigid and controlled empirical studies and objective statistical analysis, still served analysts in their struggle to remain relevant in the field. The data base accumulated over the years by individual psychoanalysts, some of the pioneers in the field of psychoanalysis and schizophrenia, served as the weapon used by these "brothers in arms" in the battle against the "empirical data" collected in studies such as the Boston Study. Müller explained why "objective" research about psychotherapy with schizophrenia was impossible, arguing:

> Let us consider the following situation: that of a psychoanalytically oriented psychiatrist working in an institution, who is in contact in the course of years with hundreds if not thousands of schizophrenic patients. He obviously

126　*The emperor's new clothes*

cannot choose any one of them at random with whom to engage in a long therapeutic combat. In only a few cases he will feel drawn to bring the best of his resources to bear and commit himself to major personal sacrifices.

(p. 619)

These motivations could stem from countertransference, but, in any case, they did not lend themselves to quantification and measurement. This claim and the argument that many factors, conscious and unconscious, which cannot be examined with statistical tools, put the mere validity of studies such as the Boston Study into question. Psychoanalysis was portrayed as a treatment method that cannot be assessed by external tools, which weakened its claim for legitimacy.

Another trend emerged, albeit a marginal one, to prove psychoanalysis's effectiveness by obtaining empirical evidence for the validity of psychodynamic theory and practice with schizophrenic patients. Subliminal stimulation was revisited, and results from this treatment were drawn from the archives as a reminder of "empirically based" evidence for the psychodynamic approach that psychiatry had been rejecting during this decade, as not implementable and ineffective in the field of schizophrenia. An article examining the results of more than 50 studies, which focused on the relationship between subliminal stimulation of unconscious phantasies and overt pathologies of adult schizophrenics, supported psychoanalytic formulations for the connection between some unconscious phantasies and psychopathology (Mendelson and Silverman 1982). One can see this as an attempt to mimic psychiatry and offer an alternative to antipsychotic drugs – in the suggestion to use the tachistoscope as a therapeutic tool for subliminal stimulation with this population.

In this era of a pharmacological monopoly over schizophrenia treatment, analysts no longer made militant arguments portraying drugs as "chemical lobotomy" or a "chemical straitjacket." Instead, the best analysts could come up with in their jurisdictional struggle was to advocate for "individualized pharmacotherapeutic strategies" that would take into account the subjectivity of the patient. Even if the therapeutic relationship was presented as a core aspect of schizophrenic patients' treatment, and even if it was advised to shy away from reductionist, biological approaches, the maximum subjectivity that these patients were allowed by many of these analysts was only in the "subjective" prescription of their drugs. Instead of administering these drugs according to some general rule, special cocktails and dosing were individually designed.

Summary

The publication of the DSM-III in the United States at the beginning of the 1980s constituted the third stage of the neosomatic revolution in psychiatry, and psychoanalysis in the United States continued to establish itself in this field as a response to both the growing force of somatic psychiatry and to being pushed, together with psychodynamic psychiatry, out of the field of severe mental illnesses. In this decade, the overall departure from the inner

The emperor's new clothes 127

psychic world and the move to the realm of observable symptoms enforced by the DSM-III, alongside the Kraepelinian approach positing the brain as the organ of the mind, constituted the most significant injury to psychoanalysis in its jurisdictional struggle over the field of schizophrenia. The presence of the DSM-III was also the basis for even more substantial strengthening of the psychopharmacological approach in psychiatry. It appears that psychiatry, which had just "divorced" psychoanalysis, was quick to find a new partner or, as Loren Mosher (1988), past editor of the *Bulletin*, said in his resignation letter to the American Psychiatric Association, "an unholy alliance" was established between the American Psychiatric Association and other institutes that promoted the drug companies.

Psychoanalysts publishing in American journals reacted in three ways to being pushed out of the field of schizophrenia. The first included criticism of and resistance to the approach of descriptive psychiatry and the narrow diagnoses it offered while coming up with its own diagnostic system. In this fight, psychoanalysts examined their own contribution to the loss of influence in the field of schizophrenia, producing two contradictory ideas. One was to emerge out of the cocoon of their analytic institutes, strengthen their relationship with medicine and return to the universities and hospitals where the new generation of psychoanalysts would be recruited. The second idea was to accept the rejection by medicine and expand the institutes so that professionals with a natural tendency to think from a psychotherapeutic perspective, such as psychologists, would gravitate toward psychoanalytic training.

The second reaction to the move to push psychoanalysis out of the field of schizophrenia was an attempt to resemble the "competitor" by viewing schizophrenia as a biological illness. Such a view served to communicate to psychiatry that analysts would accommodate the biological zeitgeist in psychiatry and that psychoanalytic treatment could serve psychiatry by instilling patients with awareness about the usefulness of medication. Moreover, this view kept borderline disorders within psychoanalysis's jurisdiction, because schizophrenia was presented as a "biological" illness that should be treated pharmacologically; borderline disorders were presented as psychological problems belonging in the jurisdiction of psychoanalysis, with its "psychological" approach.

The third reaction proposed finding new allies in the quest to decode and treat the schizophrenic state. The renunciation of psychiatry, which became increasingly biological, descriptive and technological, expressed itself in suggestions to use theories from various other fields, such as communication, cybernetics, literary criticism, the arts, anthropology and so forth, in an effort to understand and treat schizophrenia.

In this decade, American analysts publishing in the international arena walked a thin line between biological and hermeneutical explanations of the human psyche in general and the schizophrenic state in particular, both of which excluded schizophrenia from psychoanalysis. Engaging with British object-relations theories that explored pre-Oedipal development, American psychoanalysts found a theoretical haven, both from the biological "offenses" that saw schizophrenia as

128 The emperor's new clothes

an illness of the brain and from the hermeneutic escape that aimed to rid itself of the concepts of "disorders" and "patients" altogether.

Psychiatry also attacked the efficiency of psychoanalysis with empirical research and statistics. Faced with this data base, psychoanalysis retorted with a different type of theoretical and clinical data, accumulated from analysts' experience of working with schizophrenic patients for decades around the world. As in the previous decade, theoretical and clinical progress in psychoanalysis occurred when psychoanalysts found solutions from within their discipline. Exploring the inner psychic world, theorizing about it and finding technical solutions for working with disturbances afflicting it were an alternative to the narrow and limiting DSM-III of descriptive psychiatry, and to treatment methods that addressed only the symptoms and not their causes.

References

Alger, I., 1982. Editorial. *Journal of the American Academy for Psychoanalysis and Dynamic Psychiatry*, 10, pp. 329–336.

Anscombe, R., 1981. Referring to the unconscious: A philosophical critique of Schafer's action language. *International Journal of Psychoanalysis*, 62, pp. 225–241.

Appelbaum, A., 1985. A review of *Psychotherapy of schizophrenia. The treatment of choice*, by Bertram P. Karon and Gary R. Vandenbos. *Journal of the American Psychoanalytic Association*, 33, pp. 715–718.

Arieti, S., 1981. Presidential address: Psychoanalytic therapy in a cultural climate of pessimism. *Journal of the American Academy for Psychoanalysis and Dynamic Psychiatry*, 9, pp. 171–184.

Asch, S. S., and Marcus, E. R., 1988. The current status of psychoanalysis in medical student education in the United States: A preliminary overview. *Journal of the American Psychoanalytic Association*, 36, pp. 1033–1057.

Barahal, H. S., 1982. Review of *Intrapsychic and interpersonal dimensions of treatment, a clinical dialogue*, by Robert Langs and Harold Searles. *Journal of the American Academy for Psychoanalysis and Dynamic Psychiatry*, 10, pp. 321–323.

Bemporad, J. R., 1981. In memoriam. Silvano Arieti 1914–1981. *Journal of the American Academy for Psychoanalysis and Dynamic Psychiatry*, 9, pp. iii–vii.

Brady, D., 1984. Review of *Psychiatrist of America: The life of Harry Stack Sullivan*, by Helen Swick Perry. *Journal of the American Academy of Psychoanalysis and Dynamic Psychiatry*, 12, pp. 289–292.

Chodoff, P., 1984. 1984, utopia, dystopia and psychiatry. *Journal of the American Academy for Psychoanalysis and Dynamic Psychiatry*, 12, pp. 459–470.

Easton, K., 1984. Psychoanalytic principles in psychosocial rehabilitation. *Journal of the American Academy for Psychoanalysis and Dynamic Psychiatry*, 12, pp. 569–584.

Emde, R. N., 1988. Development terminable and interminable – I. Innate and motivational factors from infancy. *International Journal of Psychoanalysis*, 69, pp. 23–42.

Engel, M., 1990. Psychoanalysis and psychosis: The contribution of Edward Kempf. *Journal of the American Academy for Psychoanalysis and Dynamic Psychiatry*, 18, pp. 167–184.

Faust, D., and Miner, R. A., 1986. The empiricist and his new clothes: DSM-III in perspective. *American Journal of Psychiatry*, 143, pp. 962–967.

The emperor's new clothes 129

Forrest, D. V., 1984. The art in analysis: The analyst's art. *Journal of the American Academy for Psychoanalysis and Dynamic Psychiatry*, 12, pp. 321–340.

Forrest, D. V., 1987. Dreams of the rarebit fiend: Neuromedical synthesis of the unconscious meaning. *Journal of the American Academy for Psychoanalysis and Dynamic Psychiatry*, 15, pp. 331–363.

Forrest, D. V., 1988. Nerds, or neuroevolutionary rostral developers. *Journal of the American Academy for Psychoanalysis and Dynamic Psychiatry*, 16, pp. 491–511.

Forrest, D. V., 1991. Mind, brain, and machine. *Journal of the American Academy for Psychoanalysis and Dynamic Psychiatry*, 19, pp. 555–577.

Freud, S., 1926. The question of lay analysis. In: *The standard edition of the complete psychological works of Sigmund Freud*, Volume 20. London: Hogarth Press. pp. 177–258.

Fromm-Reichmann, F., and Silver, A. L., 1990. The assets of the mentally handicapped: The interplay of mental illness and creativity. *Journal of the American Academy for Psychoanalysis and Dynamic Psychiatry*, 18, pp. 47–72.

Frosch, J., 1983. *The psychotic process.* New York: International Universities Press.

Frosch, J., 1988. Psychotic character versus borderline (II). *International Journal of Psychoanalysis*, 69, pp. 445–456.

Garfield, D. A., 1988. Paranoia and the ego ideal: Death of a salesman's son. *Journal of the American Academy for Psychoanalysis and Dynamic Psychiatry*, 16, pp. 29–46.

Gomez, E. A., 1986. Some psychoanalytic thoughts about King Lear, Dante, and Don Quixote. *Journal of the American Academy for Psychoanalysis and Dynamic Psychiatry*, 14, pp. 545–556.

Grob, G., 1987. The forging of mental health policy in America: World War II to the New Frontier. *Journal of the History of Medicine & Allied Sciences*, 42, pp. 410–446.

Grotstein, J. S., 1985. The evolving and shifting trends in psychoanalysis. *Journal of the American Academy for Psychoanalysis and Dynamic Psychiatry*, 13, pp. 423–452.

Grotstein, J. S., 1990. The "black hole" as the basic psychotic experience: Some newer psychoanalytic and neuroscience perspectives on psychosis. *Journal of American Academy of Psychoanalysis and Dynamic Psychiatry*, 18, pp. 29–46.

Grünbaum, A., 1984. *The foundations of psychoanalysis.* Berkeley: University of California Press.

Hall, L., 1993. The biology of mental disorders. *Journal of the American Medical Association*, 266, p. 844.

Healy, D., 1997. *The anti-depressant era.* Cambridge, MA: Harvard University Press.

Jung, C. G., 1961. *Memories, dreams, reflections.* New York: Vintage Books.

Kafka, J. S., 1981. Review of *Borderline personality disorder: The concept, the syndrome, the patient*, edited by Peter Hartocollis. *Journal of the American Psychoanalytic Association*, 19, pp. 236–247.

Kantrowitz, J. L., 1986. Review of *The broad scope of ego function assessment*, edited by Leopold Bellak and Lisa A. Goldsmith. *Journal of the American Psychoanalytic Association*, 34, pp. 747–751.

Karon, B. P., 1984. The fear of reducing medication, and where have all the patients gone? *Schizophrenia Bulletin*, 10(4), pp. 613–616.

Kernberg, O. F., 1986. Identification and its vicissitudes as observed in psychosis. *International Journal of Psychoanalysis*, 67, pp. 147–158.

King, M. V., 1990. Review of *The primitive edge of experience*, by Thomas H. Ogden. *International Journal of Psychoanalysis*, 71, pp. 733–735.

130　*The emperor's new clothes*

Klerman, G. L., 1984. Ideology and science in the individual psychotherapy of schizophrenia. *Schizophrenia Bulletin*, 10(4), pp. 608–612.

Kotin, J., 1986. The ideal patient. *Journal of the American Academy for Psychoanalysis and Dynamic Psychiatry*, 14, pp. 57–68.

Kubie, L. S., 1971. The retreat from patients. *Archives of General Psychiatry*, 24, pp. 98–106.

London, N. J., 1985. An appraisal of self psychology. *The International Journal of Psychoanalysis*, 66, pp. 95–107.

Mayes, R., and Horwitz, A. V., 2005. DSM-III and the transformation of American psychiatry: A history. *American Journal of Psychiatry*, 150(3), pp. 399–410.

Mendelsohn, E., and Silverman, L. H., 1982. Effects of stimulating psychodynamically relevant unconscious fantasies on schizophrenic psychopathology. *Schizophrenia Bulletin*, 8(3), pp. 532–547.

Menninger, K., 1963. *The vital balance: The life process in mental health and illness*. New York: Viking Press.

Mosher, L. R., 1998. A letter of resignation from the American Psychiatric Association addressed to Rodrigo Munoz, President of the APA [online]. Available at: <www.oikos.org/Mosher.htm> [Accessed on October 20, 2014].

Muller, C., 1984. Psychotherapy in schizophrenia: The end of the pioneer's period. *Schizophrenia Bulletin*, 10(4), pp. 618–620.

Niederland, W. G., 1986. Review of *Hoelderlin. Weder die These vom edlen Simulanten*, by Uwe Henrik Peters. *Journal of the American Psychoanalytic Association*, 34, pp. 209–212.

Oelman, R.,1981. Experiential innovations within the psychoanalytic movement. *Journal of the American Academy of Psychoanalysis and Dynamic Psychiatry*, 9, pp. 71–99.

Ogden, T. H., 1983. The concept of internal object relations. *International Journal of Psychoanalysis*, 64, pp. 227–241.

Ogden, T. H., 1985. On potential space. *International Journal of Psychoanalysis*, 66, pp. 129–141.

Ogden, T. H., 1989a. On the concept of an autistic-contiguous position. *International Journal Psychoanalysis*, 70, pp. 127–140.

Ogden, T. H., 1989b. *The primitive edge of experience*. Lanham, MD: Jason Aronson.

Oldham, J. M., 1988. Patterns of change. *Journal of the American Psychoanalytic Association*, 36, pp. 209–213.

Olinick, S. L., 1984. Psychoanalysis and language. *Journal of the American Psychoanalytic Association*, 32, pp. 617–635.

Orr-Andrawes, A., 1987. The case of Anna O.: A neuropsychiatric perspective. *Journal of American Psychoanalysis Association*, 35, pp. 387–419.

Popper, K., 1959. *The logic of scientific discovery*. New York: Routledge.

Reiser, M., 1988. Are psychiatric educators "losing the mind"? *American Journal of Psychiatry*, 141, pp. 148–153.

Robbins, M., 1983. Toward a new mind model for the primitive personalities. *International Journal of Psychoanalysis*, 64, pp. 127–148.

Rogow, A. A., 1985. The wolf-man: Sixty years later. Conversation with Freud's controversial patient. *Journal of the American Psychoanalytic Association*, 33, pp. 200–203.

Rosen, A. M., 1986. Review of *The regressed patient*, by L. Bryce Boyer. *Journal of the American Academy for Psychoanalysis and Dynamic Psychiatry*, 14, pp. 142–143.

Satinover, J., 1986. Jung's lost contribution to the dilemma of narcissism. *Journal of the American Psychoanalytic Association*, 34, pp. 401–438.

Schafer, R., 1976. *A new language for psychoanalysis*. New Haven, CT: Yale University Press.

Schwartz, D. P., 1984. Review of *Schizophrenic disorders*, by Ping-Nie Pao. *Journal of the American Psychoanalytic Association*, 32, pp. 667–674.Shapiro, L. N., 1983. Book notices: *A biopsychological perspective*, by Andrew Crider. *Journal of the American Psychoanalytic Association*, 31, pp. 325–351.

Shapiro, T., 1989. Editorial: Our changing science. *Journal of American Psychoanalytic Association*, 37, pp. 3–6.

Sharfstein, S., 2005. From the president of APA – Big pharma and American psychiatry: The good, the bad, and the ugly. *Psychiatric News*, p. 3 [online]. Available at: <http://pn.psychiatryonline. org/cgi/content/full/40/16/3> [Accessed October 21, 2014].

Silverman, M. A., 1985. A secret symmetry. Sabina Spielrein between Jung and Freud. *Journal of American Psychoanalytic Association*, 33, pp. 205–209.

Simons, R. C., 1987. Psychoanalytic contribution to psychiatric nosology: Forms of masochistic behavior. *Journal of the American Psychoanalytic Association*, 35, pp. 583–609.

Spiegel, A., 2005, January 3. The dictionary of disorder: How one man revolutionized psychiatry. *New Yorker* [online]. Available at: <http://www.newyorker.com/magazine/2005/01/03/the-dictionary-of-disorder> [Accessed on October 21, 2014].

Spitzer, R., and Endicott, J., 1978. Medical and mental disorder: Proposed definition and criteria. In: D. Healy. *The anti-depressant era*. Cambridge, MA: Harvard University Press, pp. 233–234.

Spitzer, R. L., and Fleiss, J. L., 1974. A re-analysis of the reliability of psychiatric diagnosis. *British Journal of Psychiatry*, 125, pp. 341–347.

Stanton, A. H., Gunderson, J. G., Knapp, P. H., Frank, A. F., Vannicelli, M. L., Schnitzer, R., and Rosenthal, R., 1984. Effects of psychotherapy in schizophrenia: I. Design and implementation of a controlled study. *Schizophrenia Bulletin*, 10(4), pp. 520–562.

Stone, M. H., 1986. *Essential papers on borderline disorders: One hundred years on the border*. New York: New York University Press.

Strahl, M. O., 1983. Review of *Psychotherapy of schizophrenia – The treatment of choice*, by Bertram P. Karon and Gary R. Vandenbos. *Journal of the American Academy for Psychoanalysis and Dynamic Psychiatry*, 11, pp. 632–634.

Volkan, D. V., 1987. Psychological concepts useful in the building of political foundations between nations: Track II diplomacy. *Journal of the American Psychoanalytic Association*, 35, pp. 903–935.

Waites, E. A., 1986. The princess in the tower: Zelda Fitzgerald's creative impasse. *Journal of the American Psychoanalytic Association*, 34, pp. 637–662.

Wallerstein, R. S., 1986. Review of *Severe personality disorders: Psychotherapeutic strategies*, by Otto F. Kernberg. *Journal of the American Psychoanalytic Association*, 34, pp. 711–722.

Westen, D., 1990. Towards a revised theory of borderline object relations: Contributions of empirical research. *International Journal of Psychoanalysis*, 71, pp. 661–693.

Willick, M. S., 1983. On the concept of primitive defenses. *Journal of the American Psychoanalytic Association*, 31, pp. 175–200.

132 The emperor's new clothes

Willick, M. S., 1990a. Review of *Essential papers on borderline disorders: One hundred years at the border*, edited by Michael H. Stone. *Journal of the American Psychoanalytic Association*, 38, pp. 842–847.

Willick, M. S., 1990b. Psychoanalytic concepts of the etiology of severe mental ill. *Journal of the American Psychoanalytic Association*, 38, pp. 1049–1081.

Wilmer, H. A., 1982. Vietnam and madness: Dreams of schizophrenic veterans. *Journal of the American Academy of Psychoanalysis and Dynamic Psychiatry*, 10, pp. 47–65.

6 The last battle of psychoanalysis? The Decade of the Brain (1990–2000)

Many studies regarding the human brain have been planned and conducted by scientists at the National Institutes of Health, the National Institute of Mental Health, and other Federal research agencies. Augmenting Federal efforts are programs supported by private foundations and industry. The cooperation between these agencies and the multidisciplinary efforts of thousands of scientists and health care professionals provide powerful evidence of our nation's determination to conquer brain disease.

(George H. W. Bush, Presidential Proclamation 6158 1990)

As a practicing psychiatrist, I have watched with growing dismay and outrage the rise and triumph of the hegemony known as biologic psychiatry. Within the general field of modern psychiatry, biologism now completely dominates the discourse on the causes and treatment of mental illness, and in my view this has been a catastrophe with far-reaching effects on individual patients and the cultural psyche at large. It has occurred to me with forcible irony that psychiatry has quite literally lost its mind, and along with it the minds of the patients they are presumably supposed to care for. Even a cursory glance at any major psychiatric journal is enough to convince me that the field has gone far down the road into a kind of delusion, whose main tenets consist of a particularly pernicious biologic determinism and a pseudo-scientific understanding of human nature and mental illness.

(David Kaiser, "Against Biologic Psychiatry" 1996)

George H. W. Bush's proclamation, declaring the 1990s as the "Decade of the Brain," heralded the fourth and final stage of the neosomatic revolution in the field of schizophrenia. Schizophrenia was labeled as a brain disease to be "conquered" by the sciences, and federal funds were transferred from the treatment of the mentally ill to biological research in the field. This process had begun in the 1980s, when a small group of neuroscientists collaborated with politicians to promote neurological studies of mental illnesses. This direction raised the question of whether to operate in an open format, in terms of time, similar to cancer research, or to format the work as a "super project" that would be time sensitive, such as the human genome project (Goldstein 1994). One result of these debates

134 *The last battle of psychoanalysis?*

was the conception of the "Decade of the Brain," which became a national, time-limited research endeavor aimed at better understanding the brain and the nervous system. The program was constructed around critical neurological questions regarding the "developing brain": that is, developmental anomalies, the "injured brain," which was the result of traumatic brain injuries, the "dysfunctional brain," as in multiple sclerosis, and the "sensing brain," as in pain disorders. After the program was presented, and in response to a report by the national advising committee of the National Institute of Neurological Disorders (NINDS) and the National Institute of Mental Health (NIMH), President Bush signed Proclamation 6158 on July 25, 1989, stating that millions of Americans were affected by brain disorders, in which he included Alzheimer's, autism, speech impediments, hearing problems and schizophrenia. He further argued that the affected individuals and their families were hoping for a new era of discoveries in brain research and solutions based on new brain imaging technologies, a new understanding of brain biochemistry and the ability to design new and improved medications. This wording indicated that schizophrenia was a brain disease which could be diagnosed with technological tools and treated by somatic medical means.

The crusade to conquer illnesses of the brain

The studies that allegedly enabled brain observations, as the President noted, were supported by NIMH and other federal agencies, as well as by private industry and collaboration among entities. This, according to Bush, was a testimony to the "national effort to conquer illnesses of the brain," and his rhetoric was much like President Kennedy's challenge to scientists and engineers in 1961 to conquer space. In fact, a summary of the decade at its half point (in the mid-1990s) argued that neurological research was a success story: "Four decades of support brought about achievements that were difficult to imagine" (Goldstein 1994, p. 241). This effort to delve into the biology of normal and pathological behavior and cognition indicated a decline in interest in the mind, and it signaled a reductionist, organic approach to thought. The subtext in the President's message was that disciplines respecting the functional autonomy of mental processes, such as psychoanalysis, were anachronistic and indirectly placed psychoanalysis outside the field of mental health. This fact, together with the growing body of literature associated with what came to be called the "Freud Wars" (Gomez 2005), constituted a blow to American psychoanalysis during the 1990s in general and in the field of schizophrenia in particular.

Although Freud had been criticized systematically in America as early as the 1970s, especially by feminist writers, only in the Decade of the Brain did such criticism become a "war" in the United States. Some argue that the official date of the beginning of Freud Wars is November 1993, when the *New York Review of Books* published a piece by Frederick Crews, an English professor from Berkley, California, titled "The Unknown Freud," which summarized all the findings of Freud's critics. Much of the psychoanalytic establishment responded to this article as if it were a declaration of war. However, many agree that the article itself

The last battle of psychoanalysis? 135

was not the cause for the war, but rather where it was published. The *New York Review of Books* was considered to be the "home journal" of liberal American intellectuals and was known for its sympathetic alignment with psychoanalysis. The publication of an article attacking Freud "from within" evoked extreme reactions. After the publication of Crews's article, the Freud Wars intensified, and when a group of intellectuals signed a petition against a planned exhibition dedicated to Freud in the Library of Congress, the war escalated even further. Freud was accused of being dishonest and hypocritical, and psychoanalysis was blamed for being harmful to its patients (Brunner 2001).

This chapter explores American analysts' reaction to the two blows they suffered – one caused by the declaration of the Decade of the Brain and the other by the Freud Wars. The presidential proclamation, which officially identified schizophrenia as an illness of the brain, in essence declared schizophrenia to be under the jurisdiction of the brain sciences and put its treatment under the jurisdiction of psychopharmacology. Although this proclamation had the potential of marginalizing psychoanalysis in the field of schizophrenia, psychoanalysts proved they were willing to continue struggling for jurisdiction. They tapped a few strategies from the previous decade: first, they used the discourse of the sciences, which was more and more dominant, even at the cost of losing their own "father tongue;" second, they strove to preserve psychoanalysis's unique discourse while proving its relevance and effectiveness for schizophrenia, especially through evidence of effective clinical work; third, they gave up schizophrenia altogether in favor of other areas of mental health that were not yet marked as "brain disorders," such as the borderline disorders, and appropriated them exclusively for their jurisdiction.

Arguing for a dualistic view of schizophrenia etiology

During the decade of the 1990s, analysts in the *Journal of the American Psychoanalytic Association* (*JAPA*) showed their concern about the expansion of the somatic medical model in the field of schizophrenia, and this concern was also reflected in new psychiatric publications such as *Schizophrenia Bulletin* and *Schizophrenia Research*. There was also concern with the decrease in the number of psychoanalysts treating schizophrenics and the decline in psychoanalytic research on schizophrenia. Since most of the research on schizophrenia was produced by biological psychiatry and psychosocial studies, analysts such as Michael Robbins (1992), known for his writing on the analytic treatment of schizophrenia, voiced their concern about the further growing body of biological evidence, not only for the psychoses but also for neuroses.

Robbins addressed these trends, arguing that biology and psychoanalysis were not mutually exclusive and, in fact, were complimentary to and necessary for each other. He suggested that mental illness benefited from the use of a dual perspective – organic and psychological. He argued that both points of view, the neurological and the psychoanalytical, should have a place in psychoanalytic discourse. Robbins's suggestions were promising: that both neurobiology and psychoanalysis respect their limitations and each other's autonomy and avoid

136   *The last battle of psychoanalysis?*

assumptions or postulations that crossed their respective lines of expertise or produced reductionist rhetoric. However, his view raises the question of why he kept biology within the purview of psychoanalytic discourse at all. Robbins's writings included both explorations of the inner psychic world and of the "inner brain world." Thus he wrote, "the preschizophrenic has difficulties maintaining self-object boundaries, differentiation, or mental representations" (Robbins 1992, p. 438). At the same time he used concepts from biological discourse on mental health, such as

> studies suggestive of gross and microscopic pathology in the limbic system, which is responsible for gating of incoming stimuli and psychophysiological changes in ERP [evoked brain potential] and SCOR [skin conductance orientation response] suggest an organic substrate for this problem.
> (Robbins 1992, p. 439)

His explanations of schizophrenia remained at the meeting point of biology and primary interpersonal relationships. However, he seldom addressed the inner psychic processes occurring at that meeting place, and these processes are considered to be the core of psychoanalytic insight and clarification.

Use of neuroscience to explain schizophrenic symptoms

Analysts' attempts during this decade to insert into their discourse concepts from the world of neuroscience are reflected most tellingly in Martin Willick's writings. Willick (1993), who, as shown in previous chapters, is an example of an analyst who relegated schizophrenia to the biological sciences while keeping the borderline disturbances within psychoanalysis, argued that the deficit in schizophrenia, known from the DSM-III as one of the "negative symptoms" (flat affect; loss of motivation, initiative and drive; paucity of speech; lack of insight and judgment; psychomotor retardation), was related to frontal lobe dysfunction. Although his general psychoanalytic model was perceived as fitting with the conceptualization of decathexis of mental representations proposed by Freud's unique theory, Willick's model also reflected an attempt to reconcile with the triumphant discipline, and psychoanalysis abandoned schizophrenic patients in favor of strengthening its jurisdiction with borderline patients. Thus, such assertions as "most schizophrenic states are the result of biochemical, physiological illness of the brain" and "psychological conflicts are the result of impaired ego functions due to biological abnormalities" (Willick 1993, p. 1135) reflected an attempt to align psychoanalytic theory with the growing forces of biology in psychiatry. In the spirit of neurobiology, the deficit is identified as the only aspect differentiating schizophrenia from other psychoses, and this deficit is presented during the Decade of the Brain in solely neurological terms. What psychoanalysts referred to up until that moment as deficits in the psychic structure of schizophrenic patients – meaning a loss of libidinal hold in mental representations – were now presented unequivocally as defects in brain structures and neurological functioning. In addition,

The last battle of psychoanalysis? 137

schizophrenia was divided into two types of disorders, supposedly according to its biology, and the dopamine hypothesis was recruited to support this argument:

> Functional abnormalities have been further correlated with impairments or deficiencies in neurotransmitter systems. It has been known for some time that alterations in dopamine receptor activity play an important role in the appearance of delusions and hallucinations. Now, however, there is evidence that there is diminished dopamine activity in the prefrontal cortex, and that this abnormality may be associated with the deficit syndrome.
>
> (Willick 1993, p. 1142)

Willick added that while frontal lobe dysfunction was indicative of schizophrenia with negative symptoms, positive symptoms, such as delusions, hallucinations and bizarre behaviors, were related to "temporal-limbic structures" (Willick 1993, p. 1148). Odd mannerisms, bizarre or stereotypical movements, odd gait and other abnormal psychomotor movements described in schizophrenia were, according to Willick, the direct result of "neurobiological changes in the Basal Nuclei" (Willick 1993, p. 1152).

Analysts' movement toward "brain discourse" in the field of schizophrenia had practical consequences, as it brought them closer to drug treatments as well. For example, the works of three prominent ego psychologists, Hartmann, Rappaport and Bellak, are presented by Eric Marcus (1999), a psychiatrist and psychoanalyst from Columbia University, as forming the basis for a description of a combined regimen of analysis and medication (p. 846). By aligning psychoanalytic concepts with concepts from the realm of cognitive science, the technique of free associating, to cite one example, was presented as "neural pathways of random episodic memory" (Marcus 1999, p. 866). In what seemed like an attempt to avoid appearing to be swayed by the changing trends in psychiatric fashion, some argued that all conceptions of affect symbolization in neurobiology began in a psychoanalytic model, which was presented as a neurophysiological developmental model. Such assertions seem indicative of a desire that analysts like Marcus had to be recognized for psychoanalysis's alleged contributions to neuroscience.

Using the discourse of biological psychiatry, analysts tried to claim that they were relevant to the field, but in fact they achieved the exact opposite effect. When they replaced psychoanalysts' depth of insight into the working of the psyche with a wide range of concepts from different domains, especially those from cognitive science, they conceded that the key to understanding schizophrenia was in neurology. If this were the case, it could be rightly questioned why psychoanalysts, who specialized in the inner psychic world, were needed in this field. Moreover, psychoanalysts did not appear to offer any advantage, superior knowledge or even a unique perspective on the schizophrenic condition, in comparison with neurological explanations presented by somatic psychiatrists, neurologists and brain researchers, and, therefore, their use of biological discourse seems to be self-defeating.

138   *The last battle of psychoanalysis?*

The shift from "parent blaming" to "brain blaming" (Valenstein 1998) was accompanied by additional criticism of psychoanalysis from intellectuals, journalists and various organizations. "Freud bashing" threatened to further exclude psychoanalysis from the field of mental illness. During this decade, an attack of this kind, published by Edward Dolnick (1998), a journalist for the *Boston Globe*, argued that relying on psychoanalysis and family pathology while ignoring biological impairments was detrimental to the patient. Dolnick fiercely criticized Frieda Fromm-Reichmann's concept of "the schizophrenogenic mother," Lidz's model of schizophrenic families with high expressed emotions and Harold Searles's reports of successful psychoanalytic treatments with schizophrenic patients. Dolnick's indictment not only attacked psychoanalysis in the field of schizophrenia but also suggested, almost casually, that somatic psychiatry's theory and treatment were the correct options. He argued that psychoanalysts continued to treat schizophrenic patients despite the weakening in evidence supporting their treatment's effectiveness, notwithstanding the effectiveness of drugs and regardless of the accumulation of evidence supporting the hypothesis that genetics played a part in the disease.

Attacks on psychoanalytic theories from without and within

Analysts attempted to address Dolnick's criticism, but their arguments seemed weak. They argued, for example, that analysts offered psychodynamic treatments to schizophrenic patients when no alternative treatment was yet available. The Menninger Clinic in Topeka, Kansas, was known for its interest and investment in psychoanalysis, yet Richard Munich, an analyst there, argued that psychoanalysis was offered because the effectiveness of antipsychotic drugs had been accompanied with severe side effects, some symptoms had not been addressed by the drugs and cognitive, behavioral, psycho-educational and rehabilitation therapies had not yet been available. Moreover, the unique contribution of psychoanalysis itself to the treatment of schizophrenic patients and its advantage over other psychotherapeutic treatments were questioned by analysts themselves, according to Munich (1999). Furthermore, analysts who treated schizophrenic patients did not consider their efforts to be potentially healing, he said, but rather saw their relationships with patients as palliative care with a long-term commitment, if not for life. These analysts were portrayed as unambitious in their goals, even more so than in Dolnick's portrayal, and when they accepted the effectiveness of neuroleptic drugs, they claimed, according to Munich, that psychoanalysis could address the "missing pieces" of their patients' ability to adapt and their interpersonal repertoire (Munich, 1999). When facing the grand promises of somatic psychiatry, these modest goals of "filling in the blanks" during "life-long treatment" did not constitute a significant claim over jurisdiction.

In addition to facing external criticism and attacks, psychoanalysts working with schizophrenic patients also faced attacks from within. In an article that summarized the decade, psychoanalysis's connection with schizophrenia was presented as a cautionary tale. Again, Willick (2001) promoted the biological approach to schizophrenia, positing that three decades of psychoanalytic writing about the etiology of schizophrenia, from the 1940s to the 1970s, were proven incorrect. Willick named three erroneous assumptions in the theory: that the damage to the ego occurred within the first two years of life; that the main cause of the damage was an inadequate caretaking person; and that there were no underlying, biological abnormalities at the core of the illness. Willick (2001), who leaned on somatic psychiatry's findings and technology, argued that technological advances enabled brain studies to identify these errors. Although he attacked mainly the psychoanalytic theory of the etiology of schizophrenia, he clearly proposed the use of medications with schizophrenic patients and a supportive psychotherapy.

As Willick (2001) attacked all the psychoanalytic theories addressing schizophrenia, from ego psychology through all the British theories, he also challenged the common knowledge, arguing that analysts such as Klein, Winnicott, Fairbairn, Bion and Guntrip actually never treated patients with schizophrenia (insinuating that only Rosenfeld treated such patients) and that the reason that many assume that these analysts did actually treat schizophrenics was due to erroneous diagnoses. Willick stated that he could not similarly doubt American analysts who claimed to have worked with schizophrenics because they presented detailed case studies of four to five weekly sessions with patients, mainly in hospital settings. He did criticize their fascination with the supposedly destructive role of the first caregiver, which he said was extreme.

Willick's arguments were yet another blow to psychoanalysis's already tottering claim of jurisdiction in the field of schizophrenia. He too posited that psychoanalysis was a stand-in until neosomatic psychiatry arrived, and analysts believed it was more humane than the alternative treatments at the time: "no effective medications were available. . . . biological studies had failed to consistently reveal any organic abnormalities in schizophrenia. . . . [a] psychotherapeutic approach might be both more effective and more humane than psychosurgery or multiple insulin shock treatments" (Willick 2001, p. 38). But that was in the past, and during his lifetime, Willick was troubled by psychoanalysts' refusal to prescribe medications and warned that psychoanalytic theories of etiology might cause analysts not to give medications, due to the belief that the psychological roots of the disorder should be explored and that drugs might obscure this study. In fact, Willick's warnings exemplify how psychoanalysts themselves weakened their jurisdiction by supporting the neosomatic trend in psychiatry. Clearly, the relationship between attacking psychoanalytic etiological theories and the indication to use drugs and only supportive treatment in schizophrenia is unequivocal.

Willick's criticisms of the role psychoanalysis assumed in treating schizophrenia and, specifically, his claim that schizophrenia was a biological disorder were criticized, in turn, by other analysts. Michael Robbins (1996) argued that the hereditary explanation of schizophrenia was not a sufficient reason to ignore psychologically distinct factors in the disease's etiology. By way of comparison, he posited that although there is a wide range of agreement regarding biological differences between the sexes and that neurochemical exams would most likely

140 *The last battle of psychoanalysis?*

identify more accurately whether one is male or female than if one has schizophrenia, there is still room for discourse about the development of gender identity in the literature. Robbins suggested that prevailing social attitudes and values played a role in what analysts viewed as data and how they construed that data. According to sociocultural premises in the Decade of the Brain, schizophrenia was assumed to be an organic disorder. However, Robbins noted that the lack of indisputable organic findings was ignored by analysts. Thus, due to sociocultural biases, the biological basis of schizophrenia became a given, despite the absence of solid findings.

Psychoanalysts examine why they lost ground

Since analysts were trying to understand why psychoanalysis had lost prestige in psychiatry and why they were losing schizophrenic patients, much like in previous decades, they examined psychiatric training and the commonly used texts in psychiatric residencies. Thus, George Ginsberg (1992), a psychiatrist from New York, argued that medical schools "manufacture" residents in psychiatry who complete their training without adequate experiences in, and knowledge of, dynamic psychotherapy. These residents do not learn that human suffering is the result of coping with different types of conflicts that are inevitable in human beings, but rather that it is a result of a brain dysfunction devoid of psychological meaning.

The questions of whether psychoanalysis was a medical discipline or, more broadly, whether there was any purpose in reading 100-year-old texts, which is not the case in any other medical specialty (Winer 1997), become relevant during the Decade of the Brain. Analysts who were still trying to prove their relevance to the field emphasized that psychoanalysis was needed for understanding the relationship between therapists and patients. This approach seems to further weaken the status of psychoanalysis, as it offered itself not as a theory of mental disorders or a treatment method but rather as a way to understand the therapeutic dyad. Once again psychoanalysis was cast as a supportive practice to the main somatic treatment method. This tendency to produce "psychoanalysis-lite" reflected analysts' attempt to return to psychiatry by keeping to their "appropriate place" as dictated by the psychiatric zeitgeist. While doing so psychoanalysts created a simplistic kind of psychoanalysis, taking what was easy to understand and delivering it to "quick, efficient, and economic" psychiatrists.

Psychoanalytic institutes were suffering because of contemporary trends to use quick and cost-effective treatment methods that would be funded by managed care. Financial considerations, it was claimed, forced doctors to use economic approaches that put the focus on business instead of humans. During the Decade of the Brian the history of psychoanalysis was recruited to refute this assertion, and once more the Schloss Tegel sanatorium in Berlin was held up as an example (Danto 1999). The radical notion of allowing patients from all layers of society, including schizophrenic and other psychotic patients, to receive free psychoanalytic treatment, as was offered in the Schloss Tegel, was a distant ideal in the Decade of the Brain. Psychoanalysts lamented managed care intervention in treatment, relegating psychoanalysis only for patients with the financial means to pay for it privately. Those who lacked such funds and who were reliant on the managed care insurance companies would have to settle for the somatic treatment aimed at symptom relief, but would remain handicapped in their psychological functioning (Pardes 1997, p. 938).

JAPA calls for research on psychoanalytic treatment of schizophrenia

Since treatment outcomes were the focus of managed care, and since psychoanalysis's Achilles' heel was its inability to produce such data, the American Psychoanalytic Association supported empirical studies both of etiology and treatment and offered funding for such research projects. The Association's intention to establish a psychoanalytic research culture in general, and one that studied schizophrenia in particular, reflected two interests: first, the struggle over psychoanalysis's prestige in comparison to other, more "scientific" domains that received sponsorship during the Decade of the Brain, and second, the struggle to be acknowledged by insurance companies who paid for only empirically proven treatments. Psychoanalysis's endeavor to become an empirically proven, clinical discipline was cumbersome and posed many challenges. However, the multiple appearances of "empirical" papers in the Association's journal during this decade reflected the willingness to face these challenges. These research papers were intended to bring psychoanalysis into the public eye, support the next generation of analysts and clarify the unique value of psychoanalytic treatment in comparison to other treatment modes.

Understanding the challenge of proving treatment effective, but also acknowledging that psychoanalysis was different from other therapeutic modalities in the field of mental health, two well-known psychoanalysts, John Gunderson, director of McLean Hospital in Boston, and Glen Gabbard from the Menninger Clinic, demonstrated the difficulty of empirically studying the efficacy of psychoanalysis (Gunderson and Gabbard 1999). They explained that once psychotherapeutic approaches were rigidly manualized and the therapist could not shift flexibly according to the patients' needs as she could in a naturalistic setting, symptom relief wrongly became the desired goal or outcome of study. Moreover, studies about treatment outcome tended to focus on a specific frame of time, contrary to "real life" in which treatment duration was dictated by the patient's needs. Likewise, many patients, especially the difficult ones, were excluded from studies, and those who did partake in research were well aware and inclined to respond to "subject required for research" advertisements, as they were more motivated and mindful of their mental health. Thus, they were not a representative sample. But Gunderson and Gabbard (1999) did not discourage psychoanalysts; they simply offered them an alternative data base – that is to say, case studies and the accumulated clinical wisdom. This enabled psychoanalysis and those who argued that it did not lend itself to empirical studies to demonstrate its unique contribution with its own tools rather than those of somatic psychiatry.

142 *The last battle of psychoanalysis?*

In the political and economic climate surrounding mental health treatment, these analysts cautioned from the "worst case scenario" in which the market paradigm controlled health care policy and decision making. The free market competition dictated by managed care replaced the professional paradigm and threatened to exclude psychoanalysis if it could not prove its effectiveness empirically. Although case study reviews could potentially show the value of psychoanalytic treatments and its long-term cost-effectiveness, Gunderson and Gabbard (1999) claimed that psychoanalysts were not keen to cooperate with the demand to produce empirical proofs for their treatment value, claiming they did not have the time to involve themselves in research, methodologies, data, results and evidence. Gunderson and Gabbard, who believed psychoanalytic therapy remained compatible with the traditional rehabilitative/restorative medical mission within which it arose, recommended psychoanalysts not to desert the medical community "that needs our knowledge and skills, as well as the deeply afflicted mentally ill who continue to need our help" (p. 699). They suggested that in order to reclaim the credibility they "dramatically lost with the advance of biological psychiatry and of other psychosocial therapies" (p. 697), analysts should mobilize efforts, via their organizations and institutions, to ensure that treatment guidelines will specify when psychoanalytic therapy is needed. These guidelines, they argued, could be offered even without the empirical support of controlled outcome research. To find a more secure and appropriate place for psychoanalytic therapy within future psychiatric services, and more generally within mental health services, these authors suggested that the efficacy of psychoanalytic therapy would be systematically assessed by using the available knowledge and potential data bases and by making explicit efforts to locate the role of psychoanalytic therapies alongside other modalities. Their overall feeling was that the "worst case scenario" could be avoided, in which psychoanalytic therapy would be practiced only by very few and marginalized in the treatment of the mentally ill (p. 697).

Schizophrenic processes in psychoanalysis

Alongside analysts who were trying to prove the efficacy of psychoanalytic treatment for patients with schizophrenia were others who were attempting to strengthen their hold on borderline disorders, the most severe form of mental pathology analysts were treating, by touting their work with schizophrenics. They argued that by working with severe cases of schizophrenia, their intuition developed and enabled them to bridge between their own worlds and that of the "exotic, eerily disturbing world of their borderline patients" (Stone 1994). Since analysts believed they had lost the struggle over schizophrenia, and since borderline patients appeared to be the next candidates for the neosomatic "takeover," the profession made great efforts to defend its territory. Searles (1975), for example, who was known as a psychoanalyst devoted to the psychoanalytic treatment of schizophrenics, warned psychoanalysts against giving borderline patients shorter and less intensive analytic treatments (p. 287). Vamik Volkan, a psychiatrist from Virginia who wrote about "madness," suggested six steps for the psychoanalytic treatment of borderline

The last battle of psychoanalysis? 143

cases (Kulchycky and Munich 1995). British psychoanalyst Herbert Rosenfeld, who was also dedicated to analytic treatment of schizophrenic patients, is actually quoted in *JAPA* as saying that in the generation prior to medication, the results of psychoanalytic treatments with schizophrenics were "heart breaking," and in many cases the course of the illness did not change. However, because the therapists learned from those treatments, they could implement their knowledge in the analysis of less difficult patients – that is, with borderline patients or those with severe personality disorder (Modell 1991).

That psychoanalysts themselves were pushing schizophrenia out of their jurisdiction became apparent when schizophrenia was identified with psychiatric texts such as the DSM, while borderline disorders received significant attention in the psychodynamic counterpart to the DSM, the *Psychodynamic Diagnostic Manual* (PDM). As already mentioned, *JAPA* articles during the Decade of the Brain were concerned with adapting to biological/empirical fashion or with recounting their treatment of borderline disorders. Even analysts like Louis Sass, a psychology professor at Rutgers University in New Jersey who wrote two books related to the topic of schizophrenia, *Madness and Modernism* (1992) and *The Paradox of Delusions* (1994), were criticized because their writing seemed to reveal that they had not worked with schizophrenic patients and were not versed in psychoanalytic theories about schizophrenia. As Michael Robbins (1998) wrote in his review of Sass, it was difficult to imagine how "anyone who has worked with schizophrenics could have failed to observe how common it is for those who are not withdrawn and apathetic to act on their delusional thinking" (p. 960).

Despite theoretical interest in schizophrenia, many analysts from the American Psychoanalytic Association, judging by their texts, did not practice psychoanalysis with schizophrenics. The lack of case studies of such treatments and the limited number of reported treatments with schizophrenic patients raised the question of how rare this kind of treatment became in the 1990s. Vamik Volkan (1997), whose book, *The Seed of Madness*, was widely reviewed in *JAPA*, confessed that the book was his "memorial" to his grief over the loss of practicing analysis with difficult patients, which was precious to him. Similarly, Michael Robbins's (1993) book, *Experiences of Schizophrenia*, also reviewed in *JAPA*, reads as a lamentation for psychoanalytic treatment with schizophrenic patients as a dying art. Robbins had a provocative thesis, arguing that attempts to scientifically understand the most common elements of schizophrenia reflected primitive thinking, characteristic of the illness itself. Robbins wrote that the failure to use a pluralistic and integrative approach that included organic, psychological, interpersonal, familial, social and cultural aspects reflected the unintegrated, fragmented psyche of the schizophrenic patient. He posited that psychoanalysts had overreacted to their disappointment about treatment success because their expectations had been too grandiose; thus, they moved to a reductionist approach to schizophrenia, reducing it to an organic illness.

In the same vein as Robbins, Arnold Goldberg, a psychoanalyst from Chicago, also viewed psychoanalysts' scientific thinking about schizophrenia as potentially psychotic (Smith 1999). According to Goldberg, any synthesis of biology and

144   *The last battle of psychoanalysis?*

psychoanalysis that sought to answer the mind-brain question central to the Decade of the Brain produced an illusory solution. Attempts to eliminate the dichotomy between the two distinct fields were similar to an attempt to eliminate thinking itself, according to Goldberg (Smith 1999). The tension between the two fields was irreconcilable: although psychoanalysis and biology study the same object, psychoanalysis studies it through an internal approach and biology through an external approach (Smith 1999, p. 348).

Psychoanalysis and schizophrenia in the McDonald's culture

In contrast to what seemed like the distress of psychoanalysts' publishing in the *JAPA*, the *Journal of the American Academy of Psychoanalysis and Dynamic Psychiatry*, against all odds, celebrated pride in psychoanalysis in the 1990s. The Academy dedicated a special issue of its journal to the integration of psychoanalysis with neurology, or in the words of the Academy's past president Samuel Slipp (2000), "to refining and gaining exciting new knowledge to help our patients in dynamic psychotherapy and psychoanalysis as well as fulfilling Freud's longstanding dream for psychoanalysis to become a truly scientific psychology" (p. 200). But despite this and even though quite a few symposiums were held by the Academy on the same topic, the *Journal* still presented the pace of research related to schizophrenia in the fields of biology and genetics as too rapid to be covered in one issue.

One of the attempts at integration was published in an article by David Forrest (1991), a psychiatrist and psychoanalyst from New York who suggested using computerized models of neurological webs that could manufacture computational neural networks that model psychopathological states in aging, dyslexia and schizophrenia (p. 555). Forrest suggested that computerized applications that could model the brain might show schizophrenics' unique cognition and could be used to examine how defenses, in the psychodynamic sense, were neurologically represented and how they were affected from a neurological standpoint.

Alongside these integration efforts, and like many articles published in *JAPA*, albeit not as frequently, the analysts in the *Journal of the Academy* also used biological terminology to explain the schizophrenic state, while abandoning psychoanalytic discourse. In what seemed like an attempt to find refuge in the safety of neuroscience, a neologism typifying this perspective – "neuropsychodynamics" – was used in articles about topics such as "Brain and Self" (Miller 1991) or "Freud's Brain" (Miller 1993). It appears that the "slippery slope" manifested in the use of biological concepts in psychoanalytic discourse and resulted in a hybrid language that led analysts to strange propositions – for example, that endorphins were involved in ego defense processes (Battegay 1991). In the same vein, analysts were mixing clinically derived psychoanalytic theories, such as ideas about the significance of the early relationship of the infant with the caregiver, as offered by Winnicott and Kohut, with neurological concepts. Thus, an article about the significance of early parenting in the development of psychosis suggested

The last battle of psychoanalysis? 145

that "early failures in these dyadic relationships result in orbitofrontal organizations that are associated with insecure attachment styles, chronic difficulties with
affect regulation, and a predisposition to psychiatric and psychosomatic disorders" (Solano, Toriello, Barnaba, Ara, and Taylor 2000, p. 102). Although some
analysts wanted "to expose the dehumanizing level of practice promulgated by
for-profit-driven managed-care companies. . . . to reveal the limitations of drug
therapy in the treatment of many psychiatric problems. . . . to speak out about
the beneficial results of our practice and the importance of human contact in
psychiatry. . . . [and] to educate the public in the great classical tradition that we
proudly preserve and perpetuate" (Bemporad 1996, p. 363), they still sometimes
found themselves on the same slippery slope, even when they pointed in a different direction for the causality of psychosocial events and somatic structures.
Thus, when suggesting that the right hemisphere matures during the first three
years of life and that attachment patterns are crucial to its development, they were
implying that relationships and psychology are shaping the brain and not the
other way around (Slipp 2000). Also problematic was when brain locations were
proposed for psychodynamic concepts, as in "the right hemisphere is the home
of the pleasure/unpleasure principle" (Slipp 2000, p. 198) or "the *unconscious*
seems to be located in the subcortical system (including the amygdala) and the
right hemisphere, while the *conscious* involves the hippocampus and the frontal
lobe (the prefrontal, cingulate, and orbital cortex)" (Slipp 2000, p. 193). The
conflation of abstract psychoanalytic discourse with concrete neurological terms
did little to further understanding of either psychoanalysis or neurobiology. In an
attempt to claim jurisdiction, Slipp (2000) stated, "we stand on the threshold of
achieving an empirical basis for psychoanalytic treatment and theory" (p. 199),
and in doing so proposed that brain imaging techniques, the technology of the
competitors, could serve as important tools in the development of an empiric
basis for clinical and theoretical psychoanalysis.

The evidence of the environment's influence on the brain, especially during
early development, allowed analysts a foothold in the field of schizophrenia during the Decade of the Brain, but also created the old risk of confusing the world
of abstract ideas with that of the concrete material. Although psychoanalysis was
recognized as a branch of psychiatry invested in the subjective, the experiential
and that which was not measureable, the articles of American analysts in the *Journal of the Academy* discussed schizophrenics as suffering from dysfunction in their
dopamine system and particularly in the limbic, cortical and dopamine projection
fields (Glucksman 1995). These patients' condition was argued as consisting of
"enlarged ventricles, smaller amygdala/hippocampal, prefrontal cortical volumes,
and diminished frontal lobe metabolic activity" (p. 182). Such descriptions, as
well as suggestions that schizophrenia was related to "unilateral hemispheric dysfunction" (Wasserstein and Stefanatos 2000), led to conclusions that schizophrenics could better benefit from increasing "metacognitive awareness and social skills
counseling" (p. 388). In other words, psychoanalysts explained in neurological
terms why psychoanalysis was *not* a viable treatment for schizophrenia. Clearly,
when psychoanalysis tried to align itself with neosomatic psychiatry without

146 *The last battle of psychoanalysis?*

appropriate caution, it created theoretical concoctions that weakened psychoanalysis, both as a theory in the field of mental health and as a treatment method for mentally ill patients.

Some analysts publishing in the *Journal of the Academy* aimed at a broader, more holistic viewpoint of the human psyche and the schizophrenic condition that could take in neosomatic discourse without destabilizing psychodynamic ground. A diagnosis of schizophrenia was constructed by placing it in a social, affective, lingual and neurobiological context. The talking cure was, therefore, perceived in this light as a process that shapes identity and involves reconnecting to language, affect, environment, society and biology without excluding any of them (Sanfilippo 1998). In this spirit, another attempt was made to distance psychoanalysis from psychiatry, which became more and more somatic, and enrich it with other disciplines' viewpoints without losing the vision of the human psyche's richness. This attempt was done by aligning with theories that share a holistic understanding of man's place in the world, and with an emphasis on relationship as the basic characteristic of human life. The theories that were suggested for use in this context were theories of the unconscious, such as that of the Chilean psychoanalyst Ignacio Matte Blanco; Gregory Bateson's theory of the soul's place in nature; David Bohm's theory derived from physics regarding the relationship between matter and consciousness; Rupert Sheldrake's evolution theory; René Thom's new catastrophe theory; and James Gleick's chaos theory (Ullman 1998). Those who took this approach did not address the question of whether these theories coincided with psychoanalysis; rather, the significance of incorporating them lay in the possibility of creating new allies outside of psychiatry and the new fashion it adopted. As Michael Stone (1999) offered,

> With therapy, as with food, America has gone the way of McDonald's: fast food, fast cure. Fast food is at least digestible, even if tasteless. But there is no fast cure for schizophrenia. And even though analysis by itself may not be enough to effect big improvements in our schizophrenic patients, therapists who have analytic training bring a richness and depth of human understanding – including awareness of the often strange and eerie world of the schizophrenic – that therapists lacking this training seldom bring to their patients.
>
> (p. 598)

Analysts point out the limitations of drugs and the cost-effectiveness of analysis

Despite the agreement that medications alleviated positive symptoms of schizophrenia, there was also a conviction that unlike psychoanalytic treatment, they did not influence the course of the illness. Somatic treatments were directly criticized in this context. Ann-Louise Silver (1993), a psychiatrist and psychoanalyst who had worked at Chestnut Lodge and actively implemented psychoanalytic treatments with patients diagnosed with schizophrenia, argued that in the era of medications, the work with patients is silenced, while economic and governmental forces caused analysts to feel victimized and helpless themselves with their own "bitter pill to swallow" (p. 637). She noted that analysts were under constant threat, as they could not control the nature and length of treatment. Silver expressed her concern for the survival of mental health institutions, since they might collapse under the organizational and economic pressure applied to them. The psychoanalytic approach she was promoting comes across in her rhetoric, as she used psychoanalytic concepts to shed light on analysts' experiences of working with patients diagnosed with schizophrenia in the political and economic atmosphere of the 1990s. Silver wrote about analysts' experience of "attacks" from insurance companies, as similar to the experience of many of their schizophrenic patients, and accompanied her arguments with vignettes, as was common in the psychoanalytic writing tradition. She described a treatment with a patient diagnosed with schizophrenia who had been hospitalized for 10 years at Chestnut Lodge and had been in psychoanalytic treatment with her for five years: "We met for four sessions weekly. Our work has been under the gun of economic uncertainty" (Silver 1993, p. 640).

Like Silver, others analysts who published in *Journal of the Academy* protested that not only was countertransference in such treatments difficult, but the therapist also had to face the tremendous complication posed by insurance companies in their refusal to cover long-term treatments with challenging patients. Insurance companies were criticized because, although symptomatic treatments were proven to be ineffective in the long run, insurance still tended to pay for short-term hospitalizations, and after discharge the individual was left alone with his or her struggles, which often caused re-hospitalizations and additional financial investment. Presenting psychoanalytic treatment as more cost-effective over time in comparison to short-term neosomatic treatments targeting symptoms, which resulted in multiple, expensive hospitalizations, helped build a case for psychoanalysis's claim for jurisdiction. Psychoanalysis, in this context, was proudly displaying itself, not as a "supportive" practice to the neosomatic treatment, but rather as the treatment of choice for schizophrenia, even if only based on cost-effective considerations.

This stance is evident in an article by the Massachusetts psychiatrist and analyst Ronald Abramson (2001). Abramson stated that the American Psychiatric Association's guidelines from 1997 were combining medications with short-term psychotherapeutic treatment with measureable behavioral goals, because psychoanalytic treatment was considered by paying parties to be expensive and "indulgent" with few useful outcomes, and more appropriate for those who had minor "problems of living." In his article Abramson used data to show that when looking at long-term costs, psychoanalytic treatment in fact proved to be less expensive. He used a vignette describing a patient diagnosed with schizophrenia whom he saw for eight years, four times per week. Before her treatment with him, she was deemed psychotic and hospitalized multiple times in state hospitals' psychiatric units. Abramson showed that psychoanalysis decreased the cost of her treatment, as the number of hospitalizations she had to go through was reduced to zero after analysis began. In the past, this patient had been hospitalized 30 times

148　*The last battle of psychoanalysis?*

in nine psychiatric institutes due to self/other endangerment. She had been subjected to multiple and expensive therapeutic procedures, including various medications, which she stopped taking because of their side effects. Dialectical behavioral therapy (DBT) was also ineffective, according to Abramson, and in fact, only psychoanalysis created sustainable results for this patient. Abramson showed that after her analysis, the cost of her treatment decreased by $31,000; that, overall, psychoanalytic treatment cost $50,000 less than other treatments; and that, without it, this patient might not have survived at all (Abramson 2001).

Abramson did not use ethical arguments, such as Frieda Fromm-Reichmann's statement that "to redeem one person is to redeem the world" (Horenstein 2000, p. xvi). He did not explain the complexity of clinical processes to those who would not understand the value of psychoanalytic treatment. Instead he took the financial standpoint of paying parties. He used the financial incentives argument of employing the most cost-effective treatments, an argument that had the potential of raising far less resistance among the paying parties. By consenting to the cost-effective discussion used by insurance companies, Abramson could claim that the paying parties were mistaken about which treatment method was cheapest and most efficient. He presented data proving that the behavioral and pharmacological treatments, typically considered to be the cheapest, were in fact not superior in financial terms to psychoanalytic treatments. Ironically, he stated, only after repeated hospitalizations, when the patient showed no improvements, and after significant financial investment did medical insurance companies consider paying for analytic treatment.

Analysts in the Academy, much like their colleagues in the American Psychoanalytic Association, displayed concern for the next generation of psychiatrists. They acknowledged that psychiatry residents should be exposed to psychoanalysis if psychoanalysis were to be used for actual healing and not only for analyzing philosophy, art, literature and history. Clarice Kestenbaum (1995), in her presidential address at the annual meeting of the American Academy of Psychoanalysis in May 1994, presented a clinical vignette proving that psychoanalysis is a healing agent just as medication and cognitive therapies are. She presented a case of a young woman showing schizophrenic psychotic symptoms who was treated with medications. The patient refused to continue taking the medications and began psychoanalytic psychotherapy. As a result, her thought disorder stopped, her IQ test scores showed a significant increase in comparison to when she was hospitalized and she regained her functioning. Kestenbaum argued that the Academy had a major role to play in the future:

> to educate young psychiatrists lacking the necessary psychotherapeutic skills in working with patients, to teach the public about concepts in psychoanalysis today, and [to] conduct research in treatment efficacy and psychotherapeutic outcome[s]. If we can continue to help all those in need of psychoanalytic psychotherapy in the way we were trained and not give up our birthright, the doctor's dilemma will be solved.

(pp. 513–514)

The last battle of psychoanalysis? 149

The ethical dimension of treating schizophrenia

Although a majority of psychoanalysts gave up the struggle on schizophrenia during the Decade of the Brain, others insisted that psychoanalysis would engage in theoretical, clinical and interdisciplinary debate in this field. The substance of this debate was an attempt to study the schizophrenic condition, understand it and plan for its treatment, but in the process it also exposed the obstacles, confusion and misunderstandings that challenged analysts. At times, the therapeutic role appeared so difficult that it led to the question of why analysts would even want to face this challenge. As a response to this question, Peter Giovacchini (1993) suggested that the paradoxes inherent in the schizophrenic state – most likely due to the power of primary processes – made these patients extremely appealing. The paradoxes they live with, their multiple realities and the difficulties inherent in their treatment are also, according to Giovacchini, what enriches therapists with a perspective completely unlike their own. The emphasis on the experience of nothing, meaninglessness, chaos, "black holes," "falling through space" or the infantile catastrophe – all experiences characteristic of patients diagnosed with schizophrenia – was brought up in the context of the challenge these patients pose for the therapist's capacity for emotional and experiential understanding.

It seems that these kinds of articles reflect analysts' desire to remind themselves why they should continue to struggle for including schizophrenia in their jurisdiction. This is apparent in a review of the work of one of the most influential voices in the Academy on the subject of schizophrenia, Silvano Arieti (Bacciagaluppi 1999). Arieti is remembered as an analyst who criticized the "American way of life," which was more oriented to success than to a "subtle realization of oneself, predisposed more toward conformity than toward divergence, not very disposed to value isolation and inactivity, both of which are necessary requisites for creativity in any field" (Bruschi 1999, p. 536). He argued that pain and malice cannot be escaped, and demand our response. Arieti saw the therapist in a Dantesque role, vis-à-vis the schizophrenic patient, on a quest for spiritual meaning in the midst of chaos (Bruschi 1999). It is clear that analysts publishing in the *Journal of the Academy* were not romanticizing the schizophrenic condition; they differentiated between genius and madness, poets and schizophrenics, creative processes and schizophrenic processes, and leaders' charisma and pathological states. Although schizophrenia is neither art, nor poetry, nor genius, it was understood that analysts were drawn to these patients because of their unique condition and radical "otherness."

Unlike the articles on schizophrenia published in *JAPA* during the Decade of the Brain, almost all of those published in the *Journal of the Academy* used vignettes from treatment of schizophrenic patients from all strata of society, from the upper-middle class to immigrants and those in poverty. The focus was on psychoanalytic treatment of schizophrenia, and the theoretical emphasis was on the uniqueness and strangeness of the schizophrenic state. Thus, efforts were clearly made to design specialized analytic treatment suited to this unique disorder. Gaetano Benedetti (1999), who was influenced by Arieti and reviewed

150 *The last battle of psychoanalysis?*

his *Interpretation of Schizophrenia*, presented the study of psychoses as research of the human phenomenon in its other facets and the treatment of psychoses as a humane effort (p. 555). He quoted Arieti, who wrote in his book about schizophrenia – "it is as though I had written this book not only with ink, but with blood" (Benedetti 1999, p. 557) – to emphasize the dedication it takes to be engaged in the analytic process with patients who are at war with the world. Benedetti, like Arieti, did not see the patient as a "baby" in need of maternal care, but rather as a radical other who "may go to the point of destroying the world by altering deeply this symbolic and cognitive understanding of it" (p. 559). Even though the schizophrenic patient was depicted as a destructive individual and not as a helpless baby, and maybe precisely for this very reason, the analysts in the Academy stressed the ethical commitment to care even for those patients from the "back buildings" of the hospitals. The schizophrenic process was understood to be reversible, and thus the analysts' investment in this healing process was warranted.

Relational psychoanalysis marginalizes schizophrenia

In one of his letters to Ernst Simmel, Freud wrote that psychoanalysis is like the hydra: every time it is beheaded, it grows a few new heads. And, indeed, in the beginning of the 1990s and under the threat of the neosomatic trend, psychoanalysis spawned a new American publication, *Psychoanalytic Dialogues*, the journal of the relatively new school of relational psychoanalysis. This journal's publication was the result of a process that started in the 1980s of institutionalizing the relational approach in American psychoanalysis. It was the outcome of a few converging elements: first, Sullivan's interpersonal psychoanalysis, established through the William Alanson White Institute in New York and the School of Psychiatry in Washington; second, the growing presence of British object-relations theories in American psychoanalysis, discussed since the 1970s through the work of Guntrip, Fairbairn and Winnicott; third, the work of John Bowlby, the British analyst and pioneer of attachment theory, and Heinz Kohut, who wrote on narcissism at the end of the 1970s; and finally, psychoanalytic feminism, which developed in American psychoanalysis at the end of the 1970s and was greatly influenced by the work of Dorothy Dinnerstein, Nancy Chodorow, Carol Gilligan and Jessica Benjamin.

The establishment of the relational approach was accelerated with the formation of Division 39, the division of psychoanalysis in the American Psychological Association (APA); New York University's postdoctoral program in psychotherapy and psychoanalysis, the first to offer a relational curriculum; and, finally, the journal *Psychoanalytic Dialogues*, which offered a platform for the development of integrative psychoanalysis in general and for theorizing relational psychoanalysis in particular. The relational model was considered to be an alternative to the classic drive theory. Although the relational model could have been perceived as a simple expansion of Freud's conceptualization that object relations and internalized relations were expansions of drive processes and operated as a result of

The last battle of psychoanalysis? 151

drives, relational analysts chose to view their school as an alternative to Freud. One of the main characteristics of their approach was the constructive spirit. Relational analysts insisted on the existence of two individuals in their "two-person psychology." They acknowledged that the therapist's and the patient's psyches were distinct and separate, with their unique histories and inner worlds. However, their goal was to emphasize the third reality co-constructed in the unique interaction between the two individuals in the analytic encounter. Similarly, mental development was also argued to be the result of structuring, which could not be established ex nihilo, but out of specific natural materials, such as the body. Relational psychoanalysis's relevance to the discussion of psychosis and schizophrenia is in its self-declared aspiration to deconstruct misleading dichotomies and exaggerated polarizations; to maintain tension between the extremes; to emphasize ambiguity, dialogue, dialectic and paradox (Mitchell and Aron 1999) and to argue for the existence of a "insane-sane" self nucleus in every individual (Eigen 1993). These psychoanalysts further argued that "sanity alone provides a shadowy empty existence" (Mitchell 1995, p. 23).

Psychoanalytic Dialogues was launched in 1991 and published six issues per year dedicated to paving the way to a dialogue between theoreticians with varying perspectives: relational, interpersonal, British object relations, American ego psychology, the empirical tradition of infant and child observations and certain medleys of contemporary Freudian theories. Articles published in the *Psychoanalytic Dialogues* suggested that relational psychoanalysts were not invested in boundary work (Gieryn, 1983) with psychiatry in the field of schizophrenia. Moreover, analysts publishing in the *Dialogues* appeared to be less interested in schizophrenia than writers in other journals, and in their writings there is no evidence of jurisdictional struggles with somatic psychiatry, as was apparent in other journals. As such, relational psychoanalysis is an example of both creating distance from psychiatry and abandoning the field of schizophrenia. Analysts who were also psychiatrists wrote only seven of the 30 articles mentioning schizophrenia. The distance of relational psychoanalysis from psychiatry and from its neosomatic trend in this decade allowed those writing in *Psychoanalytic Dialogues* to avoid biological discourse, which had not been the case with the other journals. However, analysts publishing in *Dialogues* did not offer an alternative approach in the service of holding onto the field of schizophrenia. Only one article published during this decade, written by a British psychoanalyst, presented clinical work with a schizophrenic patient (Williams 1998a).

As has been shown, psychoanalytic work with schizophrenic patients greatly influenced the development of psychoanalytic theory. Just as Freud's paper on Schreber contributed significantly to his metapsychological papers, especially those on narcissism, repression and instincts, analysts publishing in the *Psychoanalytic Dialogues* during its first decade were influenced by the work of analysts who developed their theories based on their clinical encounters with schizophrenic patients. Harry Stack Sullivan's emphasis on the interpersonal dimension of the analytic encounter seems central to relational thought, just as Harold Searles's view of countertransference as a potential source of viable analytic knowledge,

152 *The last battle of psychoanalysis?*

rather than a pathological distortion to be clarified, seems to strike a chord with relational analysts' sensibilities (Mitchell 1999). In addition to Sullivan and Searles, Jung's contribution adopted by this school was described as stemming from his work on psychological approaches to psychosis (Sedgwick 2000). Clearly, psychoanalytic encounters with psychotic patients were central to the development of the relational approach, especially in the shift from viewing the therapist as a "detective-archeologist" to viewing him or her as a "collaborator-writer," or "participant-observer." This perspective emphasized the importance of countertransference analysis and undermined the analyst-patient binary, as reflected in Searles's article, "The Patient as Therapist to His Analyst" (1975), written about treatment with schizophrenic patients.

Beyond the deconstruction of the therapist-patient dyad, relational psychoanalysts also seemed to undermine binaries such as "psychosis-neurosis," "madness-sanity" and "primitive-mature." The difference between health and pathology is quantitative, and even too much sanity is considered unhealthy in their view. Aspects of human experience formerly perceived as pathological (psychotic/schizophrenic) were deemed in *Dialogues* not only as universal aspects of any human psyche but also as vital to its wholeness and richness. However, analysts in *Dialogues* showed far less interest in the healthy parts of schizophrenics. In other words, their overall narrative clarified that every healthy person had sick parts of the self, but there was no evidence that relational analysts also saw the healthy parts in the schizophrenic patient, those that might indicate analytic treatment. In contrast to the emphasis on the uniqueness and otherness of schizophrenic patients, seen in the Academy and used as an ethical argument to bring them back into the fold, the relational approach, which seemed to be more egalitarian by emphasizing similarities, actually neglected these patients almost entirely.

Freud's own neglect of these patients stemmed from his specific theory, which viewed schizophrenic patients as radically different from neurotics. Given that relational psychoanalysts assumed that "we are all more human than otherwise" (following Sullivan 1953, p. 62) and that psychotic elements are always to be found in their patients, why did so few analysts in this school report analysis with schizophrenic patients? It seems that one reason stemmed from the difficulty in analyzing the countertransference experience in such treatments and the lack in psychoanalytic training in preparing candidates for such work. When Thomas Ogden was asked in an interview (1991) with *Psychoanalytic Dialogues* why he was one of the few psychoanalysts who worked with severely disturbed patients, he replied that it was rare for psychoanalytic candidates to be required to treat such patients as part of their practical training and thus they did not have to face the countertransference they evoked. "It is tempting to conclude from unsuccessful work with borderline and schizophrenic patients that the patient is unanalyzable rather than considering the question of whether the analyst is properly equipped to conduct the analysis" (p. 363). Ogden criticized the tendency to offer these patients "supportive therapy," because he believed these therapies infantilized patients, treating them as if they could not

The last battle of psychoanalysis? 153

understand an explanation, in words, of the anxiety that prevented them from managing their lives and from connecting to objects in a more mature manner. He argued that "to deny a patient access to the transformative potential of symbols is to deny him the means by which he might attempt to achieve psychological change" (p. 364).

In this interview, Ogden was pinpointing the decline of psychoanalytic work with schizophrenic patients, which he saw as harmful both to patients with schizophrenia and to the analysts' clinical techniques. The eighth issue of *Psychoanalytic Dialogues* (1998), although not explicitly dealing with the questions Ogden raised, included one study of the relational theoretical and clinical approach to severely disturbed patients such as schizophrenics. This *Dialogues* issue was dedicated to a clinical and theoretical discussion between American and British analysts (the Americans are identified with the relational approach, also known as "the American middle school of psychoanalysis," and the British are identified with "the British middle school," also known as "the independents"). The issue opened with an unusual article for the time, by the British psychoanalyst Paul Williams (1998), presenting a detailed case study of a female patient diagnosed with schizophrenia. Despite the title, which defined her as a borderline who survived sexual abuse, the woman is referred to as schizophrenic in the body of the article. Given what seems to be a disinterest of relational analysts in schizophrenic patients, it is probably not a coincidence that this article, which received the Rosenfeld Award of the British Analytic Society for an outstanding clinical paper, came from London, where psychoanalytic treatment had been common with mentally ill patients. Williams, who is known for his work with psychotic patients, described a "heroic" treatment and a successful clinical intervention, which brought significant reduction in medication use. (While most psychotic or schizophrenic patients take an average of seven different drugs, including antipsychotic medications, this patient went down to a minimal dose of an antidepressant drug.) In his article Williams focused on the dynamics and the content of psychotic ideas, transference and countertransference, and placed an emphasis on the fact that even in psychotic states there exists an ongoing connection with reality, which explains the presence of neurotic phenomena in psychotic patients. As in Freud's later works, Williams argued that the ego maintains some connection to reality even in psychotic states, implying the existence of nonpsychotic elements in the otherwise psychotic individual. He differentiated between the psychotic and nonpsychotic parts of the patient's personality and saw the interpretation of the symbolic meaning of these parts in the nonpsychotic transference as the basis for psychotherapy with psychotic patients.

As mentioned, this issue became a source of information about relational analysts' theoretical and practical views of psychosis and schizophrenia. Generally, all the responses to Williams's article coming from the United States identified the mechanism of dissociation as the core of psychotic disorders. Dissociation is a defense mechanism, described by the French analyst Pierre Janet, evoked as a response to trauma, in which the self is split in an effort to contain the trauma which

154 *The last battle of psychoanalysis?*

threatens to overwhelm the individual. Although the perception of "psychotic and nonpsychotic personality parts" originated in British psychoanalytic thought, especially Bion's work, it has an American version in the form of multiple ego states, some of which are silenced, frozen or exiled by dissociation. The two approaches differ in that relational analysts view these various states as a preview to an ultimate integration of all the splits, followed by change in all personality aspects, while the British believe that the psychotic parts will never change. Thus, relational analysts aspire to rid patients of their psychotic component, whereas their British colleagues assume that although the analyst should speak to the delusional objects, s/he should not aim at integration of psychotic and nonpsychotic personality aspects. Instead, through the patient's identification with the analyst's sane parts and his or her capacity for empathy, reflected in the interpretations offered, the patient can approach the interaction sanely and, thus, his or her cathexis of the sane parts would increase.

Despite what appears to be clear differences between the two approaches, at times concepts from these approaches are confused, especially the term "psychosis," which is used differently by analysts and psychiatrists. The psychiatric definition, based on symptomatic evidence of delusions and hallucinations, seems to be preferred by Williams, while the relational psychoanalysts responding to him seem to use the term more flexibly. More generally it seems that, in this debate, different basic assumptions about human nature are evoked. Relational analysts view the human psyche as aspiring for integration and see only external traumas as the cause of breakdowns, splits and pathologies (for example, psychosis and schizophrenia). They perceive even the most bizarre symptoms as defensive attempts, creative at times, to make meaning, to control and to survive the traumatogenic, primary environment. The British approach as presented by Williams, however, conceptualizes two initial drives – one striving for integration and the other for fragmentation – and schizophrenia is the result of a victory of the psychotic, the death drive, aggression and destruction over the life drive. Williams insisted that schizophrenic patients were qualitatively different in their make-up – detached, lost and completely trapped in their own world. Williams also disagreed with relational analysts regarding the use of technique. While some of the American writers believed that working with schizophrenia called for adjusting the technique, such as moving from the "rule of abstinence" to a stance of nurturing and optimal provision, Williams assumed that the original analytic technique should be preserved and advocated for understanding the psychotic apparatus rather than working to eradicate it.

One of the responses to Williams in this special issue was from John Muller (1998) of the Austin Riggs Hospital in Massachusetts, known for its analytic approach to schizophrenia. Muller's use of a Lacanian perspective represented the position of psychosis as "otherness." This "otherness," explored in the Academy's attitude to the schizophrenic person, was dismissed by relational analysts. In contrast to the emphasis on radical otherness, the relationals insisted on similarity, perhaps in the spirit of egalitarianism.

The return of the seduction theory

Unlike other journals, *Psychoanalytic Dialogues* linked traumatic experiences to psychoses, framing psychoses as attempts to self-heal and as another way to cope with traumatic reality. This attitude seemed to stem from a basic tenet of relational theory which views the connection with significant others as the basis for health and pathology. The theory is based on infant studies that find the human baby to be a social creature, striving first and foremost to adjust to the social reality and only then seeking pleasure and avoiding pain. Mitchell (1988), a prominent proponent of this approach, advocated a shift from a "zoological" metaphor of the human baby to a "botanic" one (Mitchell 1988, p. 130): rather than thinking of a baby as an instinctual, pleasure-driven animal, Mitchell compared the baby to a plant seeking light to promote its growth. When something goes wrong, relational analysts tend to look for the cause in the environment. Due to this emphasis on trauma, the articles in *Psychoanalytic Dialogues* implied that the fault was in the mothering, an idea that conflicted with the feminist spirit that contributed to the relational approach's development. The "difficult" cases, a term previously reserved for patients diagnosed with schizophrenia – that is, patients who felt frozen, detached, out of place and so forth – were depicted in the *Dialogues* as those who suffered early trauma, and to judge from the articles in this relational journal, they all had schizophrenic, depressed or severely insecure mothers (Kiersky and Beebe 1994). Thus, even when relational analysts discussed schizophrenia, they mainly talked about the mothers, and sometimes the fathers, of their patients and not the patients themselves.

Since the *Dialogues* had a paucity of articles on schizophrenia, it was necessary to go further afield and look at the terms "psychosis" and "madness" to formulate a clear idea of how relational psychoanalysis approached severe mental illness. The use of the term "psychosis" in the *Dialogues* is flexible, and this fluidity created a great distance between "psychosis" as a phenomenon and psychotic patients. The 69 articles touching on psychosis published in this journal of relational psychoanalysis, in its first decade, attempted to use psychosis to redefine mental health. Additionally, in discussion on psychosis, the emphasis on trauma as related to pathology brought back to life the "seduction theory," and with it the insinuation of "parent blaming." Articles published in *Dialogues* that dealt with psychoses were influenced, even more than those that dealt with schizophrenia, by the link relational psychoanalysis saw between trauma and psychosis. In their view, the goal of analysis was not to make the unconscious conscious, but rather to reestablish connections between mental states that became dissociated from each other as result of trauma. This approach was influenced by the work of Sándor Ferenczi, whose work was revived by relational psychoanalysis.

Relational psychoanalysis's interests in the interpersonal world and in trauma that resulted in pathology were reflected in the case studies presented in *Dialogues*, mostly describing the psychotic parents of patients rather than psychotic patients themselves. Gender identity pathologies and transsexuality were presented as resulting from a mother's psychosis (Coates, Friedman, and Wolfe

156 *The last battle of psychoanalysis?*

1991; Stein 1995). Other difficulties patients experienced stemmed from "mother's grief and agitated depression [which] were probably of psychotic proportions" (Foster 1996, p. 113); "massively indifferent and psychotic parents" (Rustin 1997, p. 77); being "the child of a psychotic mother, for example, . . . doomed to psychosis" (Lichtenberg-Ettinger 1997, p. 397); a mother suffering from affective-psychotic disorder who caused her daughter's multiple personality disorder (Davies 1998, pp. 208–209); traumatic memories from a psychotic mother (Bach 1998, p. 669); and so forth. The etiological argument regarding trauma in early interpersonal relationships was somewhat reductionist, even if implicitly insinuating that all pathologies were the result of an unhappy childhood, during which the child has been beaten, seduced or neglected. Leonard Shengold (1992), a psychiatrist and analyst from New York, mostly known for his work on Schreber's trauma and psychosis, warned analysts away from this tendency to reduce all pathological factors to only one – relational trauma. He recommended that analysts refrain from the notion that people become mechanically misshapen as a result of what was presumably done to them.

Another characteristic of the discussion of psychosis in the *Dialogues* was the notion that the various pathologies were "versions of psychosis." Concepts such as "psychotic dynamic and psychotic-like process" (Eigen 1991), "psychotic elements" (Coltart 1991), "psychotic anxieties" (Gehnt 1993), "quasi-psychotic idealizations" (Stein 1995), "psychotically intense anxiety" (Kennedy 1996), "psychotic layer" (Peltz 1998), "psychotic experience" (Sweetnam 1999), "psychotic style" (Adams 2000) and so forth were common in the *Dialogues*. Such fluid use of the term created a significant gap between the psychiatric diagnosis of psychosis and the phenomenon of schizophrenia as was described by psychiatry and more traditional psychoanalysis. When the use of the term psychosis is so flexible, a thinker such as Erich Fromm (1954) was quoted as saying: "we are all crazy, we are all neurotic, we are all children and the difference between us is only quantitative . . ." (Stern 1992, p. 338). It appears that in the relational view the difference between psychotic and nonpsychotic individuals is unclear. Despite the extensive and varied interest of the *Dialogues* in psychoses, not one of the 69 articles presented a case study with a "truly psychotic" patient. Thomas Ogden, mentioned previously, is the only author reporting work with patients diagnosed with schizophrenia, while others, even if working with severe pathologies, rarely worked with psychotic patients (Blechner 1994). In addition to these somewhat slipshod definitions of psychosis, psychoanalysts in the *Dialogues* were discussing madness as a philosophical construct, detached from the suffering individuals. Thus, madness became a focal point of the scuffles between different philosophical orientations (Barrat 1995; Sass 1995), or it was argued that madness was nothing more than a construct within the psychoanalytic fiction and that it did not exist outside of it (Geha 1993).

The somatic trend crosses the ocean

In comparison to analysts publishing in American journals, American analysts publishing in the *International Journal of Psychoanalysis* in the 1990s had to cope

The last battle of psychoanalysis? 157

with biology, even though *IJP* had historically been a safe haven for Americans wishing to maintain their analytic identity. Martin Willick (1994) used the international arena to criticize the psychoanalytic emphasis on developmental factors in the etiology of schizophrenia, arguing that there was sufficient evidence that genetic factors and biological abnormalities were the main cause of these disorders. Unlike his manner of presenting his views in *JAPA*, in the international sphere he expressed his hope that psychoanalysis, which had lost its interest in the psychopathology of psychoses, would recommit itself; however, he assumed that this would be possible only if psychoanalysis was equipped with the new neurobiological findings. In other words, within the tradition of mixing the discourses, Willick suggested implementing psychoanalytic concepts of ego structure, ego functions and levels of mental organization in an attempt to better understand the neurobiological factors at play, as if psychoanalysis should serve the neurobiological research (Willick 1994). In a review he conducted, Willick found that only 11 out of the 24 main psychoanalytic institutes providing training gave any courses on psychoses, and those that did were using old formulas, in his opinion, regarding etiology (Willick 1994).

Another illustration of the growing influence of biology on American psychoanalysis, as it is reflected even in the international sphere, was a panel presentation in 1995 at the 39th Congress of the International Psychoanalytic Association in San Francisco, titled "Mental Reality in Psychotic States" (Marcus 1996). The panel focused on changes in psychoanalysis in the field of schizophrenia during the Decade of the Brain and opened with a presentation of the main controversies within psychoanalysis regarding psychoses – especially in the context of psychogenesis versus the biological approach. In the panel's summary, an argument was made that to remain relevant, analysts should maintain psychoanalytic concepts from various schools but also acknowledge developments in neighboring fields. In contrast to the unifying efforts taking place within the different schools of psychoanalysis, at the conference it was suggested that different schools could address different aspects of the patient. Thus, ego psychology could bridge psychoanalysis and neuroscience, supposedly allowing for the exploration of the influence of medication on ego dysfunctions, object relations could be used to better understand the experience of the individual in psychosis and the interpersonal approach would be used to understand the relationship between the therapist and the patient and its therapeutic potential (Marcus 1996, pp. 573–574). Unlike the efforts to integrate psychoanalysis, which were done during the 1970s and proved to be practically useful, it seems that this offer to split and divide the analytic worldview, just as the schizophrenic individual was dissected according to his or her biology, subjective experience and interpersonal experience, served to weaken psychoanalysis in its jurisdictional struggles. This wish for integration with other disciplines created a pseudo-cohesion within the different schools of psychoanalysis that created an even deeper schism within the profession.

As part of the effort to incorporate biology into psychoanalysis, Freud's abandonment of the "project" was presented, not as a willful decision, but as the

158   *The last battle of psychoanalysis?*

result of a limitation – either financial restrictions as a result of the need to make a living, or the limitation of means for scientific exploration in Freud's time. When this limitation was presented as related to technological means, it was argued that through the techniques of molecular biology, brain imaging, genetic studies and other computerized models, psychoanalysis could reconnect to the brain and pick up where Freud left off. Two questions are raised by this suggestion: "What could brain studies contribute to psychoanalysis?" and "How could psychoanalytic insight about mental functioning direct empirical studies of cognition and neurology?"

In 1997, an entire issue of the *IJP* was dedicated to articles designed to inform analysts of scientific knowledge from other disciplines. The issue opened with an article by David Olds and Arnold Cooper (1997), two New York-based psychiatrists and psychoanalysts who stated that psychoanalysis was never isolated, and in fact had always been rooted in the humanities and the scientific community. The assumption that all the relevant knowledge in psychoanalysis should "come from the couch" was criticized as they argued that infant studies about babies' cognitive abilities, self-development, ability to imagine what was in others' psyches (Theory of Mind) and attachment fluctuations could all provide psychoanalysis with new models to enrich its understanding of clinical data. Their concern that psychoanalysis might be cutting itself off from other disciplines brought up the notion that psychoanalysis needed to be assimilated into the general culture, which included, among other things, philosophy, infant research, social psychology, cognitive neuroscience and literature. However, in contrast to all these other disciplines that psychoanalysis ignored, it appears that cognitive neuroscience evoked the most substantial motivation for this initiative, as the article concluded with: "Psychoanalysis can only be enriched by more intimate contact with our *scientific neighbors*, and we hope the series of review articles that we are now beginning will achieve that goal" (Olds and Cooper 1997, p. 223). To this American analysts in the international arena offered a renaissance to the "scientific," pre-analytic Freud. If schizophrenia was one of the entry tickets to psychiatry used by psychoanalysts in the early years in the United States, once again, by being on the borderland of soma and psyche, psychoanalysts could reestablish their discipline's link to psychiatry, and especially to its powerful neosomatic trend.

In their attempts to partake in "extraordinary discoveries about the human brain" (Pally 1997, p. 587), American analysts tried to use neurology to justify their existence. They used findings of brain research to prove psychoanalytic theories. For example, the long held analytic assumption that early experiences shaped future psychological functioning was "proved" by findings indicating that maternal behavior influenced infants' brain development (Pally 1997, p. 592). However, this struggle to prove what analysts already knew appeared to be self-defeating. The idea that the first few years of life greatly influenced one's early mental development and that meaningful relationships during those years impacted psychological health or pathology had been pivotal in psychoanalysis prior to the technological possibility of observing the living brain. Looking to support these psychoanalytic hypotheses with empirical evidence by using

The last battle of psychoanalysis? 159

the tools of somatic psychiatry, though intended to strengthen psychoanalysis, seemed to work against this aim. The "slippery slope," where psychoanalytic concepts were replaced by terms from somatic psychiatry, is notable here as well. Thus, it was proposed that schizophrenia resulted from functional insufficiency of the right hemisphere, related to early emotional experiences in combination with subtle brain damage (Pally 1998, p. 574). Another idea was that the negative symptoms of schizophrenia (that is, disturbances of attention, distortion of self-image, deficits in relating socially, blunting of affect and concreteness of thinking) were related to hypoactivity of the right hemisphere and compensatory hyperactivity of the left hemisphere, which leads to delusions (p. 575). The dopamine hypothesis was reinstated, and its link to "proper" treatment was insinuated as it was argued that the dopaminergic system was more active in the left than in the right hemisphere; thus, medications that reduced dopamine improved symptoms related to left-side hyperactivity, but would have little effect on negative symptoms (p. 575). Alongside these biological data about schizophrenia, analysts were cautioned (by neuroscientists) against overzealous attempts to make specific correlations between psychoanalytic theory and observations from neuroscience, and even when their explicit wish was to study the mind, the conclusion was taken from the somatic discourse, as was suggested by the assertion that "comprehension of the world around us depends on the integrated function of both hemispheres" (p. 575).

Other attempts to maintain relevancy in the field of severe mental illness were made by American psychoanalysts in the international arena. Psychoanalysts encouraged their peers to engage in research and in incorporating psychoanalysis in universities. In his comprehensive article dedicated to the correspondence between Adolph Meyer from John Hopkins and Sandor Rado from Columbia University, Craig Tomlinson (1996) from Weill-Cornel Medical Center in New York suggested that the interaction between these two prominent analysts represented an important crossroad in relationships between medicine, academic psychiatry and North American psychoanalysis. Rado, who believed psychoanalysts should work in hospitals, insisted on a natural science approach in psychoanalysis. He argued that psychoanalytic theories should be supported by physiological theories and research. Among the evidence of scientific/biological history in psychoanalysis was Rado's coining of the term "schizotype" as the manifestation of the schizophrenic phenotype (p. 971). Rado also tried to implement psychoanalytic concepts outside of the analyst's office, while taking into account the biosocial history and functioning level of the individual, an approach he adopted from Meyer's clinic. However, the mainstream psychoanalytic approach during Rado's time was described by Tomlinson (1996) as hostile to academic- and research-oriented psychology, neuroscience and pharmacology, thus leaving Rado and his collaborators outside of psychoanalytic publications. Rado, who is said to have been edited out of the history of psychoanalysis, becomes relevant during the 1990s, as he predicted the risk of psychoanalysis's place in psychiatric academic departments and the difficulty analytic institutes would face in recruiting candidates from psychiatric residency programs (p. 997). Tomlinson (1996) warned that if psychoanalysis continued to ignore clinical, biological, epidemiological

160   *The last battle of psychoanalysis?*

and empirical studies about the connection between body and mind, it would be further alienated from governmental institutes, scientific institutes and the academic-medical establishment that supported these studies, as well as the public discussion elicited by scientific research. The article presented the scientific advancements in technology, imaging, genetics and molecular biology as leading different scientific fields, including academic-medical psychiatry, to declare psychoanalysis as irrelevant. The article suggested that to address the problem of departing from medicine, psychoanalysis should return to the integrative efforts known from the work of Rado and Meyer, not only between mind and body but also between psychoanalysis and medicine.

Whether schizophrenia is a completely unique state that can be treated but never fully resolved – as argued in the *Journal of the Academy* – or similar yet quantitatively different from so-called normal states – as presented in *Dialogues* – continued to occupy psychoanalysts throughout the decade of the 1990s. The confusion among analysts in the field of schizophrenia was discussed at the International Psychoanalytic Association in 1995, where a panel attempted to address criticism over psychoanalysis's lack of conceptual differentiation among psychosis, psychotic states and psychotic parts (Marcus 1996). The discussion seemed to be less for the purpose of better understanding these conditions and more to communicate and possibly integrate psychoanalytic ideas with neurophysiological, biochemical and neuroanatomical information (Marcus 1996, p. 574).

Alongside these efforts for integration, a criticism of this tendency and its relation to the naiveté of American psychoanalysis (and especially self-psychology) comes from Louis Sass (2001). Sass argued that American psychoanalysis is too naïve in its efforts to integrate, too optimistic, and relies on unrealistic ideals about mental health that are reflected in the so-called cohesive self (p. 1015). In contrast, he presents French psychoanalysis as emphasizing the impossibility of wholeness and as committed to the limitations of men, while the Americans were demanding complete satisfaction of their wishes (p. 1016).

Aside from the pressure during this decade to compete with somatic psychiatry, analysts were concerned when the Freud Wars reached the international arena. In a review of Edward Dolnick's *Madness on the Couch* (1998) many contradictions and inaccuracies were noted, including the deceptive book title, as psychoanalysis, it was argued, had been largely against treating madness – that is to say, patients diagnosed with schizophrenia – on the couch (Rosenfeld 1999). Dolnick perceived Seymour Kety's genetic findings in the field of schizophrenia as a significant achievement in somatic psychiatry, as well as an important weapon in debunking the psychoanalytic approach to schizophrenia. Yet, Rosenfeld, the reviewer of Dolnick's book, noted that Kety greatly appreciated Frieda Fromm-Reichmann and her psychodynamic work with patients diagnosed with schizophrenia. So while Dolnick perceived psychoanalysts as small-minded, provincial and unscientific, his scientific hero, Seymour Kety, found psychoanalysts to be cultured and thoughtful (p. 1253).

That said, psychoanalysts such as Martin Willick (1994) continued to criticize the treatment of schizophrenia with psychoanalysis, and in his review of his

The last battle of psychoanalysis? 161

colleague's new book (by Eric Marcus), Willick argued again and again that biological abnormalities in schizophrenia were related to impairments in ego functions. When he wrote that analysts should integrate biological findings into their understanding in order to "maintain a credible position within the psychiatric community" (Willick 1994, p. 632), it was clear that these efforts had more to do with the jurisdictional struggle and the need to be acknowledged by the psychiatric profession than with searching for psychoanalytic answers to the difficult questions schizophrenia was posing.

In response to the criticism of using analysis with patients diagnosed with schizophrenia, an attempt was made in this decade to conceptualize psychotherapy as affecting the brain. Regina Pally (1998), a psychoanalyst from California, argued for psychoanalytic effectiveness, using the discourse of the competitor – somatic psychiatry. She argued, for example, that the use of metaphors in treatment could lead to better integration between the left and right hemispheres. Since metaphors contained sensory elements and emotional and verbal images, they activate various brain centers simultaneously. Pally was using neuroscientific terminology (e.g., cortical areas, subcortical areas, dendrites and more) to show how psychoanalysis was in fact healing the brain. These various attempts to use somatic terminology, to call for reengagement in medical schools and academic research and to give diagnoses that fit the current psychiatric viewpoint of mental illness were accompanied with very little clinical work with patients diagnosed with schizophrenia, and the little vignettes used in articles were mostly of historical treatments (Shapiro 1991).

Danger! Psychoanalysis! Or psychoanalysis in danger

The decrease in psychoanalytic publications on schizophrenia during the Decade of the Brain was even more apparent in the *Schizophrenic Bulletin*. Nonetheless, as the limitations of antipsychotic drugs came to light, a renewed interest in psychological interventions arose. That said, most psychological treatments for schizophrenia discussed during this decade were not psychoanalytic or psychodynamic in nature. The treatments of interest were cognitive and behavioral interventions, psychosocial treatments related mainly to rehabilitation, cognitive recovery, occupational therapy, family therapy, behavioral therapy, high expressed emotion-focused family interventions, personal therapy interventions (designed to help the patient gain insight, recognize early warning signs and increase compliance with medications), social skill training, supportive therapy and so forth. Not only was the psychodynamic approach unpopular, but during the Decade of the Brain the question was no longer whether psychoanalytic treatments were effective, but whether they might in fact be harmful.

A paper from 1998, "Translating Research into Practice: The Schizophrenia Patient Outcomes Research Team (PORT) Treatment Recommendations" (Lehman et al. 1998), could be considered the fifth stage in the neosomatic revolution in psychiatry in the field of schizophrenia. This research, published in the "At Issue" section of the *Bulletin* – the section dedicated to controversial topics

162   *The last battle of psychoanalysis?*

that presents views not necessarily congruent with the journal editors' stand on said issues – was funded by NIHM and AHCPR (Agency of Health Care Policy and Research) and had been intended to determine treatment recommendations for schizophrenia by reviewing contemporary research findings. The study was launched in 1992, when AHCPR and NIHM created research teams in the Maryland School of Medicine and the School of Public Health at Johns Hopkins University. It had the goal of identifying treatment recommendations for patients diagnosed with schizophrenia and improving the quality of care for these patients through examining cost-effective ratios. Since the demand was to use "actual scientific evidence," the results included many more pharmacological recommendations than psychosocial ones. Studies provided categorical recommendations for antipsychotic drugs, anti-anxiety drugs, antidepressants, medication addressing aggression and hostility, electroconvulsive therapy, psychological interventions, family therapy, vocational rehabilitation and community services. Each recommendation had a letter grade, signifying the degree of its evidence. An A grade reflected good evidence from research and experts' supportive opinion; a B grade reflected acceptable evidence from research and experts' supportive opinion; and a C grade reflected mainly experts' opinion with little research evidence and mostly clinical evidence.

Recommendation 22 of this report is relevant in understanding the way psychoanalytic treatment of schizophrenia was perceived among policy makers as well as psychiatrists during the Decade of the Brain. The recommendation was given in the section dedicated to psychological treatments and stated that "individual and group psychotherapies adhering to a psychodynamic model (defined as therapies that use interpretation of unconscious material and focus on transference and regression) should *not* be used in the treatment of persons with schizophrenia" (Lehman et al. 1998, p. 7). The rationale was that

> the scientific data on this issue are quite limited. However, there is no evidence in support of the superiority of psychoanalytic therapy to other forms of therapy, and there is a consensus that psychotherapy that promotes regression and psychotic transference can be harmful to persons with schizophrenia. This risk, combined with the high cost and lack of evidence of any benefit, argues strongly against the use of psychoanalytic therapy, even in combination with effective pharmacotherapy.
>
> (Lehman et al. 1998, p. 8)

This "consensus" relied on class C evidence and was presented as an unequivocal fact without the caution called for by the low grade of evidence used. Furthermore, PORT's Recommendation 26 determined that "family therapies based on the premise that family dysfunction is the etiology of the patient's schizophrenic disorder should *not* be used" (p. 8). The rationale here was that

> Research has failed to substantiate hypothesized causal links between family dysfunction and the etiology of schizophrenia. Therefore, therapies

The last battle of psychoanalysis? 163

specifically designed from this premise are not empirically founded. Although there has been little or no randomized, controlled research on the impact of family therapies arising from this orientation, experts in the field have expressed strong caution against the use of these techniques. The presumption that family interaction causes schizophrenia, especially as an alternative to biological risk factors, has led to serious disruption in clinician/family trust without any evidence of therapeutic effectiveness. The repudiation of the theoretical premise of these therapies, the lack of empirical studies, and the strong clinical opinion raising concerns about the potential harm caused by these approaches lead to this recommendation.

(Lehman et al. 1988, p. 8)

In contrast to this vehement rejection of psychodynamic etiology and psychoanalytic treatments, Recommendation 23 noted that psychological treatments focused on support, education and development of behavioral and cognitive skills designed to address the flaws and deficits in schizophrenia could be used, at times, mainly to improve functioning and "treat other issues such as medication non-compliance" (p. 8).

In the decade of the 1990s, psychoanalysis had to face PORT's determination that psychoanalysis's etiological theory, as well as the treatment methods derived from the psychodynamic paradigm, should *never be used* with patients diagnosed with schizophrenia, as these were harmful for such patients. Instead, etiology should focus on biological factors, and psychological treatment should aim only at supporting the somatic treatment and any resistance to it, such as in non-compliance to medication.

Thus, at this point in time, analysts not only faced the risk that their theories of etiology would be dismissed or that their treatment method would not be funded or recommended, but also ran the risk of using their "harmful" etiology and conducting treatments designated as dangerous and not recommended for use. The PORT report could have been the fifth stage in the neosomatic revolution and a "knockout" punch to psychoanalysis in the field of schizophrenia, from which it would never recover. However, as severe as this blow was, so was the restorative power of analysts in this field and the vast recruitment made to address it. Beyond some sporadic responses in different journals, a whole issue of the *Journal of the Academy* was dedicated to disputing the PORT report's recommendations. The special issue, published in 2003, was called "The Schizophrenic Person and the Benefits of Psychotherapies – Seeking a PORT in the Storm." Edited by Ann-Louise Silver, this issue was based on the assumption that psychodynamic approaches were becoming no more than a part of the history of psychiatry. The exclusion of psychodynamic perspectives in favor of biological approaches was reflected in declaring schizophrenia to be an illness of the brain requiring biologically based treatment; assuming that psychological treatments were only valuable if they supported medication compliance; and perceiving psychodynamic research as anecdotal or non-scientific. The refusal of psychiatric residents to engage with psychoanalytic research and the fact that they were unfamiliar with the discourse also reflected the exclusion of

164   *The last battle of psychoanalysis?*

psychodynamic perspectives in favor of biological approaches. Psychiatrists were said to ask members of the treatment team, "why are you bothering to talk to X?" Medicating the patient seemed enough (Silver and Larsen 2003).

This special issue's goal was declared as reminding analysts and policy makers that the individual diagnosed with the illness was a human being in need of human connections and support, best provided by working hard to "strengthen his ego." The dire straits of hospitals that were being closed were lamented in this issue, along with the shift to a model of short hospitalizations. The perception of schizophrenia as a brain illness was harshly criticized, as such an approach rendered patients diagnosed with the illness to be hopeless and broken, warehoused with their suffering ignored (Silver and Larsen 2003, p. 2). Books and articles that challenged reliance on medications and criticized the growing dependency on pharmacological companies were mentioned in the issue, especially Robert Whitaker's *Mad in America* (2002). Whitaker, like Dolnick, was a journalist at the *Boston Globe* who condemned American psychiatry's history with "madness," mostly berating the harsh somatic treatments. Aligning herself with critics such as Whitaker, but also speaking on behalf of psychoanalysts who were losing this battle, Silver laments the fact that psychiatrists shun anything that cannot be quantified, such as soul, faith and intuition, which she said is like "throwing out the alienated baby in her bathwater" and leaving "practitioners maddeningly isolated, mechanical and despondent. We find many boring studies, which paradoxically are more easily manipulated" (Silver and Larsen 2003, p. 4).

In the special issue of the *Journal of the Academy*, the potential contribution of literature in the fight for psychoanalysis was acknowledged, and psychoanalysts were advised to collect written materials focused on the role of psychotherapy in schizophrenia. The task force that Silver recruited to challenge and change the PORT report's recommendations became international, and members of ISPS (the International Society for Psychological Treatment of Schizophrenia and other Psychoses) were recruited from Germany, Australia, England, New Zealand and the United States. In 2004, updated PORT recommendations were published that reconsidered the task force's original criticism (Lehman et al. 2003). As it struggled to restore the position of psychoanalysis as a possible treatment for schizophrenia, the task force was able to influence PORT to delete Recommendations 22 and 26. Although a significant accomplishment, in the explanation for the change, the revised PORT report's authors noted that this was *only* a strategic change. It was suggested that the recommendations brought about much disdain in the analytic community and, more broadly, a concern had been raised that treatments were becoming increasingly biological and reductionist, failing to take into account the importance of understanding and addressing patients and their families. Although the updated PORT canceled the recommendations to avoid psychodynamically oriented treatments for patients diagnosed with schizophrenia, this correction was not made because of a change in the evidence base for these treatments, but rather because the researchers had come to the strategic decision not to mention all the treatments of schizophrenia that had been tried and found to be ineffective.

Clearly, PORT was not retracting its claim that psychodynamic treatments derived from psychoanalysis were ineffective; however, since they were not declared as dangerous, PORT no longer warned against their use, which seemed like an achievement for psychoanalysis in the field of schizophrenia. An additional gain that the ISPS task force achieved was that PORT's updated report recommended avoiding a reductionist biological stance and advocated for combined treatments of psychosocial interventions and medication. PORT was therefore adopting the bio-psychosocial model, which moved the pendulum, even if an inch, back toward the psyche.

Summary

This book could have concluded with reflections on how fluid the definition of schizophrenia is and how it changes according to psychiatric trends, as the recommendations for its treatment are subject to pressure from different political groups. Additionally, it might have optimistically added Wayne Fenton's last article (2000), published in the *Schizophrenia Bulletin*, which offered that both somatic psychiatry and psychoanalysis could claim schizophrenia in their jurisdiction. But, two weeks after concluding the research upon which this book is based, Fenton, a dynamic psychiatrist who worked at Chestnut Lodge, was murdered in his private clinic by a psychotic patient, as Fenton allegedly was trying to persuade the patient to take antipsychotic medications. Daily newspaper reports (Carey 2006), as well as ISPS internal private communications, reported that this patient was "borderline," "a psychopath," "a drug abuser" with a history of violence who, despite all that, was denied admission to a psychiatric unit. These communications also noted that after Chestnut Lodge was closed, Fenton worked mainly in his private practice with very difficult patients, and that he had made exceptions and met with the patient who killed him outside of his working days and hours.

The tragic irony is that Fenton's paper, published two years after the publication of PORT's recommendations, offered an integrative approach that tapped both somatic and psychoanalytic schools of thought. He described the lack of faith in treatments for schizophrenia and the sense of nihilism many felt when treating patients diagnosed with schizophrenia. Fenton also showed that psychological treatments, especially those influenced by psychoanalysis, had changed the perspective of schizophrenia from an untreatable illness to a malady from which one could recover. He contrasted the psychoanalysis-based treatments with supportive psychotherapies that were preferred by biologically and pharmacologically oriented clinicians, rooted in the medical model, and argued that supportive treatments were focused on eliminating symptoms and increasing medication compliance and social and functional recovery, without any in-depth personality change.

Fenton argued that the onset of neuroleptic use, which was marked here as the first stage of the neosomatic revolution, had been a divisive event in psychiatry, splitting it into psychodynamic and biological approaches. He argued for an integrative model as the most fitting for the understanding of schizophrenia's

166 *The last battle of psychoanalysis?*

etiology, its development and its treatment. The "stress vulnerability" model he offered theorizes that schizophrenia is the result of a dynamic interaction between environmental and experiential stressors, and one's vulnerability to reacting to stress with schizophrenic symptoms. Some aspects of this vulnerability were hereditary, but some could develop in utero, during labor or due to complications after birth. The psychosocial stressors included, but were not limited to, life events, cultural milieu, social class and status, the social system and the emotional quality of the patient's environment. Schizophrenia was presented as heterogenic and so, Fenton argued, should its treatments be: those schizophrenic patients who were suffering from severe impediments might benefit from supportive treatments, avoiding stress, and having their basic human needs met; those patients with schizophrenia who were more highly motivated and better able to create a good therapeutic alliance could benefit from more in-depth psychotherapeutic encounters.

Thus, four decades of the neosomatic revolution ended with this tragic event, brought on by a psychotic patient who was not hospitalized because of the growing cuts in budgets for psychiatric admissions and length of hospital stay. That this patient murdered a psychiatrist trying to integrate dynamic and biological aspects of treatment, while he attempted to give the patient medications in his private office after hours, reflects the tragedy of this specific incident, as well as the danger that might be inherent to psychotic states. Most of all, this event is a testament to the tremendous challenges of providing adequate theoretical, therapeutic and institutional solutions to patients diagnosed with schizophrenia in the 21st century in the United States, and to therapists who are treating them.

References

Abramson, R., 2001. A cost-effective psychoanalytic treatment of a severely disturbed woman. *Journal of the American Academy of Psychoanalysis and Dynamic Psychiatry*, 29, pp. 245–264.

Adams, M. V., 2000. Compensation in the service of individuation – Phenomenological essentialism and Jungian dream interpretation. Commentary on a paper by Hazel Ipp. *Psychoanalytic Dialogues*, 10, pp. 127–142.

Bacciagaluppi, M., 1999. Evolutionary aspects of Silvano Arieti's work. *Journal of the American Academy of Psychoanalysis and Dynamic Psychiatry*, 27, pp. 575–581.

Bach, S., 1998. Two ways of being. *Psychoanalytic Dialogues*, 8, pp. 657–673.

Barratt, B. B., 1995. Review of *Madness and modernism: Insanity in the light of modern art, literature and thought*, by Louis Sass. *Psychoanalytic Dialogues*, 5, pp. 113–121.

Battegay, R., 1991. Defense and coping in the antinomy between self-maintenance and adaptation. *Journal of the American Academy of Psychoanalysis and Dynamic Psychiatry*, 19, pp. 471–483.

Bemporad, J., 1996. Caring for the psyche. *Journal of the American Academy of Psychoanalysis and Dynamic Psychiatry*, 24, pp. 353–363.

Benedetti, G., 1999. Interpretation of schizophrenia. *Journal of the American Academy of Psychoanalysis and Dynamic Psychiatry*, 27, pp. 551–562.

The last battle of psychoanalysis? 167

Blechner, M. J., 1994. Review of *The intimate edge: Extending the reach of psychoanalytic interaction*, by Darlene Bregman Ehrenberg. *Psychoanalytic Dialogues*, 4, pp. 283–291.

Brunner, J., 2001. *Freud and the politics of psychoanalysis*. Oxford: Blackwell.

Bruschi, R., 1999. Introduction. *Journal of the American Academy of Psychoanalysis and Dynamic Psychiatry*, 27, pp. 531–539.

Bush, G.H.W., 1990. Presidential proclamation 6158 [online]. Available at: <www.loc.gov/ loc/brain/proclaim.html> [Accessed October 29, 2014].

Carey, B., 2006, September 19. A psychiatrist is slain and a sad debate deepens. *New York Times, Mental Health and Behavior.*

Coates, S., Friedman, R. C., and Wolfe, S., 1991. The etiology of boyhood gender identity disorder: A model for interacting temperament, development, and psychodynamics. *Psychoanalytic Dialogues*, 1, pp. 481–523.

Coltart, N., 1991. The silent patient. *Psychoanalytic Dialogues*, 1, pp. 439–453.

Danto, E. A., 1999. The Berlin Poliklinik: Psychoanalytic innovation in Weimer Germany. *Journal of the American Psychoanalytic Association*, 47, pp. 1269–1292.

Davies, J. M., 1998. Multiple perspectives on multiplicity. *Psychoanalytic Dialogues*, 8, pp. 195–206.

Dolnick, E., 1998. *Madness on the couch: Blaming the victim in the heyday of psychoanalysis*. New York: Simon & Schuster.

Eigen, M., 1991. Boa and flowers. *Psychoanalytic Dialogues*, 1, pp. 106–119.

Eigen, M., 1993. *The psychotic core*. Northvale, NJ: Jason Aronson.

Fenton, W. S., 2000. Evolving perspectives on individual psychotherapy for schizophrenia. *Schizophrenia Bulletin*, 26(1), pp. 47–72.

Forrest, D. V., 1991. Mind, brain, and machine. *Journal of the American Academy of Psychoanalysis and Dynamic Psychiatry*, 19, pp. 555–577.

Foster, R. P., 1996. The bilingual self: Duet in two voices. *Psychoanalytic Dialogues*, 6, pp. 99–121.

Geha, R. E., 1993. On the "mere" fictions of psychoanalysis: Reply to Sass. *Psychoanalytic Dialogues*, 3, pp. 255–266.

Ghent, E., 1993. Wish need and neediness: Commentary on Shabad's "Resentment, indignation, entitlement," *Psychoanalytic Dialogues*, 3, pp. 495–507.

Gieryn, T. F., 1983. Boundary-work and the demarcation of science from non-science: Strains and interests in professional ideologies of scientists. *American Sociological Review*, 48(6), pp. 781–795.

Ginsberg, G. L., 1992. Psychodynamic psychiatry: Theory and practice. *Journal of the American Psychoanalytic Association*, 40, pp. 247–251.

Giovacchini, P. L., 1993. Schizophrenia, the pervasive psychosis. *Journal of the American Academy of Psychoanalysis and Dynamic Psychiatry*, 21, pp. 549–565.

Glucksman, M. L., 1995. Psychodynamics and neurobiology. *Journal of the American Academy of Psychoanalysis and Dynamic Psychiatry*, 23, pp. 179–195.

Goldstein, M., 1994. Decade of the brain: An agenda for the nineties. *Western Journal of Medicine*, 161, pp. 239–241.

Gomez, L., 2005. *The Freud wars: An introduction to the philosophy of psychoanalysis*. East Sussex: Routledge.

Gunderson, J. G., and Gabbard, G. O., 1999. Making the case for psychoanalytic therapies in the current psychiatric environment. *Journal of the American Psychoanalytic Association*, 47, pp. 679–704.

168 *The last battle of psychoanalysis?*

Kaiser, D., 1996. Commentary: Against biological psychiatry [online]. Available at: <psychiatrized.org/articles/psychTime-KaiserCommentary.htm> [Accessed October 29, 2014].

Kennedy, R., 1996. Aspects of consciousness: One voice or many?. *Psychoanalytic Dialogues*, 6, pp. 73–96.

Kestenbaum, C. J., 1995. Psychoanalysis and its vicissitudes. *Journal of the American Academy of Psychoanalysis and Dynamic Psychiatry*, 23, pp. 501–514.

Kiersky, S., and Beebe, B., 1994. The reconstruction of early nonverbal relatedness in the treatment of difficult patients: A special form of empathy. *Psychoanalytic Dialogues*, 4, pp. 389–408.

Kulchycky, S., and Munich, R. L., 1995. The borderline patient: Emerging concepts in diagnosis, psychodynamics, and treatment. J. S. Grotstein, M. F. Solomon, and J. A. Lang, eds. *Journal of the American Psychoanalytic Association*, 43, pp. 623–626.

Lehman, A. F., Kreyenbuhl, J., Buchanan, R. W., Dickerson, F. B., Dixon, L. B., Goldberg, R., . . . Steinwachs, D. M., 2003. The schizophrenia Patient Outcomes Research Team (PORT) updated treatment recommendations. *Schizophrenia Bulletin*, 30(2), pp. 193–217.

Lehman, A. F., Steinwachs, D. M., and the Co-Investigators of the PORT Project, 1998. Translating research into practice: The schizophrenia Patient Outcomes Research Team (PORT) treatment recommendations. *Schizophrenia Bulletin*, 24(1), 1–10.

Lichtenberg-Ettinger, B., 1997. The feminine/prenatal weaving in matrixial subjectivity-as-encounter. *Psychoanalytic Dialogues*, 7, pp. 367–405.

Marcus, E. R., 1996. Panel report: Psychic reality in psychotic states. *International Journal of Psychoanalysis*, 77, pp. 565–574.

Marcus, E. R., 1999. Modern ego psychology. *Journal of the American Psychoanalytic Association*, 47, pp. 843–871.Miller, L., 1991. Brain and self. *Journal of the American Academy of Psychoanalysis and Dynamic Psychiatry*, 19, pp. 213–234.

Miller, L., 1993. Freud's brain. *Journal of the American Academy of Psychoanalysis and Dynamic Psychiatry*, 21, pp. 183–212.

Mitchell, S. A., 1988. *Relational concepts in psychoanalysis*. Cambridge, MA: Harvard University Press.

Mitchell, S. A., 1995. *Hope and dread in psychoanalysis*. New York: Basic Books.

Mitchell, S. A., and Aron, L., 1999. *Relational psychoanalysis: The emergence of a tradition*. New York: Routledge.

Modell, A. H., 1991. Review of *Impasse and interpretation*, by Herbert Rosenfeld. *Journal of the American Psychoanalytic Association*, 39, pp. 248–250.

Muller, J., 1998. Psychosis and the other: Commentary on paper by Paul Williams. *Psychoanalytic Dialogues*, 8, pp. 519–526.

Munich, R. L., 1999. Review of *Madness on the couch: Blaming the victim in the heyday of psychoanalysis*, by Edward Dolnick. *Journal of the American Psychoanalytic Association*, 47, pp. 939–943.

Ogden, T., 1991. An interview with Thomas Ogden. *Psychoanalytic Dialogues*, 1, pp. 361–376.

Olds, D., and Cooper, A. M., 1997. Dialogues with other sciences: Opportunities for mutual gain. *International Journal of Psychoanalysis*, 78, pp. 219–225.

Pally, R., 1997. I: How brain development is shaped by genetic and environmental factors. Development in related fields neuroscience. *International Journal of Psychoanalysis*, 78, pp. 587–593.

The last battle of psychoanalysis? 169

Pally, R., 1998. Bilaterality: Hemispheric specialization and integration. *International Journal of Psychoanalysis*, 79, pp. 565–578.

Pardes, H., 1997. Psychiatric residency training and psychodynamic teaching. *Journal of the American Psychoanalytic Association*, 45, pp. 937–939.

Peltz, R., 1998. The dialectic of presence and absence: Impasses and retrieval of meaning states. *Psychoanalytic Dialogues*, 8, pp. 385–409.

Robbins, M., 1992. Psychoanalytic and biological approaches to mental illness: Schizophrenia. *Journal of the American Psychoanalytic Association*, 40, pp. 425–454.

Robbins, M., 1993. *Experiences of schizophrenia: An integration of the personal, scientific and therapeutic.* New York: Guilford Press.

Robbins, M., 1996. Nature, nurture and core gender identity. *Journal of the American Psychoanalytic Association*, 44, pp. 93–117.

Robbins, M., 1998. Review of *The paradoxes of delusions: Wittgenstein, Schreber, and the schizophrenic mind,* by Louis Sass. *Journal of the American Psychoanalytic Association*, 46, pp. 959–962.

Rosenfeld, A., 1999. Review of *Madness on the couch: Blaming the victim in the heyday of psychoanalysis,* by Edward Dolnick. *International Journal of Psychoanalysis*, 80, pp. 1250–1253.

Rustin. J., 1997. Reply to Carolyn Clement's commentary. *Psychoanalytic Dialogues*, 7, pp. 77–80.

Sanfilippo, L. C., 1998. Identity and experience. *Journal of American Academy of Psychoanalysis and Dynamic Psychiatry*, 26, pp. 573–583.

Sass, L. A., 1992. *Madness and modernism: Insanity in the light of modern art, literature and thought.* Cambridge, MA: Harvard University Press.

Sass, L. A., 1994. *The paradoxes of delusion: Wittgenstein, Schreber, and the schizophrenic mind.* Ithaca, NY: Cornell University Press.

Sass, L. A., 1995. Reply to Barnaby Barratt. *Psychoanalytic Dialogues*, 5, pp. 145–149.

Sass, L. A., 2001. The magnificent harlequin. *International Journal of Psychoanalysis*, 82, pp. 997–1018.

Searles, H., 1975. The patient as therapist to his analyst. In: H. Searles, ed., 1979, *Countertransference and related subjects: Selected papers.* Florida: International University Press. pp. 380–459.

Sedgwick, D., 2000. Answers to nine questions about Jungian psychology. *Psychoanalytic Dialogues*, 10, pp. 457–472.

Shapiro, R. L., 1991. Melanie Klein today: Developments in theory and practice. Volume I: Mainly theory. *International Journal of Psychoanalysis*, 72, pp. 730–734.

Shengold, L., 1992. Commentary on "Dissociative processes and transference-countertransference paradigms," by Jody Messler Davies and Mary Gail Frawley. *Psychoanalytic Dialogues*, 2, pp. 49–59.

Silver, A. S., 1993. Countertransference, Ferenczi, and Washington, DC. *Journal of the American Academy of Psychoanalysis and Dynamic Psychiatry*, 21, pp. 637–654.

Silver, A. S., and Larsen, T. K., 2003. The schizophrenic person and the benefits of the psychotherapies – Seeking a PORT in the storm. *Journal of the American Academy of Psychoanalysis and Dynamic Psychiatry*, 31, pp. 1–10.

Slipp, S., 2000. Subliminal stimulation research and its implications for psychoanalysis. *Journal of the American Academy of Psychoanalysis and Dynamic Psychiatry*, 28, pp. 305–320.

170   The last battle of psychoanalysis?

Smith, H. F., 1999. Arnold Goldberg – Two heads are better than one. *Journal of the American Psychoanalytic Association*, 47, pp. 343–349.

Solano, L., Toriello, A., Barnaba, L., Ara, R., and Taylor, G. J., 2000. Rorschach interaction patterns, alexithymia, and closeness to parents in psychotic and psychosomatic patients. *Journal of the American Academy of Psychoanalysis and Dynamic Psychiatry*, 28, pp. 101–116.

Stein, R., 1995. Analysis of a case of transsexualism. *Psychoanalytic Dialogues*, 5, pp. 257–289.

Stern, D. B., 1992. Commentary on "Constructivism in clinical psychoanalysis." *Psychoanalytic Dialogues*, 2, pp. 331–363.

Stone, M. H., 1994. Review of *My work with borderline patients*, by Harold Searles. *Journal of the American Psychoanalytic Association*, 42, pp. 285–287.

Stone, M. H., 1999. The history of the psychoanalytic treatment of schizophrenia. *Journal of the American Academy of Psychoanalysis and Dynamic Psychiatry*, 27, pp. 583–610.

Sullivan, H. S., 1953. *The interpersonal theory of psychiatry*. New York: Norton.

Sweetnam, A., 1999. Sexual sensation and gender experience. The psychological positions and the erotic third. *Psychoanalytic Dialogues*, 9, pp. 327–348.

Tomlinson, C., 1996. Sandor Rado and Adolf Meyer: A nodal point in American psychiatry and psychoanalysis. *International Journal of Psychoanalysis*, 77, pp. 963–982.

Ullman, M., 1998. Midwifery of the soul: A holistic perspective on psychoanalysis. *Journal of the American Academy of Psychoanalysis and Dynamic Psychiatry*, 26, pp. 636–641.

Valenstein, E. 1998. *Blaming the brain: The truth about drugs and mental health*. New York: Free Press.

Volkan, V. D., 1997. *The seed of madness: Constitution, environment, and fantasy in organization of the psychotic core*. Madison, CT: International Universities Press.

Wasserstein, J., and Stefanatos, G. A., 2000. The right hemisphere and psychopathology. *Journal of the American Academy of Psychoanalysis and Dynamic Psychiatry*, 28, pp. 371–395.

Whitaker, R., 2002. *Mad in America: Bad science, bad medicine and the enduring mistreatment of the mentally ill*. New York: Basic Books.

Williams, P., 1998. Psychotic developments in a sexually abused borderline patient. *Psychoanalytic Dialogue*, 8, pp. 459–491.

Willick, M. S., 1993. The deficit syndrome in schizophrenia: Psychoanalytic and neurobiological perspectives. *Journal of the American Psychoanalytic Association*, 41, pp. 1135–1157.

Willick, M. S., 1994. Review of *Psychosis and near psychosis: Ego function, symbol structure, treatment*, by Eric Marcus. *International Journal of Psychoanalysis*, 75, pp. 632–634.

Willick, M. S., 2001. Psychoanalysis and schizophrenia – A cautionary tale. *Journal of the American Psychoanalytic Association*, 49, pp. 27–56.

Winer, J. A., 1997. The new psychiatric texts and psychoanalysis. *Journal of the American Psychoanalytic Association*, 45, pp. 941–958.

7 The many faces of Schreber as the face of American psychoanalysis (1954–2000)

I cannot of course count upon being fully understood because these things are dealt with which can not be expressed in human language; they exceed human understanding . . .

(Schreber 1903/2000)

Flechsig's brain science is the theory and Schreber's delusions are the practice of the same traumatic collapse of the symbolic dimension of subjectivity, of the gap separating bodily cause and symbolic effect. Schreber's point would seem to be that the elimination of the gap – the attempt to fill it with neuroanatomical knowledge – is nothing short of soul murder.

(Santner 1996)

It remains for the future to decide whether there is more delusion in my theory than I should like to admit, or whether there is more truth in Schreber's delusion than other people are as yet prepared to believe.

(Freud 1911)

"This world is mine," was Y's answer to my request to tell me about himself in our first encounter in the mental hospital where I was seeing him in the early 2000s. "I am Heinrich Heine, I am Jesus Christ, I am the saintly genius from Vilnius, I am the Admor of Vishnitz, I am Ori Katz [a proper name, but literally also means in Hebrew "my light had come to an end"], I am the one who founded the Jewish state. This world is mine."

A highly articulate, intelligent and a very handsome young man, Y was committed to the hospital after threatening his mother, "the parturient," that he would make sure she burned in thousands of hells. Like Nietzsche's portrayal of himself in his letter of insanity (1889), Y too was at root every name in history or every historical personage, but on file he was just another "male schizophrenic patient with first rank symptoms and cannabis abuse," or F20.0 (paranoid schizophrenia) and F12 (mental and behavioral disorders due to use of cannabinoids), according to the ICD-10, the World Health Organization's manual that classifies and categorizes diseases. And like other F20's he was prescribed antipsychotic

172   The many faces of Schreber

medications. Since Y was not willing to comply with the pharmacotherapy he was offered, he was forced by law to receive it by injection; and because of severe side effects known as extra-pyramidal symptoms (EPS), mostly akathisia (continual restlessness), but also agitation and grand mal seizures, he also received a "cocktail" of five to seven other drugs a few times a day. Y felt these medications were killing him, and most of his treatment was characterized by his struggles with the staff, which, in his experience, wanted to reduce him entirely to a body to be medicated. Smart and eloquent, Y studied the psychiatric discourse of his time and communicated with his doctors and nurses using mainly psychopharmacological language. He would say: "I want more Lustral; I need only a therapeutic dosage of liquid THC; give me Valium, it always worked. I need antidepressants, not antipsychotics," and so forth. His communications sounded uncannily more and more like discussions during our daily morning staff meetings. One of the oldest nurses in the ward used to say in Yiddish that our concerns for the patients had been reduced to *essen, pissen, kaken* und *trinken* ("eating, pissing, shitting and drinking"). And, indeed, staff meetings more often included a dry report of patients' behavior and follow-up recommendations for adjustment of their medications.

That said, it seemed that Y's use of this kind of communication only masked a much richer, if psychotic, universe. When not communicating with the staff, I overheard Y with other patients in the yard preaching the end of the world with a prophetic rhetoric. His delusion of the end of the world and apocalyptic destruction was elaborate, consisting of the redemption and resurrection of the chosen ones. He believed that he would die and be reborn as God's son and as part of a new generation of improved human beings. Although I saw Y some 100 years after the publication of Judge Schreber's *Denkwürdigkeiten eines Nervenkranken*, or in its English translation, *Memoir of My Nervous Illness* (1903/2000), and almost 100 years after Freud published his famous paper, "Psycho-Analytic Notes on an Autobiographical Account of a Case of Paranoia" (1911), his delusions were remarkably similar to Schreber's, especially in reference to his therapist, his professed relationship with God and his apocalyptic prophesies. Inspired by Johnny Cash's song "Personal Jesus," I nicknamed Y "my personal Schreber."

Judge Daniel Paul Schreber is considered to be the paradigmatic schizophrenic, and his memoir is the most written about document in psychiatric literature (Dinnage 2000). By studying the varying interpretations of Schreber in American psychoanalytic literature, it is possible to trace American theories of madness and approaches to its treatment during the four decades of the neosomatic revolution, beginning in postwar America. During this period, Schreber went from being a conflicted individual, to a pre-Oedipal child, a person with a defect in his ego, a cultural hero, a victim of his traumatizing father and, finally, to a person who suffered a brain disease.

These shifts in perspective affect many patients with schizophrenia. My own personal Schreber was only 31 when he hanged himself a few hours after coming back from a psychiatric emergency room, where his request for Valium was denied by a psychiatrist who worked according to a protocol.

The life of Daniel Paul Schreber

Daniel Paul Schreber (1903/2000) whose specter still haunts American psychoanalysis was born in 1842, the third of five children, into a prominent Leipzig family. His father was an orthopedic surgeon and an eminent educator, the author of many popular books on physical exercise, child-rearing and mental hygiene. He died when Schreber was 19, 10 years after suffering a head injury that left him with a marked personality change and intermittent depressions. Schreber was a brilliant student who studied law at the University of Leipzig and became a district magistrate in the nearby town of Chemnitz. In 1879 he married a woman who was younger and less educated than himself, Sabine Behr. Schreber wrote about his wife, repeatedly stating that her inability to have children after six miscarriages was their only sorrow. Schreber's first nervous illness occurred when he was 42. The only symptoms he described were hypochondria and a preoccupation with weight loss, but his hospitalization at Dr. Flechsig's asylum lasted 18 months, and he returned to his previous duties in early 1886. His memoirs referred to his next eight years as "quite happy ones" (Schreber 1903/2000, p. 46). During these years Schreber had been promoted from the provincial court in Chemnitz to a more prominent position in Freiburg, and in June 1893 he was appointed Senatspräsident of the Superior Court of Appeals in Dresden. Between June and November 1893, at the age of 51, Schreber's major illness began. He suffered from severe sleeplessness, anxiety symptoms and depression. During this period, he recorded a fateful dream, or reverie, that would later turn into his famous delusion, familiar from Freud's case, of being transformed into a woman. He was readmitted to Dr. Flechsig's asylum in November 1893 as his symptoms intensified and his insomnia and depression failed to respond to the various bromides – chloral hydrate and morphine injections (Baumeyer 1956). The hospital chart describes him as "very agitated," noting that he "screams for help, throws table and chair around" (p. 62). In February of 1894, his agitation grew worse, precipitated by his wife's four-day absence. He then began to use the term "miracles" for hallucinations and to view all human beings as phantoms.

A month later, Schreber first mentioned "the beginning of my contact with God caused by somebody having committed soul murder," and Flechsig was named as the instigator of this murder (Schreber 1955/2000, p. 34). At this time, Dr. Flechsig transferred Schreber from his sanatorium to the vast state asylum at Sonnenstein, against Schreber's will. This transfer meant that his illness was considered incurable and, according to his new psychiatrist at Sonnenstein, Dr. Guido Weber, it was diagnosed as paranoia, which was then regarded as an organic disease of the brain (Lothane 1992). The first two years of Schreber's second illness marked the fullest elaboration of his delusions about his body being transformed into that of a woman by the telepathic implantation of "nerves" from Flechsig's body. He was then to be impregnated by God himself,

174 *The many faces of Schreber*

represented by the sun, through "fertilization by divine rays for the purpose of creating new human beings" (Schreber 1955/2000, p. 64). As a woman, he would bear a new generation of the Schreber family as a kind of resolution to the soul murder that Flechsig had committed. Schreber himself had discussed "soul murder" in terms of popular folklore, as well as with reference to the Faustian legends of selling one's soul to the devil, or of gaining possession of another's soul by way of sorcery. In this same spirit he had called his wing at Sonnenstein "the Devil's Castle" (p. 116). During the next few years Schreber became more talkative and accessible. He was allowed increasing freedom of movement, played chess and the piano, made lively and intelligent conversation and gained the privilege of taking his meals with Dr. Weber's family. His outward behavior became essentially normal, except for episodes of involuntary "bellowing," some grimacing and periods of gazing at himself in the mirror "with some feminine adornments" (Lothane 1992). Beginning in October 1899, Schreber wrote a series of appeals for his release from Sonnenstein and for obtaining the revocation of his incompetency status. After two appeals were turned down, opposed by Dr. Weber on the basis that paranoia was an incurable organic disease, Schreber's third appeal was accepted by Weber on the basis that the patient was showing some improvement. In July 1902, the judges granted his appeal and rescinded his guardianship. They acknowledged that a person capable of dealing with such complicated legal matters was capable of managing the simpler and less important matters of ordinary life.

The last years of Schreber's life were apparently peaceful and happy. His third and final illness began in November 1907, following his mother's death at 92 and his wife's disabling stroke. He was admitted to the new Leipzig-Dösen asylum with symptoms quite different from those which had characterized his previous illnesses. He had become deeply withdrawn and silent, with somatic delusions about lacking lungs and other organs, and he was preoccupied with bodily decay. There was no sign of the grandiose delusions or hallucinations that had characterized his second major illness. Schreber died of cardiac failure in 1911 at the age of 69.

Freud makes Schreber immortal

Although Freud was very enthusiastic about Schreber's case, he opened his account of it with the following disclaimer:

> The analytic investigation of paranoia presents difficulties of a peculiar nature to physicians who, like myself, are not attached to public institutions. We cannot accept patients suffering from this complaint, or at all events, we cannot keep them for long since we can not offer treatment unless there is some prospect of therapeutic success.
>
> (Freud 1911, p. 9)

While Freud's "account" of Schreber discussed mostly the disturbance in the flow of his libido, the analysis most relevant to the discussion here is more directly related to his interpretation of Schreber's delusion about the "end of the world." Freud believed that this delusion was based on Schreber's experience that his subjective world had come to an end, since he withdrew his love from it. And it was exactly due to this withdrawal that Freud assumed that people suffering schizophrenia were unable to establish transference to their doctors and, hence, could not benefit from psychoanalysis. Thus, psychoanalysis's paradoxical attitude towards schizophrenia began with Freud's own ambivalent stance toward individuals suffering from it. It was Jung who introduced Freud to Schreber's memoir (Lothane 1989), since, while in Vienna, Freud and his followers studied mainly neurosis, in the Burghölzli asylum in Zurich, Jung and others (notably, Eugen Bleuler, Adolf Meyer, Abraham Brill and Karl Abraham) were treating severely disturbed patients, especially those with schizophrenia. Although Freud was already analyzing patients at the time Schreber fought his psychosis and his doctors, he never made an effort to meet Schreber in person, and Schreber's two main therapists were indeed psychiatrists known rather for their somatic, forensic and very pessimistic conception of schizophrenia. Thus, while the first official psychoanalytic "encounter" with schizophrenia was exciting for Freud and led to his groundbreaking writings on narcissism (1914) and to the development of his object-relations theories, his engagement with schizophrenia remained largely theoretical. Only toward the end of his life, when he espoused a more pessimistic conception of human nature and realized that psychoanalysis was an interminable endeavor, did Freud became more optimistic about the possibility of treating people suffering from schizophrenia. He suggested that there was a piece of historical truth in insanity, and that even in the most acute psychotic disturbances, in a remote corner of the psyche, there hid a normal person with whom therapeutic efforts could yield successful results.

Ironically, in the same year that Schreber died in the Leipzig-Dösen hospital, Freud (1911) published his article on the Schreber case, which made him immortal. It was also the same year that two major psychoanalytic institutions were established in America – the American Psychoanalytic Association in Baltimore and the New York Psychoanalytic Society and Institute in New York, the place where Freud (1925) had hoped psychoanalysis would gain traction as he observed many leading psychiatrists, proprietors of institutions and directors of insane asylums endeavor to observe their patients in the light of psychoanalytic theories (Freud 1917, p. 423).

Freud had an ambivalent attitude towards America. Alongside his wish that America be the place where psychoanalysis would flourish, Freud had anti-American bias; mainly he railed against the "primitiveness" of American pragmatism and the country's broad-mindedness (Roudinesko 2001). He wrote to Fritz Wittel, the Austrian psychoanalyst who had moved to New York, that psychoanalysis and America were so ill adapted for each other that one is reminded of Grabbe's parable, "as though a raven were to put on a white shirt" (Wittel 1995). This criticism pertained to Americans' scientific spirit that was

176 *The many faces of Schreber*

devoted to dimensions, to measuring and weighing, to figures and statistics; in a word, to quantities. Quality is less well comprehended. It may be that this young civilization is not sufficiently seasoned to develop the concept of quality which dominates values in art, religion, and, as we now know, in science too.

(Wittel 1995, p. 148)

Freud's concerns about the fate of psychoanalysis in America partially became reality: the so-called "broad-mindedness" of Americans turned psychoanalysis into a dynamic, eclectic psychiatry as it struggled over jurisdiction against more narrowly specialized disciplines, just as pragmatism enticed psychiatry to turn psychoanalysis into just another of its therapeutic methods. Indeed, the close relationship between psychoanalysis and medicine in America enabled the former to be in touch with patients with schizophrenia. But both eclecticism and pragmatism were tendencies that would finally distance psychoanalysis from these very same patients. The confusion in the identity of psychoanalysis and of psychiatry caused the two disciplines to regress into more purely professional environments (Abbott 1988, p. 118): psychoanalysis regressed into psychoanalytic institutes and private practices (Leville 2002) and psychiatry regressed into the boundaries of somatic medicine.

Stage 1: Schreber as victim of a defective ego or a pre-Oedipal child (1960–1970)

In the early years of the neosomatic revolution, the massive use of antipsychotic medications enabled deinstitutionalization. This was the finest hour of somatic psychiatry, in which "the shame of the States" (Deutch 1948), namely the psychiatric hospitals, was replaced with the promise of returning a large group of patients, who could be made "easily manageable," to their own communities. In reaction to this formative event in psychiatry, American psychoanalysts of the 1960s showed two clear tendencies in the field of schizophrenia: one was an effort to adjust psychoanalysis to the trend toward re-medicalization in psychiatry; the other, along the lines Freud had laid out, was to insist on psychoanalysis's singularity as an approach separate from medicine. Analysts influenced by the first tendency presented themselves as "holier than the Pope," or in other words, as "physicians" more worthy of the name. Ego psychology, the most prominent school of thought in these circles, marked the ego as an organ that could be defective, malfunctioning or able to be afflicted by wounds. Indeed, ego psychology took even more elements from the medical "toolbox," including classification, empirical laboratory studies, etiological formulations of the schizophrenic condition and more. It even aspired to gain access to somatic psychiatry by formulating an explanation of the very mechanism that responded to neuroleptic medications. Using hybrid language, and not minding the gap, as it were, between the physical and the mental, the objective and the subjective, and the qualitative and the quantitative, ego psychologists claimed that drugs could treat the ego, that libido, originating in the basal ganglia in the brain, could be quantified on a numerical scale and that notorious electroconvulsive therapy was allegedly fusing self and object representations. Within this framework, Schreber's psychosis was portrayed as a result of "abnormal changes in a defective organ," the ego (Bergmann 1963). In contrast to this trend, other American psychoanalysts less preoccupied with the medical model based their papers mainly on psychoanalytic encounters with schizophrenic patients, but also on infant observation and on the British psychoanalysis of object relations, represented by Melanie Klein, Ronald Fairbairn and Herbert Rosenfeld. They concentrated on pre-Oedipal development and kept their research methods purely psychoanalytic, meaning that the "lab" remained the psychoanalyst's room and the only "manipulation" was the psychoanalytic method. As a result, a new interest in Schreber's conflict with his mother emerged. Until then only Fairbairn (1956), a Scottish psychiatrist and psychoanalyst, had mentioned Schreber's mother – notably her absence from his fantasies caused by the primal scene and the rage against her, which Schreber had felt when, as a child, he had imagined her betraying him with his father. But during the 1960s, American analysts, especially those who were working within psychiatric hospitals, began to show interest in this early relationship. Harold Searles (1961) from Chestnut Lodge referred to Schreber's mother in the context of the schizophrenic patient's annihilation anxiety, and Robert White (1961) suggested that her absence had a considerable place in Schreber's pathology, and that primitive oral dependency and destructive urges against the mother were significant in the dynamic of Schreber's psychosis. This renewed analysis of Schreber's memoir in this pre-Oedipal spirit suggested that hidden and symbolic representations of the mother and of such drives were a considerable part of Schreber's psychotic productions. Schreber's projections of his drives onto God – turning God into a dependent, greedy and destructive being – were none other than Schreber's own infantile yearning for his mother and his envy and possessiveness. These drives, which were represented symbolically as a "nerve-connection" and which enabled the "soul murder," threatened to destroy the whole world, including God himself. In the same vein, his delusion that his manhood would be taken away from him was simultaneously a wish to once again become a fetus in his mother's womb. Though the father was seen as a significant figure in Schreber's life, especially since Niederland's work pointed this out (1959, 1960), it was the mother who was presented as the significant figure in the earlier and, therefore, most pathogenic stages of Schreber's conflicts:

> To the infant the mother is the entire world. If a baby is forced too early in life, as Schreber was, to relinquish the subtle, life-giving, trust-endowing nurture, which only the mother can give, if he is too soon forced to learn the "art of renouncing", he comes, as Schreber did, dangerously near to losing his entire world.
>
> (White 1963, p. 72)

178 The many faces of Schreber

The emphasis on the mother's importance in early mental development was also demonstrated in the analytic technique, which emphasized the importance of the transferential relations. It was no longer only the reconstruction, interpretation and insight of the Oedipal past that served as the main tool of the psychoanalytic technique, but also the therapeutic relationship itself as nurturing that became more and more significant in the therapeutic process.

Stage 2: Schreber as tragic hero or a multidimensional analysand (1970–1980)

The second stage of strengthening the hold of neosomatic psychiatry in the field of schizophrenia included Kety's findings on schizophrenia's genetic etiology (Kety, Rosenthal, and Wender 1978) and Snyder's dopamine hypothesis (Snyder 1976). If in the previous decade somatic psychiatry offered a therapeutic technology claiming to be more efficient and cheaper than the one offered by psychoanalysis, by the 1970s mainstream psychoanalysis in America was less and less concerned with schizophrenia and schizophrenic patients. When they were writing on schizophrenia, American analysts resurrected Freud the scientist, who hoped for future biological understanding and treatment of the mind – the Freud of the "Project for a Scientific Psychology" (1895/1950) and "On Aphasia" (1891/1953). Discourse in the psychoanalytic mainstream journals turned more and more biological, and texts written by psychoanalysts began detailing brain structures, the functions of neurotransmitters and the effect of medication on different receptors. It was not uncommon to find psychoanalytic texts on schizophrenia claiming that it was stimulation of their "amygdalate nucleus" that induced rage, or that it was an excitation of the patient's "anterior cingulate gyrus" that caused intensive fear (Heilbrunn 1979). In the same spirit it was assumed that the supposedly heightened narcissism of these patients was a consequence of a disordered "noradrenergic metabolism" and that the dearth of available norepinephrine at the "pleasure centers" of the brain was responsible for the anhedonia in these conditions (Heilbrunn 1979, p. 604). In the wake of this somatization of the psychoanalytic discourse it was argued that there was "every reason to expect the eventual manufacture of drugs that allow the chemical comprehension and manipulation of specific emotions, of personality traits, and of defensive attitudes" and that "existing conflicts can be mitigated molecularly" (Heilbrunn 1979, p. 621).

Judge Schreber had no place among this type of psychoanalysis, but rather among the "rebels" against this approach. In the 1970s, the *Journal of the American Academy of Psychoanalysis and Dynamic Psychiatry* was established. The American Academy of Psychoanalysis, which came into being in the same year in which neuroleptic treatment was introduced in America (1956), had been founded in connection with the drift of rebellious analysts away from orthodox psychoanalysis. Indeed, in its earliest articles, the Academy seemed to represent the same intellectual ambiance as the "counterculture" that was its contemporary. On the one hand, the Academy turned against "psychoanalytic culture,"

The many faces of Schreber 179

which had established ego psychology, and on the other, it protested against the broader psychiatric/somatic/medical culture. The change of focus from intrapsychic power struggles to those occurring on the social scene, notably in the environment of the general counterculture of the 1970s, was demonstrated in the work of the well-known "Schreberologist," William Niederland. Although Niederland began publishing his papers on Schreber's father in the early 1950s, his major edited work including other authors' articles on the subject was published in 1974.

Like Niederland, Morton Schatzman (1973), a psychiatrist inspired by Gregory Bateson and R. D. Laing, emphasized Schreber's relationship with his father to attack certain aspects of psychiatry and modern society, such as child-rearing practices, education and religion. In this climate, psychoanalysts compared Schreber to a victim in a concentration camp, and his father was named a "Gestapo father" (Breger 1978). The allegedly bizarre aspects of his delusional system were now seen as his re-experiencing symbolically his childhood traumas (Ehrenwald 1974), and his psychosis was reformulated as a self-therapeutic process. The regression to his early childhood experiences, according to this view, meant to free him from the long-lasting influence of his traumatic education (Breger 1978, p. 140).

As an alternative to seeing Schreber as a victim, this psychoanalytic counterculture offered to see him as a hero (Wilden 1972 in Breger 1978), a great mystic and a great social utopian philosopher, whose memoir was in fact an ethical document on the organization of aggressiveness in 19th century society (Breger 1978, p. 154). Within this countercultural environment, Schreber's insanity was conceptualized as an attempt to design a new set of rules to live by, as well as a new "superior self" that would live through a more appropriate demonstration of all the aspects of its nature (Berger 1978, p. 155).

If within the borders of psychoanalysis in the United States Schreber became either a victim of his defective biology or a hero struggling to emancipate himself from his oppressors, outside the United States, American psychoanalysts maintained his status as an analysand. Instead of dealing with their opponents, American analysts publishing in the international arena put all their intellectual efforts into integrating the splits between the different kinds of psychoanalysis, just as within psychoanalysis they were trying to integrate the conflict and defect theories of schizophrenia. As part of this integrative effort, Ping-Nie Pao (1973, 1977) from Chestnut Lodge suggested that the mental condition of Schreber (that is to say, his schizophrenia) originated in the emergence of conflict around erotic or aggressive drives, as is the case with neurotics. But while the neurotic patient experienced anxiety, the schizophrenic patient experienced an "organismic panic" (Pao 1977, p. 392), paralyzing all ego functions. Thomas Ogden (1980) suggested – in the spirit of integration – that there was no need to choose between either a meaningless defect or meaningful conflicts when speaking of Schreber, as had been suggested by Nathaniel London (1973) when he first formulated Freud's unitary and specific theory of schizophrenia. Rather, the schizophrenic conflict, Ogden maintained, situates itself between meaningfulness and

180 *The many faces of Schreber*

meaninglessness. The assumption that the schizophrenic patient has both "sick" and "healthy" aspects, "neurotic" and "psychotic" parts, a "defect" and "conflicts," as it was formulated during these years, suggested that although schizophrenia is different from other conditions, some aspects of the schizophrenic patient's personality remain nonetheless "similar" to those of all other people, and that, therefore, these patients can be treated with psychoanalytic therapy.

Stage 3: Schreber as a brainsick, pre-human or complicated socio-somatic being (1980–1990)

The introduction of the *Diagnostic and Statistical Manual of Mental Disorders*, Third Edition (DSM-III), in the United States in the early 1980s inaugurated the third stage in the neosomatic revolution in psychiatry. This founding document, reflecting a paradigmatic shift in the profession, marked a transition in focus within American psychiatry from psychoanalysis – and the dynamic conception derived from it – to a focus on biology as part of the neosomatic trend. The manual became the textbook for insurance companies, for the financing of research and for the needs of pharmaceutical companies, and it documented the next phase in the process of re-medicalization of American psychiatry. The emphasis had shifted from the intra-psychic world towards visible symptoms and, hence, from Freud to Kraepelin, whose major claim was that the brain is the organ of the mind. The Kraepelinian credo declared that psychiatry was a branch of medicine and, as such, should maintain its scientific orientation and focus on the biological aspects of mental life. Thus, the "new partner" of American psychiatry became psychopharmacology. This meant, of course, that psychoanalysis was pushed away even further from the domain of schizophrenia and its treatment.

Like their colleagues from the previous decade, mainstream psychoanalysts tried once again to assimilate their competitor's rhetoric. In psychoanalytic texts, schizophrenia was presented as a biological disease; psychoanalytic treatment, it was further implied, could serve psychiatry by helping schizophrenic patients realize that they needed medication (Loeb and Loeb 1987). In the same spirit, analysts claimed that borderline patients, who were thought to suffer from "nonbiological" disturbances, should remain within the jurisdiction of psychoanalysis (Willick 1990).

The 1980s, which saw the appearance of the descriptive DSM-III together with the more formulated critique of psychoanalysis as a science (especially the one offered during the 1980s by Adolf Grünbaum), raised questions within the psychoanalytic community about what type of knowledge psychoanalysis could claim to offer. Did it belong with the natural sciences or was it a purely hermeneutic discipline, which need not bother with controlled research, since it dealt primarily with meanings and not so much with causes? The hermeneutic approach to psychoanalysis addressed subjective experiences. Unlike the DSM-III, it did not focus on behavior and did not recognize single causes for single effects. Meaning was not the product of a cause, but rather the creation of a subject. Unfortunately, both the biological explanations of schizophrenia and the hermeneutic approach

The many faces of Schreber 181

were constraining psychoanalysis's position vis-à-vis patients (Anscombe 1981). Both disputed the intelligibility of the meaning of schizophrenic symptoms: the somaticists asserted that schizophrenia derives from a meaningless biological defect, while the supporters of hermeneutics said that in the schizophrenic condition, the "person," the agency on which hermeneutic psychoanalysis had to focus, was not yet created. As a way out of this predicament, pre-Oedipal-focused psychoanalysis, based on psychoanalytic work with regressive patients and young children and on infant observation, suggested a genuine psychoanalytic response to the schizophrenic condition and offered a theoretical "asylum" to American analysts, both from the biological "attacks," which had framed schizophrenia as a "brain disease," and the hermeneutic "escape," which had aspired to get rid of the concept of "patient" altogether.

Schreber's schizophrenic psychosis had no place in biological psychoanalysis, nor did it find one in the hermeneutic alternative. But, in the course of the 1980s, it did find a home in American psychoanalytic texts that focused on very early development and were integrating British theories. Thus, although James Grotstein (1985, 1990b) suggested that Schreber's psychotic schizophrenia was a socio-psychosomatic disturbance of the central neural system, his descent into the disturbance – into the experience itself, the interruption of the "going on being," to cite Winnicott – marked Schreber's psychosis as a psychological defense against falling into the "black hole" of meaningless somatic events. Grotstein (1990a, 1990b) further suggested that without the presence of the primary identification background, the baby feels overwhelmed and inferior, as prey, a victim and a being in "another order of things," precisely as Schreber had described the psychotic experience (Grotstein 1990a, p. 390). Moreover, he suggested that a baby is born into the most archaic, depressive situation. If it is not saved in time by a benign folie à deux–inducing mother (i.e., by the strong attachment and bonding created with a meaning-supplying other), "it will fall between the cracks" into primary meaninglessness, randomness and chaos (infantile catastrophe). Its "innocence is foresworn" (Grotstein 1990b, p. 41). As a result, its mental matrix will have a deficit in primary narcissism, with low experience thresholds and a limited ability to transform experiences. This matrix, then, makes the future patient afflicted with schizophrenia vulnerable to the experience of stress, demonstrated in traumatic situations. If the traumatic situation is experienced as intolerable, the patient emotionally "disappears" from his body and experiences depersonalization, which is, according to Grotstein, precisely the decathexis Freud described in Schreber's case. According to Grotstein, the psychotic "holocaust" experienced by Schreber was the "living force" in reverse. It seems that the act of theorizing the lack, the absence and the "black hole" reflected psychoanalysis's very life force in the field of schizophrenia. Even when the neurological findings claimed that there was no meaning in the schizophrenic experience, analysts kept returning to this no-meaning. Put differently, even if the basis of the phenomenon was a meaningless brain dysfunction, psychoanalysis claimed to be the theory to bring meaning to the experience of meaninglessness, and as such it could rightly claim schizophrenia in its jurisdiction.

182 _The many faces of Schreber_

Stage 4: Schreber with or without a soul? (1990–2000)

President Bush's presidential proclamation in the Decade of the Brain in 1990 was the fourth stage in the neosomatic revolution occurring in psychiatry. The "nation's mission," Bush insisted, was "conquering brain diseases." Conquering the brain meant bracketing the soul and the phenomenology of meaning and pushing aside disciplines that assumed the functional autonomy of mental processes (Post 1991). Only three years after this proclamation, in 1993, the so-called Freud Wars broke out, with the first shot fired by the publication of Fredrick Crews's article, "The Unknown Freud," in the _New York Review of Books_, asserting that psychoanalysis failed as a mode of therapy and had proved to be nothing but a pseudo-science (Crews 1993). In this atmosphere, in which psychiatrists seemed to have "lost their mind" (Shapiro 1997), it seemed that psychiatry was more eager than ever to get rid of Freud and his followers.

As in previous decades, mainstream psychoanalysis once again desperately attempted to court psychiatry by replacing its language with the vocabulary of the sciences that had been named as the eventual conquerors of the schizophrenic territory. Siding with Kraepelin, mainstream American psychoanalysts offered that delusions were caused by a functional abnormality in the frontal lobe of the brain, especially in the dorsolateral prefrontal cortex. This neurobiological hypothesis put forth by a psychoanalyst in a psychoanalytic journal was indicative of a willingness to give up three basic analytical formulas concerning the causes of the deficit syndrome in schizophrenia: first, that the syndrome represented a psychological defense; second, that it resulted from conflicts or neglect during early childhood; and third, that difficulties relating to the aggressive drive were a primary etiological factor in schizophrenia.

Faced with the increasingly dominant role of biological explanations of mental illnesses, opposing voices began to emerge that understood Schreber's "soul murder" to be the very result of explaining his symptoms in terms of a brain disease. With his book, _My Own Private Germany_ (1996), Eric Santner, a professor of modern Germanic studies, inspired a discussion of Schreber among psychoanalysts. Santner suggested that the chronic traumas creating Schreber's bizarre symptoms and delusions were a result of his suppression, first by his father's dominance and later by the authority of his psychiatrists, Flechsig and Weber. Some of Schreber's paranoid delusions concerning Flechsig, according to Santner, were thus related to "the impersonal and completely biological psychiatric attitude of the psychiatrist," which was nothing short of "soul murdering" (Santner 1996, p. 75). Following this argument, Theodor Dorpat (1998), a psychoanalyst from Seattle, suggested that "soul murder" derived from certain psychiatrists' all too rigid and exclusive approaches to biological treatments. Furthermore, he argued that Schreber's invocation in his memoir of theologians and philosophers was only further evidence of his awareness that the causes of his disease and its meaning were not accessible to the neurobiological approach Flechsig had used.

In their attack on reductionism, psychoanalysts presented Freud not only as opposed to Flechsig in his search for meaning in psychosis, but also as contradicting

The many faces of Schreber   183

Flechsig's endeavor to reach narrow brain localization (Kravis 1992; Niederland 1968). Although Flechsig is known mainly as Schreber's psychiatrist, his other claim to fame was to have identified a neural tract, which, for a short period of time, was even named after him (Flechsig's Tract; Kravis 1992, p. 14). Indeed, Freud, in his own attempt to develop a code to decipher the riddle of psychosis, suddenly emerged in a very positive light when it was recalled, in the 1990s, that Flechsig kept a brain museum next to his hospital office, while Schreber's other psychiatrist, Weber, was a forensic specialist who wrote a dissertation on dead bodies, not on living people (Lothane 1997, 1999).

Since the Decade of the Brain was also the decade of Freud Wars, Schreber was only one of the many targets used to attack Freud in these disputes in the United States, and in the international area, Schreber was, on the contrary, recruited, notably by American psychoanalysts, to protect Freud. In this respect, the Freud Wars were a reprise of the jurisdictional struggle between psychoanalysis and somatic psychiatry. For example, Zvi Lothane (1999), the most prominent Schreberologist in the world, sought to protect Freud from the Freud bashers. Although he offered a more complex picture of psychosis than the one provided by Freud, his defense of Freud against his critics placed Freud's opponents in the camp of pharmacological reductionism, in the tradition of positivism. Thus, against Adolf Grünbaum's attack on Freud, Lothane insisted that the insight that life has meaning – just as insanity has meaning and symptoms have their own logic – was expressed most eloquently by Freud. He added that psychoanalysis was not suitable for everyone: "Some people want to remember, and for them psychoanalysis is a powerful opportunity; others want to forget, and for them pharmacotherapy is the better way" (Lothane 1999, p. 167).

Summary

Although mainstream American psychoanalysis has completely detached itself from overtly psychotic patients, during the four decades that this book covers, a small group of analysts continued to work against making themselves obsolete in the field of schizophrenia. These analysts respected the uniqueness of the schizophrenic person and the complexity of the intra-psychic world and feel ethically committed to the radical otherness provided by patients such as the mythical Schreber. These analysts seemed to declare to these patients, just as Abraham declared to the Creator at the event of the binding of Isaac, "Hineni" ("Here I am!"). These healers, in essence, said: "Driven to – and by – responsibility, ready to face your panic and your terror, I make myself available to your needs and to your sufferings. I am here to be haunted by you." Schreber, as the symbol of the schizophrenic patient, still haunts psychoanalysis with the plea to be heard as a "human being" and not to be "forsaken," as he himself wrote. And it is precisely individuals like him and like my patient Y, whose "subjective world," as Freud suggested, came to an end, who demand psychoanalysts and others treat them, not as bare life (Agamben 1998) – as biological entities – but rather as surviving subjects bearing witness, in Derrida's words, to "life beyond life, life more than life. . . . the most intense life possible" (Derrida 2004 in Fassin 2010).

184 *The many faces of Schreber*

References

Abbott, A., 1988. *The system of professions.* Chicago, IL: University of Chicago Press.

Agamben, G., 1998. *Homo sacer: Sovereign power and bare life.* D. Heller-Roazen, trans. Stanford, CA: Stanford University Press.

Anscombe, R., 1981. Referring to the unconscious: A philosophical critique of Schafer's action language. *International Journal of Psychoanalysis,* 62, pp. 225–241.

Baumeyer, F., 1956. The Schreber case. *International Journal of Psychoanalysis,* 37, pp. 61–74.

Bergmann, M. S., 1963. The place of Paul Federn's ego psychology in psychoanalytic metapsychology. *Journal of the American Psychoanalytic Association,* 11, pp. 97–116.

Breger, L., 1978. Daniel Paul Schreber. *Journal of the American Academy of Psychoanalysis and Dynamic Psychiatry,* 6, pp. 123–156.

Crews, F., 1993, November 18. The unknown Freud. *New York Review of Books,* pp. 55–66.

Deutch, A., 1948. *The shame of the states.* New York: Harcourt, Brace and Company.

Dinnage, R., 2000. Introduction. In: *Memoirs of my nervous illness.* New York: New York Review Books. pp. xi–xxiv.

Dorpat, T. L., 1998. Review of *My own private Germany. Daniel Paul Schreber's secret history of modernity,* by Eric L. Santner. *Psychoanalytic Quarterly,* 67, pp. 511–515.

Ehrenwald, J., 1974. The telepathy hypothesis and schizophrenia. *Journal of the American Academy of Psychoanalysis and Dynamic Psychiatry,* 2, pp. 159–169.

Fairbairn, D., 1956. Considerations arising out of the Schreber case. *British Journal of Medical Psychology,* 29, pp. 113–127.

Fassin, D., 2010. Ethics of survival. *Humanity,* 1(1), pp. 81–95.

Freud, S., 1911. Psycho-analytic notes on an autobiographical account of a case of paranoia (dementia paranoides). In: *The standard edition of the complete psychological works of Sigmund Freud,* Volume 22. London: Hogarth Press. pp. 1–82.

Freud, S., 1914. On narcissism. In: *The standard edition of the complete psychological works of Sigmund Freud,* Volume 14. London: Hogarth Press. pp. 67–102.

Freud, S., 1917. Introductory lectures on psycho-analysis. In: *The standard edition of the complete psychological works of Sigmund Freud,* Volume 16. London: Hogarth Press. pp. 241–463.

Freud, S., 1925. An autobiographical study. In: *The standard edition of the complete psychological works of Sigmund Freud,* Volume 20. London: Hogarth Press. pp. 1–74.

Freud, S., 1950. Project for a scientific psychology. In: *The standard edition of the complete psychological works of Sigmund Freud,* Volume 1. London: Hogarth Press. pp. 281–391. (Original work published 1895).

Freud, S., 1953. *On aphasia: A critical study.* Oxford: International Universities Press. (Original work published 1891).

Grotstein, J. S., 1985. The evolving and shifting trends in psychoanalysis. *Journal of the American Academy of Psychoanalysis and Dynamic Psychiatry,* 13, pp. 423–452.

Grotstein, J. S., 1990a. Nothingness, meaninglessness, chaos, and the "black hole" II. *Contemporary Psychoanalysis,* 26, pp. 377–407.

Grotstein, J. S., 1990b. The "black hole" as the basic psychotic experience. *Journal of the American Academy of Psychoanalysis and Dynamic Psychiatry,* 18, pp. 29–46.

Heilbrunn, G., 1979. Biologic correlates of psychoanalytic concepts. *Journal of the American Psychoanalytic Association*, 27, pp. 597–625.

Kety, S. S., Rosenthal, D., and Wender, P., 1978. Genetic relationships within the schizophrenia spectrum: Evidence from adoption studies. In: R. L. Spitzer and D. F. Klein, eds., *Critical issues in psychiatric diagnosis*. pp. 213–223. New York: Raven Press.

Kravis, N. M., 1992. The "prehistory" of the idea of transference. *International Review of Psychoanalysis*, 19, pp. 9–22.

Leville, J. J., 2002. Jurisdictional competition and the psychoanalytic dominance of American psychiatry. *Journal of Historical Sociology*, 15, pp. 265–266.

Loeb, F. F., Jr., and Loeb, L. R., 1987. Psychoanalytic observations on the effect of lithium on manic attacks. *Journal of the American Psychoanalytic Association*, 35, pp. 877–902.

London, N. J., 1973. An essay on psychoanalytic theory: Two theories of schizophrenia. Part I: Review and critical assessment of the development of the two theories. *International Journal of Psychoanalysis*, 54, pp. 169–178.

Lothane, Z., 1989. Schreber, Freud, Flechsig, and Weber revisited: An inquiry into methods of interpretation. *Psychoanalytic Review*, 76, pp. 203–262.

Lothane, Z., 1992. *In defense of Schreber: Soul murder and psychiatry*. London: Analytic Press.

Lothane, Z., 1997. The schism between Freud and Jung over Schreber: Its implications for method and doctrine. *International Forum of Psychoanalysis*, 6, pp. 103–115.

Lothane, Z., 1999. The perennial Freud: Method versus myth and the mischief of Freud bashers. *International Forum of Psychoanalysis*, 8, pp. 151–171.

Niederland, W. G., 1959. Schreber: Father and son. *Psychoanalytic Quarterly*, 28, pp. 151–169.

Niederland, W. G., 1960. Schreber's father. *Journal of the American Psychoanalytic Association*, 8, pp. 492–499.

Niederland, W. G., 1968. Schreber and Flechsig – A further contribution to the "kernel of truth" in Schreber's delusional system. *Journal of the American Psychoanalytic Association*, 16, pp. 740–748.

Nietzsche, F., 1889. Letter to Jacob Burckhardt, Turin, January 6, 1889. In: C. Middleton, trans., 1969, *Selected letters of Friedrich Nietzsche*. pp. 346–347. Chicago, IL: University of Chicago Press.

Ogden, T. H., 1980. On the nature of schizophrenic conflict. *International Journal of Psychoanalysis*, 6, pp. 513–533.

Pao, P., 1973. Notes on Freud's theory of schizophrenia. *International Journal of Psychoanalysis*, 54, pp. 469–476.

Pao, P., 1977. On the formation of schizophrenic symptoms. *International Journal of Psychoanalysis*, 58, pp. 389–401.

Post, S. C., 1991. 34th winter meeting. *Journal of the American Academy of Psychoanalysis and Dynamic Psychiatry*, 19, pp. 484–487.

Roudinesko, E., 2001. *Why psychoanalysis*. New York: Columbia University Press.

Santner, E. L., 1996. *My own private Germany: Daniel Paul Schreber's secret history of modernity*. Princeton, NJ: Princeton University Press.

Schatzman, M., 1973. *Soul murder: Persecution in the family*. New York: Random House.

Schreber, D. P., 1903/2000. *Memoirs of my nervous illness*. New York: New York Review Books.

186 *The many faces of Schreber*

Searles, H., 1961. Sexual processes in schizophrenia. *Psychiatry Supplement*, 24, pp. 87–95.

Shapiro, T., 1997. Review of *The talking cure: The science behind psychotherapy*, by Susan C. Vaughan. *International Journal of Psychoanalysis*, 78, pp. 1035–1036.

Snyder, S. H., 1976. The dopamine hypothesis of schizophrenia: Focus on dopamine receptor. *American Journal of Psychiatry*, 133, pp. 197–202.White, R. B., 1961. The mother-conflict in Schreber's psychosis. *International Journal of Psychoanalysis*, 42, pp. 55–73.

White, R. B., 1963. The Schreber case reconsidered in the light of psychosocial concepts. *International Journal of Psychoanalysis*, 44, pp. 213–221.

Wilden, A., 1972. *System and structure: Essays in communication and exchange*. London: Routledge.

Willick, M. S., 1990. Review of *Essential papers on borderline disorders: One hundred years at the border*, edited by Michael H. Stone. *Journal of the American Psychoanalytic Association*, 38, pp. 842–847.

Wittels, F., 1995. *Freud and the child woman*. New Haven, CT: Yale University Press.

Epilogue

This volume on the history of psychoanalysis in America begins with Freud, whose interest in schizophrenia focused mainly on exploring the psychosis of Judge Schreber, who claimed that his somatic psychiatrist was murdering his soul. It ends with the murder, almost 100 years later, of Wayne Fenton, a psychiatrist who was a proponent of psychoanalytically driven approaches to treating schizophrenia. This book explores the question of whether psychoanalysis "fell, pushed, or jumped" from the treatment of severe psychoses in the United States and concludes that it probably jumped.

Contrary to popular belief, it was not only the pharmaceutical companies, somatic psychiatrists, insurance companies or policy makers who pushed psychoanalysis away from treating schizophrenic patients. Richard Lucas (2009), a contemporary British analyst, follows David Bell's (2001) idea, and argues that when a patient jumps out of the window and commits suicide, it's his psychotic part that is pushing his non-psychotic part to its death. In extending the metaphor to psychoanalysis, we can say that it did not passively "fall" from the field of severe mental illness, just as it was not actively "pushed" by some third party. Rather, an in-depth exploration of the American psychoanalytic archive of abstract knowledge proves that it was psychoanalysis's own internal "psychotic part" that pushed it out of the field of severe mental illness and excluded schizophrenia from its domain. Moreover, the psychotic dynamics that, in the service of the death instinct, attack love and meaning and turn the human inhuman, the metaphoric concrete, the complex simple, not only afflicts patients with schizophrenia, but also can be found in analysts' attitudes and writing on psychoanalysis. The threat of reducing schizophrenia to a brain illness, the danger of understanding its symptoms as no more than a neurological "glitch" and the temptation to treat it using "McDonald's-like solutions" exist not only in the many political forces outside the profession, but also within psychoanalysis itself.

Despite the tendency of many to join the zeitgeist in reducing mental illness to a biological malfunction, some American analysts are still fighting to keep even the most severely ill patients in the jurisdiction of psychoanalysis. In the western United States they are mainly the disciples of Melanie Klein and Wilfred Bion. In the eastern United States, they are the Chestnut Lodge generation and their

188 *Epilogue*

descendants and followers who were able to conduct long-term psychoanalysis in institutions that offered the right environment and facilities so desperately needed by psychotic patients and their therapists.

Just as battles create vulnerabilities as they are waged inside the psyche, they create ruptures within disciplines and professions. The remedy for these injuries, as Joshua Durban (2008) suggests, is not only love and normalcy; to "live, dream, and heal," one should also be able to "mourn the loss of an illusion and embrace it with love and longing as it becomes a good object in our inner world" (p. 35). Those that live psychoanalysis, dream it and heal it from the injuries it suffers as it struggles in difficult therapeutic analytic encounters, as well as in its battles over jurisdiction, soldier on. They do not suffer the illusion of grandiose therapeutic expectations for the psychoanalytic treatment of schizophrenia, but they are not bitter, vengeful or cynical. These analysts are able to contain the complexities of the schizophrenic patients' otherness, and still see their similarities to other people even when patients deny it. They accept their patients' uniqueness and commonness, loneliness and connection, angst and hope. These analysts are invested in strengthening psychoanalysis's foundations and mending its internal ruptures. They also sustain psychoanalysis's vitality as a radical and courageous treatment method, concerned with threshold phenomena and the primitive edges of experiences – a method that can offer meaning where catastrophe seems to nullify it. As much as those diagnosed with schizophrenia need psychoanalysis to guide them in their quest for thinking in states of annihilation, psychoanalysis as a profession, research method, therapeutic approach and ethical practice needs these patients and the experiences they offer. Such patients, with the ongoing extreme experiences they face, challenge the defenses of the single analyst and, at the same time, confront psychoanalytic theoretical, practical and institutional stalemates. Indeed, the treatment of schizophrenia evokes extreme countertransference in analysts and within institutions; however, as psychoanalytic intellectual history indicates, these encounters create the tension essential for thinking and for developing knowledge. They prevent the stagnation and regression inherent in the effort to split off madness and expel it to faraway territories.

As Freud taught us, the nature of the repressed is to return, and Klein insisted that the nature of what is split off and expelled is to become ever more persecutory. If psychoanalysis is to survive it must reconnect with the edges of experience, with what appears to be "complete otherness" and with the death instinct and catastrophic inferno, where many schizophrenic patients exist. It is the psychoanalysis of "Beyond the Pleasure Principle" (Freud 1920) that recognizes the death instinct, violence and destruction, as part of the very nature of the human beast, which can contain madness in its jurisdiction. As Derrida (1998) wrote, it is only the psychoanalysis of the tragic Freud, who broke away from psychological, evolutional and biological sciences, the psychoanalysis that is open to the unknown and that does not police the threshold between reason and insanity, that can be an ethical practice hospitable to madness.

References

Bell, D., 2001. Who is killing what or whom? Some notes on the internal phenomenology of suicide. *Psychoanalytic Psychotherapy*, 15, pp. 21–37.

Derrida, J., 1998. To do justice to Freud. In: P. Kamuff, P. A. Brault, and M. Nass, trans., *Resistance of Psychoanalysis*. pp. 70–133. Stanford, CA: Stanford University Press.

Durban, J., 2008. *Introduction: Melanie Klein – Ktavim nivcharim (Melanie Klein – Selected writings)* (In Hebrew). Tel Aviv: Tolat Sfarim.

Lucas, R., 2009. *The psychotic wavelength*. East Sussex: Routledge.

Index

Abbott, Andrew 2, 4, 20, 28, 30, 31, 45
Abraham, Karl 107, 175, 183
Abramson, Ronald 147–8
Agency of Health Care Policy and Research (AHCPR) 162
Alexander, Franz 77
Alger, Ian 114–15
American Academy of Psychoanalysis and Dynamic Psychiatry 6, 10, 33, 76–7, 78, 79, 92, 109, 110, 114, 144, 148, 149, 150, 152, 178; dissidents 80–4
American Association for Psychoanalysis 33
American Journal of Insanity 32
American Medical Association 39
American Medico-Psychological Association 99
American Psychiatric Association 34, 36, 39, 97, 127, 147; committee on Nomenclature and Statistics 99
American Psychoanalytic Association 6, 30, 39, 45, 46, 48, 52, 56, 71, 76, 77, 92, 114, 141, 143, 148, 175
amphetamines 70
Anscombe, Roderick 117
anti-psychiatry 77, 80–4, 109, 110
Arieti, Silvano 77, 80, 83, 109, 115, 149–50; *Interpretation of Schizophrenia* 82, 150
Arlow, Jacob 60
Asch, Stuart 104, 105, 106
Association of Biological Psychiatry 41

Bak, Robert 52
Basaglia, Franco 91
Behr, Sabine 173
Bell, David 187
Bellak, Leopold 102, 137
Benedetti, Gaetano 90–1, 125, 149–50
Bernays, Martha 13

biological psychiatry 41, 101, 112, 135, 137, 142, 181, 182
Bion, Wilfred 51, 59, 84, 119, 139, 187
Bleuler, Eugen 15, 16, 175
Bohm, David 146
Boston Psychotherapy Study 122–6
Boyer, Bryce 60–1, 112
Brenner, Charles 60
Brill, Abraham 31, 46, 175
British Psychoanalysis Society 56
Buber, Martin 83
The Bulletin see Schizophrenia Bulletin
Bulletin of the American Psychoanalytic Association 46
Burghölzli Clinic 62, 124, 175
Bush, George H.W. 2, 8, 133, 134, 182; *see also* Decade of the Brain
Bychowski, Gustav 62

Carter, Jimmy 124
Center for Advanced Study of the Psychoses 60
Chestnut Lodge 1, 11, 37–8, 55, 74, 84, 107, 124, 146, 147, 165, 177, 179, 187
child development: scientific study 50–1, 58
chlorpromazine 43, 74
Chodoff, Paul 115
Clark University 30, 31
Community Mental Health Act 45, 50
community psychiatry 4, 46, 62, 72, 74, 90
Cooper, Arnold 158
Cooper, David 77
Cornelison, Alice 50
counterculture 6, 82, 178–9; approach to schizophrenia 76–9, 92
Crews, Frederick: "The Unknown Freud" 134–5, 182
cultural model 33

192 Index

Decade of the Brain 2, 8, 9–10, 133–70, 182, 183; arguing for a dualistic view of schizophrenia etiology 135–6; attacks on psychoanalytic theories from without and within 138–40; ethics of treating schizophrenia 149–50; illnesses of the brain 134–5; *JAPA* calls for research on psychoanalytic treatment of schizophrenia 141–2; limitations of drugs and the cost-effectiveness of analysis 146–8; neuroscience use to explain schizophrenic symptoms 136–8; psychoanalysis in danger 161–5; psychoanalysts examine why they lost ground 140–1; relational psychoanalysis marginalizes schizophrenia 150–4; schizophrenic processes in psychoanalysis 142–4; seduction theory 155–6; somatic trend crosses the ocean 156–61
defective organ 47, 48, 64, 177
defect theory 4, 107, 118, 179
deficit theory 75, 76, 84, 86
Deleuze, Gilles: *Anti-Oedipus* 78
delusions 17, 18, 21, 23, 27, 88, 91, 121, 137, 154, 171, 172, 173, 174, 175, 182
dementia praecox 15, 16, 37
depression 156, 173
Derrida, Jacques 183, 188
Diagnostic and Statistical Manual of Mental Disorders see DSM
dialectical behavioral therapy 148
Dialogues see Psychoanalytic Dialogues
Dolnick, Edward 138, 164; *Madness on the Couch* 160
"dopamine hypothesis" and evidence of genetic factors in schizophrenia 69–96, 113, 137, 159, 178
Dorpat, Theodor 182
DSM 143; history 98–9
DSM-II 108, 122
DSM-III 6, 7, 9–10, 93, 98, 104, 105, 108, 109, 118, 119, 120, 122, 126, 127, 128, 136, 180; development 99–101; game changer 101–3
dualism 1, 109
dual view of schizophrenia 2, 13–26, 84–8
Durban, Joshua 188
dynamic psychiatry 3, 6, 28, 30, 31, 32, 36, 40, 98, 99, 110, 124, 125, 126, 140, 144; eclectic 35; vs. ego psychology 33–4

early psychiatry in medical institutions 28–9
ECT *see* electroconvulsive therapy
ego function assessment (EFA) 102
ego psychology 30, 32, 40, 56, 61, 64, 77, 107, 120, 157, 176; drugs 177; vs. dynamic psychology 33–4; object relations 57–9, 65; schizophrenia 46–9, 55
Eigen, Michael 20
EIO *see* exploratory, insight-oriented psychotherapy
Eissler, Kurt 63
electroconvulsive therapy (ECT) 31, 36, 38, 40, 49, 54, 62, 63, 124, 162, 177
Emde, Robert 120
Emerson, Ralph Waldo 78
Engel, Milton 115
exploratory, insight-oriented psychotherapy (EIO) 123, 124
extra-pyramidal symptoms (EPS) 172

Fairbairn, Ronald 119, 139, 150, 177
Federn, Paul 47, 124
Fenton, Wayne 1, 11, 165–6, 187
fixation 18, 20–1, 106, 107, 120
Flechsig, Paul 17, 171, 172, 173–4, 182–3
Fleck, Stephen 50
Forrest, David 111, 115, 144
Forrester, John 15
Foucault, Michel 1, 77–8
Freeman, Thomas: *Psychopathology of the Psychoses* 51
Freud, Anna 58, 59, 109
Freud, Sigmund 1, 2–3, 5, 9–10, 12, 34, 36, 56, 65, 77, 92, 98, 100, 105, 107, 109, 110, 111, 115–16, 117, 144, 151, 171, 183; American eclecticism 27, 30–1; "Analysis Terminable" 22–3; "An Autobiographical Study" 27; "Beyond the Pleasure Principle" 18, 188; biology and psychoanalysis 157–8, 178; Clark University visit 30, 31; "Constructions in Analysis" 22, 23; criticism 134–5, 138, 183; dreams 49, 51; dual view of schizophrenia 13–26, 84–8; ego 153; *The Ego and the Id* 18; "Fetishism" 16, 19; lay analysis 79; "Loss of Reality in Neurosis and Psychosis" 18; *Moses and Monotheism* 19; "Negation" 18; "Neurosis and Psychosis" 18; "On Aphasia" 178; "On Beginning the Treatment" 16; "On Narcissism"

69; *An Outline of Psycho-Analysis* 19, 43; "Project for a Scientific Psychology" 51, 52, 178; psychoanalysis 53; "Psycho-Analytic Notes on an Autobiographical Account of a Case of Paranoia (Dementia Paranoides)" 17; *The Question of Lay Analysis* 14, 79; schizophrenia theories 6, 47, 55, 57, 75, 81, 136; Schreber paper 151, 174–6; seduction theory 78; and Simmel relationship 54, 150–1; somatic psychoanalysis 72–4; split theory of schizophrenia 84–8; translations of works 46, 57; treatment of psychotic patients 16–17; unitary theory 55, 60, 75, 179

Freud Wars 9, 134, 135, 160, 182, 183

Fromm, Erich 156

Fromm-Reichmann, Frieda 37, 77, 107, 112, 123, 125, 138, 148, 160

Frosch, John 46, 118

Gabbard, Glen 141, 142

Galton, Francis 29

Garfield, David 114

Gay, Peter 22

genetic findings 6, 92, 160

Ginsberg, George 140

Giovacchini, Peter 149

Gitelson, Maxwell 53–4

Gleick, James 146

Goffman, Erving 78

Goldberg, Arnold 143–4

Gomez, E.A. 116

Great Depression 33, 54

Green, Hannah (Joanne Greenberg): *I Never Promised You a Rose Garden* 37

Greenacre, Phyllis 48, 54

Grob, Gerald 98

Grotstein, James 84–6, 87, 110, 111, 112, 113, 181; "The Psychoanalytic Concept of Schizophrenia: I. The Dilemma" 85; "The Psychoanalytic Concept of Schizophrenia: II. Reconciliation" 85

Grünbaum, Adolf 39–40, 116–17, 180, 183

Guattari, Felix: *Anti-Oedipus* 78

Gunderson, John 141, 142

Hale, Nathan 29, 30, 31, 32, 33, 34, 35, 36, 38, 40, 45

Haley, Jay 74

Hartmann, Heinz 47, 137

Healy, David 70

Heilbrunn, Gret 73, 74

Hollos, Istvan 22

hysterical clients 15, 16

illusion 78, 81, 188

International Journal of Psychoanalysis (*IJP*) 4, 46, 56, 71, 82, 101, 156–7

international psychoanalytic arena (IJP) 8, 9

International Psychoanalytic Association (IPA) 45–6, 47, 53, 56, 57, 160; "Mental Reality in Psychotic States" 157

International Society for the Psychological Treatment of Schizophrenia and Other Psychoses (ISPS) 10, 90, 125, 164, 165

Janet, Pierre 153–4

JAPA see Journal of the American Psychoanalytic Association

Jelliffee, Smith Ely: *Diseases of the Nervous System* 32

Joint Commission on Mental Illness and Health: "Action for Mental Health" 44

Jones, Ernest 56–7, 105

Journal of the American Academy of Psychoanalysis and Dynamic Psychiatry (*Journal of the Academy*) 4, 6, 7, 10, 71, 76, 77, 78, 79, 92, 101, 109, 110, 111, 112, 114–15, 144, 146, 149, 160, 163, 164, 178; dissidents 81, 82

Journal of the American Psychoanalytic Association (*JAPA*) 4, 7, 9, 48, 50, 51, 53, 55, 56, 57–8, 61, 64, 71, 72, 73, 74, 76, 101, 103, 104, 105, 107, 108, 135, 143, 144, 149, 157; calls for research on psychoanalytic treatment of schizophrenia 141–2; history 45–6

Jung, Carl 16, 62, 112, 152, 175

Kafka, John 74

Kaiser, David 133

Karon, Bertram 125; *Psychotherapy of Schizophrenia* 103

Katan, Morris 58

Kaufman, Ralph 113–14

Kempf, Edward 115

Kennedy, John F. 44–5; "New Frontier" 4, 45; "ounce of prevention" 50; space frontier 134

Kernberg, Otto 55–6, 102–3, 107, 121, 122

194 *Index*

Kestenbaum, Clarice 148
Kety, Seymour 5, 71, 80, 84, 85, 160, 178
Klein, Melanie 58, 59, 63, 107, 119, 120, 139, 177, 187, 188
Klerman, Gerald 124
Kraeplin, Emil 6, 15, 30–1, 37, 48, 99, 100, 104, 127, 180, 182
Kris, Ernst 47, 107
Kuhn, Thomas: *The Structure of Scientific Revolutions* 53

Lacan, Jacques 84, 119
Laing, R. D. 71, 77, 80, 119, 179
Lehmann, Heinz 43
Leveille, John 38, 39
libido 5, 21, 47, 52, 63, 177; theory of schizophrenia 17–19
Lidz, Ruth 50
Lidz, Theodore 50, 71, 91, 138
Loewald, Hans 58
Loewenstein, Rudolph 47
London, Nathaniel 20–2, 84, 118, 179
Lothane, Zvi 183
Lucas, Richard 187
Lynn, David 16–17

Mahler, Margaret 58, 81, 107; *On human symbiosis and vicissitudes of individuation* 50
Marcus, Eric 104, 105, 106, 137, 161
Matte-Blanco, Ignacio 84, 146
McDonald's-like solutions 10, 146, 187
Menninger, Karl 90, 98
Menninger Clinic 36, 54, 55, 59, 138, 141
Menninger Foundation 31, 53, 108
Mental Health Study Act 44
mental illness: in the body 29–30; severe 34–8
Meyer, Adolf 30, 31, 75, 99, 110, 115, 159, 160, 175
Modell, Arnold 59
Müller, Christian 125
Muller, John 154

National Commission on Mental Hygiene 99
National Institute of Mental Health (NIMH) 35–6, 40, 71, 72, 88–9, 108, 133, 134
National Institute of Neurological Disorders 134
National Mental Health Act 35

neosomatic psychiatry 3, 4, 8, 9, 45, 47, 49, 55, 139, 145, 178
"Neurobiology and the Unconscious" 111
neurologists: mental illness treatment 29, 30, 31; views vs. psychiatrists views 31–3
New York Academy of Medicine 99
New York Psychoanalytic Institute 48
New York Psychoanalytic Society and Institute 175
New York Review of Books 134, 135, 182
Nietzsche, Friedrich 171
NIMH *see* National Institute of Mental Health
nosographic model 32, 48

object-relations theories 6, 58, 81, 118–22, 127, 175
Ogden, Thomas 84–5, 86–7, 119–20, 152–3, 156, 179; *The Primitive Edge of Experience* 120
Olds, David 158
One Flew Over the Cuckoo's Nest 31
oppression 78
Ostow, Mortimer 62–3; *Drugs in Psychoanalysis and Psychotherapy* 52
otherness 10, 83, 149, 152, 154, 183

Pally, Regina 161
Pao, Ping-Nie 84, 102, 107, 179
Papini, Giovanni 116
Patient Outcomes Research Team (PORT) 10, 161, 162, 163, 164–5
personal problems 15, 28, 30
PET scans *see* positron emission tomography (PET) scans
Pfister, Oskar 16
pharmaceutical companies 8, 70, 101, 180, 187
philosophical/phenomenological model 33
Pinel, Philippe 45
Popper, Karl 116
PORT *see* Schizophrenia Patient Outcomes Research Team
positron emission tomography (PET) scans 110, 111
pre-Oedipal development 8, 119, 120, 121, 127, 172, 176, 177, 181
psychiatrists views vs. neurologists views 31–3
Psychiatry 35
psychoanalysis: American 56–7; American turns to British object-relations

theory 118–22; between biology and hermeneutics 8, 116–18; distinguishing from medicine 108–12; identity crisis 53–4; jurisdictional struggles 14–16; "light" 88–91; limitations of drugs and the cost-effectiveness of analysis 146–8; McDonald's culture 144–6; medicalization of American 27–42; moves away from its roots 51–2; object-relations theory 118–22; place in a changing therapeutic landscape 38–9; psychiatry revisits the role 39–40; psychopharmacology and community psychiatry 43–68; schizophrenia treatment 112–16; scientific method 49; unique contributions 61–2

psychoanalysts: borderline patients 106–8; examine their role in the narrowing of their jurisdiction 103–6; examine why they lost ground 140–1

Psychoanalytic Dialogues (*Dialogues*) 4, 9, 150, 151, 152, 153, 155, 156

Psychoanalytic Institute (Columbia University) 77

Psychoanalytic Institute (New York) 60

Psychoanalytic Institute (Washington-Baltimore) 50, 90

psychoanalytic method 4, 5, 6, 16, 36, 55, 61, 108, 177

psychodynamic model 33, 99, 100, 118, 162; attack on 97–8

psychological psychoanalysis 72–5; specific vs. unitary theory 75–6

psychotherapeutic model 32

psychotic patients: splitting 19–20; treatment of 16–17

Rado, Sandor 77, 159, 160

reality-adaptive supportive psychotherapy (RAS) 123, 124

Reik, Theodore 14

Rey, Henri 11, 88

Rinsley, Donald 59

Robbins, Michael 117, 135–6, 139–40, 141, 143; *Experiences of Schizophrenia* 143

Rosen, Arnold 112

Rosen, John 36–7

Rosenfeld, Herbert 51, 59, 139, 143, 160, 177

Rosenfeld Award 153

Rosenthal, David 71

Ross, Nathaniel 52

Roudinesco, Elizabeth 32

Ryle, Gilbert 110

Santner, Eric 171; *My Own Private Germany* 182

Sass, Louis 160; *Madness and Modernism* 143; *The Paradox of Delusions* 143

Schafer, Roy 116, 117, 120

Schatzman, Morton 179

schizophrenia: arguing for a dualistic view of schizophrenia etiology 135–6; counterculture approach 76–9; dopamine and genetic connections 69–72; "dopamine hypothesis" 69–96; ego psychologists' view 46–9; ethics of treating 149–50; Freud's dual view 13–26, 84–8; *JAPA* calls for research on psychoanalytic treatment 141–2; libido theory 17–19; McDonald's culture 144–6; neuroscience to explain symptoms 136–8; neuroscience use to explain schizophrenic symptoms 136–8; processes in psychoanalysis 142–4; relational psychoanalysis marginalizes 150–4; theories 20–2; treating with psychoanalysis 54–6, 112–16

Schizophrenia Bulletin (*The Bulletin*) 4, 6, 8, 46, 71, 88–9, 90, 122, 124–5, 127, 135, 161, 165

Schloss Tegel 3, 54, 140

Schreber, Daniel Paul: brainsick, pre-human or complicated socio-somatic 180–1; *Denkwürdigkeiten eines Nervenkranken* 172; Freud makes immortal 174–6; life of 173–4; *Memoirs of My Nervous Illness* 17, 172; soul 182–31; tragic hero or multidimensional analysand 178–80; victim of a defective ego or a pre-Oedipal child 176–8

Schultz, Clarence 90

Schwartz, Morris: *The Mental Hospital* 37

Searles, Harold 55, 56, 58–9, 62, 63, 69, 82, 107, 123, 138, 142, 151–2, 177; "The Patient as Therapist to His Analyst" 152

Sechehaye, Marguerite 112

seduction theory 78, 155–6

Segal, Hannah 107, 119

severe mental illness 12, 30, 34–8, 45, 106, 108, 118, 120, 126, 155, 159, 187

Shapiro, Theodore 105–6

196 Index

Sheldrake, Rupert 146
Silver, Ann-Louise 146–7, 164; "The Schizophrenic Person and the Benefits of Psychotherapies" 163
Simmel, Ernest 3, 54, 124, 150
Slipp, Samuel 144, 145
Smith, Kline and French Laboratories 43
Snyder, Solomon 5, 69–70, 178
Social Security Amendment 89
somatic psychiatry 1, 3, 5, 6, 7, 8, 9, 36, 37, 38, 43, 44, 48, 49, 51, 52, 53, 54, 56, 61, 62, 63, 64, 71, 72–5, 81, 84, 87–8, 90, 92, 102, 103, 106, 107, 108, 110, 113–14, 115, 117, 120, 123, 124, 126, 137, 138, 145, 151, 159, 160, 161, 165, 176, 178, 183; McDonald's-like approach 10, 146, 187
specific theory 2, 6, 20, 21–2, 75, 85, 89, 152, 179; vs. unitary theory 75–6
Spitzer, Robert 97, 99–100, 101
split theory of schizophrenia 84–8
splitting 19, 75, 85, 90
Stanton, Alfred: *The Mental Hospital* 37
Stoller, Robert: *Splitting* 88
Stone, Michael 106, 146
Strecker, Edward 31
Sullivan, Harry Stack 33, 34–5, 76–7, 83, 115, 120, 125, 150, 152
superego 19, 20, 60, 102
Szasz, Thomas 77

Tannenbaum, Samuel 56
Thompson, Clara 77
Thoreau, Henry David 78
treatment, worth of 52–3

unitary theory 2, 20, 21, 55, 60, 74, 85; vs. specific 75–6
University of California 36

Vandenbos, Gary R.: *Psychotherapy of Schizophrenia* 103
Virchow, Rudolph 109
Volkan, Vamik 142–3; *The Seed of Madness* 143

Waelder, Robert 52
Wallerstein, Robert 47, 53, 72, 108
Washington School of Psychiatry 35, 107
Weber, Guido 173, 174, 182, 183
Weill-Cornell Medical College 104, 159
Wender, Paul 71
West Chester University 38
Westen, Drew 119
Western New England Psychoanalytic Society 20
White, Robert 177
White, William Alanson 31, 115, 150; *Diseases of the Nervous System* 32
WHO *see* World Health Organization
Williams, Paul 153, 154
Willick, Martin 106–7, 108, 136–7, 139, 157, 160–1
Willmer, Harry 113
Winnicott, D.W. 107, 119, 121, 139, 144, 150, 181
Winter, Sarah 14
Wittle, Franz 27, 175, 176
World Health Organization (WHO) 171; *International Classification of Diseases* (ICD-6) 99, 122
World War I 33; post- 32
World War II 35, 46, 97; post- 38, 39, 52, 99; pre- 98

Zilboorg, Gregory 44